DATE DUE

JUN 13 1990			

DEMCO 38-297

The Origin of British Field Systems:
An Interpretation

The Origin of British Field Systems: An Interpretation

ROBERT A. DODGSHON
University College of Wales, Aberystwyth

1980

ACADEMIC PRESS

A Subsidiary of Harcourt Brace Jovanovich, Publishers

London • New York • Toronto • Sydney • San Francisco

ACADEMIC PRESS INC. (LONDON) LTD
24/28 Oval Road
London NW1

United States edition published by
ACADEMIC PRESS INC.
111 Fifth Avenue
New York, New York 10003

British Library Cataloguing in Publication Data
Dodgshon, R A
    The origin of British field systems.
    1. Land tenure — Great Britain — History
    2. Agricultural systems — Great Britain —
    History
    I. Title
    333.2   HD594   80-49987

    ISBN 0-12-219260-5

Printed in Great Britain by
John Wright & Sons, Ltd., at the Stonebridge Press, Bristol

For Katherine

Acknowledgements

The author wishes to thank the editor of the *Transactions of the Institute of British Geographers* for permission to reproduce Figs. 2, 7 and 10 from "The Nature and Development of Infield-outfield in Scotland", 59(1973), pp. 1-23: the Chief Editor of the Victoria County Histories for permission to reproduce Fig. 11 from M. D. Lobel (ed.), *A History of the County of Oxford* vol. VI (London, 1959), p. 98 and the Keeper of the Scottish Record Office for permission to reproduce Fig. 14. Grateful acknowledgement is also made for permission to use material from the author's papers on "The Landholding Foundations of the Open Field System" in *Past and Present*, 67(1975), pp. 3-29: "Scandinavian 'Solskifte' and the Sunwise Division of Land in Eastern Scotland", in *Scottish Studies*, 19(1975), pp. 1-14: "The Origin of the Two- and Three-Field System in England", in *Geographia Polonica*, 38(1978), pp. 49-63 and "Changes in Scottish Township Organization During the Medieval and Early Modern Periods" in *Geografiska Annaler*, 58B(1977), pp. 51-65. The author also wishes to thank D. Murison for the transcription of the extract from Craig's *Jus Feudale* cited on p. 33 and B. R. S. Megaw for the reference to an early land division at Haliburton (Berwickshire), also cited on p. 33.

Preface

The aim of this book is to present an interpretation of how British field systems originated. Some of the ideas have already been published in various British and European journals. My intention in repeating them here is to show how they can be integrated into a single, coherent argument. Although these connections have been implied or stated in my papers, it is clear to me that only by bringing them together in book-form can this point be adequately conveyed. I have also taken this opportunity to discuss at length those aspects of the argument which I have previously neglected, so as to make it more comprehensive. Put simply, my approach has been to concentrate on structuring the ideas from which my argument is fashioned, rather than to produce a heavily substantiated text; nor have I bothered too much with establishing the broad geographical sweep of different types of field system or with analysing individual townships in depth. The subject already has sufficient and admirable examples of this sort of case-study. What is now needed — and what this book is uncompromisingly about — is more exploratory discussion of origins; this is not to say that appearances are neglected: far from it. Much of what I have to say has not been gleaned from a careful sifting of the skeletal forms or carcases of early systems in the hope of discovering nascent forms or discerning different stages of growth; rather is it based instead on understanding what lies behind the character and operation *of field systems at the point when we are permitted to view them in detail.* This is not a book, therefore, in which fresh evidence about their early antecedents will be unveiled, but an attempt to shift or alter opinion on how we interpret what is already familiar, a case of playing the part of a physiologist on what we see as living or functioning systems rather than a palæontologist ransacking the archives for extinct fossil forms.

In writing a book about my ideas on field systems, I have become more acutely conscious of how they have altered over the years. From an initial stance of seeing them, rather simplistically, as the systems of husbandry devised and adopted by communities out of choice, I am now more appreciative of *external* influences at work on their choice and the vital importance of tenure. With the latter has naturally come a greater regard for the early pioneer work of scholars like F. W. Maitland and P. Vinogradoff. As someone who began his research on Scotland, it was my reading of their work and the realisation that they had formulated similar thoughts about England, that led me to search for a more general basis for my ideas. From this has flowed a definite pattern in my work, with ideas developed in regard to Scotland being _.ien applied to England, a sequence which I developed in respect of my views on sub-divided fields, infield-outfield, split townships and the two- or three-field system. Equally significant, and apparent throughout the book, is my conviction that field systems were not the consciously-contrived institutions of field layout and husbandry which they have been made out to be; to put this another way, it was not a case of early communities sitting down with the simple question in their minds of how they might best farm their lands, and then devising a system of communal open-field husbandry as the answer. Such a system may have been what early communities had to put up with, but it was not necessarily a direct match for their expectations. A range of formative influences were at work; some had no immediate bearing on the basic tasks of farming, whilst others were matters over which the ordinary husbandman had little real control. What this means is that field systems cannot be treated as free-standing institutions — as mere collections of strips and ploughteams — that can be neatly or surgically lifted out of their context for analysis: they had too many ramifications to be treated in such a tidily discrete way and their nature demands a broader, comprehensive approach that searches beyond the problems of husbandry *per se*. This book is offered as a contribution to this broader debate.

Although it has been written over the winter and spring of 1978/79, it can boast a much longer gestation period. It began with my postgraduate research work on south-east Scotland under Professor Richard Lawton at Liverpool University, 1963-66. Although this work was ostensibly concerned with the agrarian changes wrought by the eighteenth-century Improvers Movement, it was my concern with establishing pre-Improvement conditions that led to an interest in field systems. My interest developed whilst at Reading University, 1966-70. Working in a multi-disciplinary department — in contact with scholars like Eric Jones, Ted Collins and Andrew Jewell — encouraged me to take a methodologically less constrained, more problem-oriented approach to my work. Arguably though, working on the data-scarce conditions of early Scotland also encouraged me to be less hide-bound in my point of view and to see my problems in a more rounded-fashion. It is for this reason that readers may find relatively little historical geography in this book; instead, they will find an attempt to see my kind of history as made up of problems to be solved or explored rather than of particular methods to be applied. Since 1970, I have been on the staff of the Geography Department at the University College of Wales, Aberystwyth, and it is here that all my papers on field systems, as well as this book, have been written. Despite its remoteness in the minds of those who feel themselves at the centre of the academic world, there can be few more satisfying environments in which to live and work than Aberystwyth. I am grateful to all those colleagues who have helped to make it so. Special thanks are due to Donald Williams and Michael Gelly Jones who drew the maps, David Griffiths for all the photographic work and Miss Gaynor Hamer for typing the final text. Put together over the busiest time of the year from a teaching point of view, most of the text has necessarily been written during evenings and weekends. My wife, Katherine, and children, Clare and Lucy, have borne my desk-bound and mentally-absorbed condition patiently. They are, no less than my College, the benefactors of my research work.

R. A. DODGSHON   Aberystwyth, 1979.

Contents

———————————

List of Illustrations

Chapter 1

Field systems: a review of past interpretations

The term field system has a broad, generic meaning. It is applied to early patterns of landholding and husbandry that wove groups of farmers together into communities of mutual or related interests and resources. But if there is one essential qualification to be met before the term can be legitimately used, then it must surely be the intermixture of land between landholders in the form of strips or parcels, an arrangement described throughout this book as sub-divided fields. Other characteristics usually associated with field systems, such as a communally-regulated system of cropping or rights of common grazing over arable after harvest, lose their *raison d'etre* if there were no sub-divided fields to promote agrarian interaction and the need for cooperation. But although, in essence, a question of farm economy, field systems had linkages or connections extending outwards to all aspects of the rural community. Herein lies much of their interest for the historian and the reason why the study of their nature and origin is a long and distinguished one.

Yet despite their impressive lineage as a subject of debate amongst historians, problems still remain. No more striking indication of this can be cited than the fact that the debate over them has not been a progressive one, with each contribution adding to, or refining, a single line of argument. Instead, one has had a plethora of independent viewpoints put forward, each one tending to add uniquely to the debate. Since so little has been resolved to everyone's satisfaction — as ongoing contributions to the debate so clearly demonstrate — an introductory review of the problem faces the daunting task of reiterating a long list of ideas still considered relevant, some of which were first expressed nearly a century ago; nor can the task be made easier by an act of bold categorisation of like interpretations. Field systems have been increasingly portrayed as complex rather than simply-structured institutions, with interpretations likewise taking on a complex form, a form which cuts across any neat, exclusive categorisations. For these reasons, the following review of past work adopts an approach based on the personalities involved, grouping them together where scholars have clearly entered a dialogue over particular issues or views.

The foundations of the field systems debate were first laid down during the late nineteenth century. Without question, the first substantive offering was that by F. Seebohm.[1] Like other scholars of his generation, Seebohm boasted a breadth of knowledge and skills only rarely matched today. Although he relied heavily on the example of Hitchin (Herts) for his representation of what an English field system constituted as regards layout, his discussion of field husbandry, land tenure and origins drew upon a much wider array of data. An important feature of his argument was the way he discounted the organic unity of field systems, or the view that they were somehow born into a state of full maturity. Their parts were seen by him as having separate histories and therefore, requiring separate explanations. Seebohm responded to this need with some well-argued, if now questionable ideas. Looking back, the most durable of these ideas have been those regarding how sub-divided fields evolved; they were, he proposed, the product of co-aration or joint-ploughing. Assuming the use of a heavy mouldboard plough, with teams of up to eight oxen, he envisaged a situation in which individual landholders contributed an ox or plough part to each team, thereby creating the need for a division of ploughed land. Apart from references to church tithes accounting for the produce of every tenth rig, his most explicit support for this idea was taken from the Welsh law codes; these framed clear guidelines over how rigs (Welsh = *erw*) should be allocated, with the persons who subscribed the plough irons, the oxen and looked after the plough timbers, each being given their strips or selions in a strict sequence.[2] Even the use of strips as the unit of allocation is accommodated by Seebohm's scheme, for they were seen as the equivalent of a day's ploughing. Furthermore, the annual renewal of the entire exercise during the early growth of field systems meant that as new land was taken into cultivation, new landholders and plough teams could easily be absorbed to work it. In short, many of the key questions concerning the root cause and adopted-methods of land division within sub-divided field systems were reduced by Seebohm to simple matters of plough technology and technique. Since sub-divided fields were a feature of Celtic areas like Wales as well as Saxon areas, he saw no difficulty in extending back their date of inception to at least the late prehistoric period. Indeed, as an instance of an institution that thrived before the Saxons arrived in England, it formed part of his wider notion that when it came to farms and fields, the Saxons inherited more than they actually devised themselves.[3]

Subsequent writers have dealt more harshly with those aspects of his argument that concerned field husbandry. One particularly flawed aspect was his belief that manorial systems (with their juxtaposition of demesne and villeinage) and the three- (or two-) field system(s) were formatively linked together, so much so, that 'the community in villeinage fitted into the open field as into its shell — a shell which was to long survive the breaking up of the system of serfdom which lived within it.'[4] It was villeinage that conferred the 'peculiar form' (or three-field cropping) on English open fields.[5] Such an exclusive association between the manor, villeinage and the three-field system did not convince subsequent writers. However, we must be careful exactly what we discard. His suggestion that manors and villeinage were present during the earliest stratum of Saxon settlement[6] has a distinctly modern ring about it.[7] But many scholars would be less enthusiastic if such a concept is used as a Trojan horse to instate the three-field system with an equally early appearance on the grounds that the one was contained within the other. Even fewer would accept his assertion that not only did the three-field system pre-date the coming of the Saxons, but that it was a Roman innovation. In his own words, what the Romans added to transform it (the pre-existing sub-divided field system) into the manorial three-field system was probably the three-course rotation of crops, the strengthening of the manorial element on British estates, and the methods of taxation by 'jugation', rather than any radical alteration in the land-divisions or in the system of co-operative ploughing.[8] The logic behind this conclusion was founded on the simple fact that the three-field system was more likely to be found in the Roman rather than non-Roman parts of Germany. The common denominator with those parts of Britain which shared the same field system was the fact that they were at some point Romanised.[9]

At roughly the same time that Seebohm was fashioning his theories on field systems, another distinguished scholar, or Sir Paul Vinogradoff, must have been formulating his. Surprisingly though, few modern writers have acknowledged the contribution made to the debate by Vinogradoff. Admittedly, his treatment of field systems was incidental to his main theme, or the institutional structure of medieval rural society; however, it was still a substantive one and this was especially true of his views on how sub-divided fields developed: they were based on the notion of shareholding. They were, he wrote, "a system primarily intended for the purpose of equalising shares, and it considered every man's rights and property as interwoven with other people's rights and property: it was therefore a system particularly adapted to bring home the superior right of the community as a whole, and the inferior, derivative character of individual rights".[10] Contained in this statement is the very kernel of his argument. It answered what he thought was an essential requirement of any explanation. A sub-divided field system could not be explained away as a convenient means of smoothing over the consequences of joint ploughing, since it was "no lax or indifferent system, but stringent and highly peculiar. And so it cannot but proceed from some pressing necessity".[11] What more "pressing necessity" can be imagined than one which strikes at the very heart of the community's tenurial structure. For Vinogradoff, the hides, carucates and virgates out of which rural vills were fabricated in England connoted shares in the whole vill. Such "shares are not formed at random as indifferent arithmetical parts of the aggregate, but form organic units and stand in organic relation to the composite unity of the tun".[12] Landholders then, held so-much land *of* the *tun* and not just so-much land within it. Nor did it matter whether their shares were unequal in size. They could form a mixture of half-hides, quarter-hides or virgates or even half virgates, but it did "not destroy its fundamental idea — the proportional adjustment of rights and duties, though it be effected not on a uniform but on a graduated scheme".[13] All that was of the essence was that "whatever their arithmetical variations (as units of landholding) they are always equal against each other within the limits of one and the same *tun* at one and the same time!"[14]

Of course, such shares could still logically be laid out as consolidated holdings. For sub-divided fields to have resulted requires some extra piece of logic: this missing logic was seen by Vinogradoff as a question of how shares were interpreted when it came to equating hide with hide, or carucate with carucate. He inclined to construe the problem in practical rather than theoretical terms. Each *tun* "was not like a homogeneous sheet of paper out of which you may cut lots of every desirable shape and size".[15] Rather was each possessed of variety. "Over the irregular squares of this rough chessboard", he wrote, "a more or less entangled network of rights and interests must be extended. There seem to be only two ways of doing it: if you want the holding to lie in one compact patch you will have to make a very complicated reckoning of all the many circumstances which influence husbandry, will have to find some numerical expression for fertility, accessibility, and the like; or else you may simply give every householder a share in every one of the component areas . . . This second method leads necessarily to a scattering and intermixture of strips".[16]

Vinogradoff set these ideas in a framework of land law which arranged the different types of sub-divided field along an evolutionary continuum. At the more primitive or archaic end of this continuum were communal, tribal systems of tenure. To use his own words, "the communalistic origin of property in land has been lately much contested. But in so far as agriculture is historically developed out of pastoral husbandry, there seems to be hardly anything more certain in the domain of archaic law than the theory that the soil was originally owned by groups and not by individuals".[17] In Britain, this stage was thought to be exemplified by the landholding system of the Celts. It not only involved the joint-holding of land by tribal or kindred groups, but also, the temporary rather than permanent occupation of strips by individual members of these groups. "The point in this system", he wrote, "was that the soil was not allotted once for all to particular owners, but remained in the ownership of the tribal community, while its use for agricultural purposes was apportioned according to certain rules to the component households, strips for cultivation being assigned by lot".[18] He went on to argue that in terms of tenure as opposed to mere occupation "individual appropriation is the result of a slow process of development".[19] The Romans had some influence in "furthering private property and private appropriation in land".[20] However, their impact reflected itself in more permanent layouts rather than any change in tenure. Indeed, Vinogradoff was careful not to rush the individualisation of tenure, arguing that "even when the shifting, 'ideal', share in the land of the community had given way to the permanent owner- ship by each member of certain particular scattered strips, this permanent ownership did by no means amount to private property in the Roman or modern sense".[21] Only with the eventual enclosure of the open fields did private property in the modern sense finally establish itself in relation to such land.[22] This slow but always ongoing decay of communalism, both in tenure and behaviour, was prejudicial to Vinogradoff's thoughts on other aspects of the early English village community. What he termed somewhat mystically as the "superior right of the community"[23] was seen as an invisible hand behind the organisation of the village field economy. Fundamental practices like the communal regulation of cropping or common grazing were seen as deriving not just from practical need, but also, from the spirit of communalism that pervaded tenure, a spirit that became more and more diluted or transparent as time went by.

Vinogradoff was much less forthcoming on the question of how the cropping arrangements of early open-field communities developed. Ad- mittedly, he was in little doubt that the temporary cropping of land (which he termed runrig not outfield) was associated with the Celts, since it fitted in with their temporary allocation of use-rights to members of the tribe or kindred. Nor was he in any doubt that the Saxons were associated with the more intensive and stable two- or three-field systems. However, when it comes to dating or explaining the appearance of the two- or three-field system, he tends to gloss over the matter. There are clues that he saw their emergence as a function of the more enlarged, nucleated settlements that were spawned by the Saxon invasion,[24] and the need that stable field layouts created for orderly cropping; but nowhere is he really explicit.

To some extent, Vinogradoff's greater concern over the web of tenurial interest that bound open-field systems together and its contrast with his reluctance to comment in equal depth on how the various forms of regulated cropping developed, mirrored the priorities present in a wider debate. Foremost in this debate were scholars like Sir Henry Maine and G. L. Gomme. Like Vinogradoff, they were interested in devising evolutionary schemes covering the growth of jurisprudence and land law; they sought to do so by looking at the nature of primitive farming communities. Their work intersected the field-systems debate on the thorny issue of how tribal or collective tenures decayed into severalties. The main source of contention centred on their choice of community or example, for they relied heavily on early English and Scottish boroughs or burghs whose burgesses cultivated surrounding waste, such as those of Malmesbury (Wiltshire) and Lauder (Berwickshire). They asserted that such communities depict land tenure at a mid-way stage of development between collective and individual tenure, since land was shared out between burgesses on a temporary, annual basis.[25] Gomme, in particular, provided numerous examples of these communities suspended between one stage and another in the history of tenure, arguing throughout, the formative influence which it had on their agrarian character. Like Vinogradoff, he was convinced of the link between shareholding and sub-divided fields, as well as the origin of the former in tribal or collective systems of tenure.[26] In fact, scholars have continued to assert the tribal or communal roots of sub-divided field tenure down to the present-day, interpreting the diverse forms of the latter as signifying different stages in the pulling apart of these roots.[27]

One notable voice of dissent to such an interpretation was that of F. W. Maitland. To see open fields as engendered by communal tenure was he declared, "a fashionable doctrine", but it confused co-ownership with ownership by *communitates*.[28] This was a criticism directed above all at those arguments buttressed mainly by the evidence for early boroughs. Not only did he see the tenure of cultivated land by their burgesses as decidedly non-communal, but he also considered it to be a relatively recent growth. Lauder (Berwickshire), for instance, only began cultivating its common waste in the sixteenth century, yet it was held up by scholars like Maine as the primitive community *par excellence*.[29] "Here if anywhere the danger of mistaking the new for the old was an ever besetting danger" was his verdict on such communities.[30] But Maitland's interpretation of open fields did have some common ground with that of Vinogradoff *et al*. He accepted their share-holding character, but strongly rejected the idea that this shareholding character could only be explained as an adjunct of communal or tribal tenure. To help prove his point, he published a detailed analysis of Aston and Cote (Oxfordshire). His study concluded that "open field husbandry has shown itself to be not incompatible with a very perfect individualism, a very complete denial that the village has any proprietary rights whatever or even any legal organisation".[31] "Each landholder", he reasoned, "holds his arable land by a separate title, a title that is in no sense communal":[32] a conclusion later written up as a general interpretation.[33] This attempt to demolish the notion of open field communities as a sort of *personna ficta* whose rights were superior to those of the individual by using the example of Aston and Cote, was very much a reply to Vinogradoff's comparable study of nearby Great Tew, also in Oxfordshire. In the latter study, Vinogradoff had tried to depict his ideas in more concrete form, stressing throughout the role of shareholding as a system of equalised rights, measure for measure, and the continuity of such a system from very early times.[34] This dialogue between these two great scholars charged the debate on field systems with considerable meaning, making it an issue central to the history of land law and not just a matter of antiquarian interest.

The next milestone in the debate was marked by the publication of H. L. Gray's book on *English Field Systems* in 1915. There are many ways in which Gray's book altered the debate. Not the least was the sharpness of definition which he brought to all sides of the problem. His more searching and questioning approach is exemplified by his reconstruction of the regional types of field system. Scholars like Seebohm and Vinogradoff had contented themselves with the somewhat crude distinction between Celtic and Saxon areas, Highland and Lowland. In its place, Gray postulated a much more elaborate pattern. Altogether, he identified six different, regional types. The two- or three-field system, which had hitherto been cast in the role of being the archetypal system of all parts of England, was confined by Gray simply to the Midlands. This was not achieved by any sleight of definition, for like other scholars before him, the essential characteristic was seen as the grouping of a township's shots or furlongs into two or three large fields or zones for the purpose of cropping, with the former having a half and the latter, a third, under fallow yearly (see Fig. 1). Rather was its more restricted distribution established by a more critical examination of available sources. Even within the Midlands, but notably along its western fringes, he isolated another type which he called systems with "irregular fields". These consisted of townships whose sub-divided fields had been arranged into more than three cropping zones, or which had been subjected to partial enclosure or had become surrounded and over-shadowed by assarted land that had been laid out directly into several parcels and enclosures. Around the southern and eastern edges of these two Midland types, Gray recognised three others: that of East Anglia possessed three distinguishing characteristics on which he placed great stress. First, holdings or tenements tended to be either compact or more localised in their spread between fields; their balanced distribution between

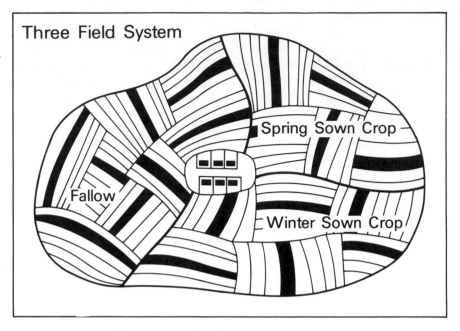

Fig. 1. Layout of a three-field cropping system.

the different cropping zones of the township, such as one had with the two- or three-field systems of the Midlands, was absent. Secondly, cropping itself was more flexible, varying locally or within the different parts of the township; and thirdly, East Anglian townships were generally divided between two or more manors. Each manor usually had specific part of the township set aside as its fold-course, an area over which its lord had exclusive grazing rights for his sheep from February to September. As Gray himself put it, such "particularism, antagonistic as it was to action by the whole township, proved irreconciable with the practice of the two- and three-field system of tillage".[35] He depicted the field systems of Kent as broadly similar in so far as some holdings were sub-divided but were not sprawled systematically through-out the township. Furthermore, cropping lacked any communal regulation; but it acquired distinction from the prevailing shape of fields — or the iuga, dolae or tenementa on which rents and services were assessed — for many were impressed with a regular, rectangular form. Midway between those of the Midlands, East Anglia and Kent, both geographically and typologi-cally, the field systems of the lower Thames Basin shared characteristics of all three, causing Gray to separate them out as another, albeit hybridised type, of field system.

The sixth and most extensively distributed type recognised by him was his Celtic system. As with so many other aspects, his definition of this type was much more all-embracing than any offered before. Its most immediate characteristic was its relatively small scale, with fewer landholders (rarely more than six) and fewer acres (rarely more than 100, or 50 ha), when compared with the large village-based systems of the Midlands. Unlike Seebohm and Vinogradoff, he was not persuaded to see the periodic re-allocation of strips between landholders as the distinguishing mark of sub-divided fields in Celtic areas. The terms generally used of such fields, or runrig and rundale, carried no such meaning as this. In his opinion, "more characteristic of runrig or rundale were the size of the farm or township, its occupation by co-tenants or co-heirs, the manner in which it was tilled, and the distribution of the tenants' acres throughout the arable fields".[36] He took an equally independent line as regarding cropping arrangements. Whereas earlier writers had inclined to stress only the periodic or temporary cropping of outfield, he left his readers in no doubt that there was also an intensive, permanently cropped sector called infield. At one point, he even likens infield to the cropping structures of the Midlands, since it had three breaks or sectors in some townships, but goes on to underline the absence of fallow as a source of real difference[37] (see Fig. 2).

One of the real pleasures of reading Gray is that he shirks none of the more difficult questions on how field systems came to be. One is left with a comprehensive set of answers on how their various parts were brought together. Yet curiously, his views on the central question of how the two- or three-field system originated are hedged with one or two doubts, an uncertainty which makes for a sharp contrast to the conviction with which he argued the origin of other types. His main argument was that the Midland type of field system was "a system of the Saxon homeland"[38] whose presence in England could be ascribed to the "thoroughgoing nature of the fifth-century subjugation".[39] But having classified it as an import, he then admits the possibility — though not with any great enthusiasm — that some examples had an alternative origin. Those he had in mind occurred along the geographical edges of the Midland system and owed their origin to the intensification of pre-existing outfield cropping systems, or runrig systems as he sometimes called them. He implies that this was how it had developed in the Saxon homeland, but felt it may be stretching the point to contrive a situation in which the Midland type was being independently invented under two quite different circumstances. Are we, he questioned, "to assume that the Germans, both in Germany and in England, had a genius for developing runrig into a more regular system?"[40] This equivocal stance seems strange, given his assumption that as outfield was intensified under population pressure, it must have come to resemble the cropping structures of the

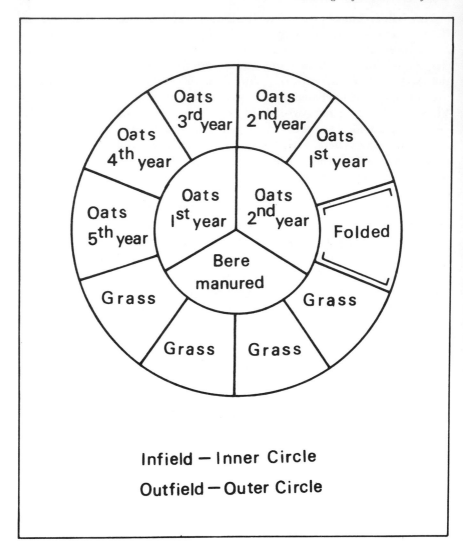

Fig. 2. Layout of an infield-outfield cropping system.

Midland system, so that no special qualities of inventiveness were being invoked.[41] Gray made no secret of the fact that direct, unambiguous evidence of two- or three-field cropping is not available before the twelfth century. Admittedly, sub-divided fields in the Midlands can be taken as far back as ninth and tenth century references to property lying "aecer under aecer" or "scattered here and there intermixedly in the common arable field"[42] or (more questionably so) to the seventh-century references in the Laws of Ine to *gedalland* or sharedland, but not so two- or three-field cropping. This lack of early evidence for the latter masks a problem which Gray seized upon, and that is, did both the two- and three-field variants of the Midland system exist from the very beginnings of Saxon settlement in England. He concluded that only the two-field variant did, and that the "three-field system may have been altogether a derived one, arising from an improvement in agricultural method".[43] He dated the "improvement" to the late thirteenth and early fourteenth centuries.

Gray's stress on the Midland type as largely an imported system that was later modified from a two- to a three-field pattern means that he omits to comment on the mechanics by which the Saxons first arrived at a system of landholding based on the sub-division of property and fields. This lacuna in his argument stands out all the more because he was at pains to explain the sub-division of fields in Celtic areas, East Anglia and Kent as caused by the progressive sub-division of property between co-heirs, but having introduced this quite novel idea, he failed to declare whether it had any relevance to the formation of Saxon sub-divided fields as well. One can only infer from other comments he made that for these, he favoured the standard cause of joint ploughing.

Gray's reliance on a cultural interpretation of the Midland type recurs in his interpretation of other types. The lack of communally-regulated cropping systems in both Kent and East Anglia meant that the weight of interpretation had to fall on their respective landholding arrangements, though in neither case were sub-divided fields widely developed as a form of field layout. In Kent, such sub-divided fields as existed were seen by Gray as produced by the operation of gavelkind — or the division of property between co-heirs — acting on holdings formed out of the "iugum, the unit of villein tenure, which, compact and rectangular in shape, had its exact counterpart nowhere else in England".[44] The origin of the iugum, he suggested, was Roman. The "Germans who occupied Kent seem to have adopted Roman arrangements and to have maintained a closer agrarian tie with Roman Britain than persisted elsewhere in the island".[45] The origin of gavelkind proved more intractable for Gray. He was not even sure whether it could be taken back beyond the Norman Conquest.[46] But he was clear in his mind that it was a force working for sub-division within the confines of each holding not within whole townships, and that this was why its impact was localised and partial.[47] He envisaged basic conditions in East Anglia to have been similar, with a *tenementum* unit that was first conceived during Roman times. However, its subsequent history diverged from the iugum of Kent. What impelled this divergence were the new social conditions introduced by the Danish settlement, which led to a higher preponderance of free landholders and a more complex manorial structure; and also froze the fragmentation of the *tenementum*. It was the combination of these factors which, for Gray, shaped the character of East Anglian field patterns, with their limited spread of sub-divided fields, lack of a truly regular cropping pattern and, most important of all, its fold-course system.[48]

Scholars working before Gray had used the field-systems of Celtic areas as a sort of primitive gene-pool from which all other forms devolved. Gray himself shared this attitude but added his own refinements. His overall verdict comes over clearest in respect of cropping arrangements. What others before him had merely implied, he made explicit, namely, that outfield was the first cropping sector to emerge. Unlike Seebohm *et al.*, he was prepared to follow this through to its inevitable conclusion by seeing infield as a later addition, an "innovation in Scotland, probably not much antedating the seventeenth century".[49] However, he also talked of there being "another escape" from "the limitations of outfield tillage", meaning its development into a two-field system.[50] As already intimated, he considered the sub-divided fields of Celtic areas, or runrig, to have been produced by the partition of property between co-heirs. Thinking specifically of Irish sub-divided fields, he drew attention to the ability of partible inheritance to produce complex patterns of intermixture within a few generations. He was also aware that it distinguished itself from joint ploughing as a cause, in so far as it achieved its effect accidentally rather than by choice or deliberation. In a statement that begs all sorts of extra questions, he declared that if "the explanation of the origin of runrig given above be correct, such subdivision was rather an accident. Farms, townships, townlands, which are found divided in the eighteenth century may well have been undivided a few generations earlier . . . . Regarding Celtic countries, then, no sweeping statement can be made as to the precise aspect of the townships at any particular time. Some of them may have been entirely in the hands of one or two tenants, with no runrig manifest; others may have been much subdivided".[51] However, as if undecided about the role which he had attached to chance, he conceded that "co-operative ploughing must . . . have been a custom complementary to the subdivision of holdings among heirs".[52] Despite the lack of a specific chronology to Gray's interpretation of runrig, he admitted its relevance to the earliest stages of sub-divided field formation. There was even the possibility that "all English field systems arose on the basis of runrig".[53] His reasoning on this point, though, commits the common error of confusing the terms runrig and outfield. To treat the terms as interchangeable, as Gray most certainly does, is to imply that the temporary cropping of one was reflected in the temporary layout or occupation of the other. Indeed, he struggles hard to avoid contradicting his own conclusion that periodic re-allocation was never an *essential* characteristic of runrig, regressing to the point of seeing or assuming that annual re-allocation was once its original condition.[54]

The next contribution of any note was published in 1935 when T. A. M. Bishop stepped aside from previous lines of argument and put forward a novel but well-supported argument on how sub-divided fields originated through assarting.[55] Using Yorkshire evidence, he demonstrated how land assarted over the twelfth and thirteenth centuries soon became incorporated into the open fields. The conditions of the region were, of course, special. Much of Yorkshire had been amongst the areas devastated by William the Conqueror. There was much to be *re*-colonised, let alone pioneered. It was the subsequent re-stocking and filling out of the landscape that afforded Bishop with such a valuable opportunity for researching the link between assarting and the open fields. The charter evidence which he uncovered left him in no doubt that "assarting, carried on by groups of cultivators, often seems to be a communal activity tending to the enlargement of the common fields".[56] He based this conclusion on the fact that land described as assart land in one charter appeared in later charters as incorporated into the open fields. Although such evidence documented only a single phase of growth, he felt confident enough to expand his argument into a more general thesis embracing whole sub-divided field systems, arguing that " the open field system of the typical Yorkshire vill has not the appearance of having simply survived from some period when it was created by a large group of settlers; it seems, on the contrary, to be the result of successive accretions of freshly cleared land, and to have expanded with the expanding numbers of the village community".[57]

But his argument did not end there. His inspection of twelfth- and thirteenth-century charters disclosed that some assarts began life as parcels held in severalty; only at a later date were they absorbed into the open fields. He derived the same conclusion from the way some open-field furlongs incorporated personal names, such as Osmundflat or Edricflat in North Cowton. In some cases, it was possible to be more specific. Thus, he cited the instance of Baldersby, where tenants "cultivated certain strips in *Gikelflat*, Gikel held land in Baldersby in the middle of the twelfth century, and was no doubt responsible for bringing into cultivation this part of the fields".[58] The widespread use of personal names in the toponymy of furlongs suggested to him that it must have been common for assarting to result initially in several parcels that were cultivated by individuals rather than the community. To then argue "that such tracts were divided up by being shared among heirs of the original assarters is no more, of course, than to connect the growth of communal agriculture with the natural increase of the community".[59]

Gray's attempt to see so much of the problem as a matter of culture was given equally scant support by the Orwins whose book entitled *The Open Fields*, published in 1938, formed the next significant offering to the debate, though there was implied support for the ideas of Bishop on the role of piecemeal colonisation. The Orwins brought a practical touch to their handling of many issues, invoking economic or technical need where others had subsumed them under the heading of cultural heritage. In their view, terms like Saxon and Celtic may serve as labels, "but the implication that they date or locate the systems to which they have been applied is hardly warranted".[60] Instead, they believed the "principles which actuated these early cultivators in the organisation of their townships and farms were economic and technical, and they were everywhere observed, in all the farming districts of England".[61] Vaguely formulated notions of cultural background or stage receded before the unmistakeable needs and necessities of the ordinary husbandman.

In regard to sub-divided fields, the Orwins endorsed Seebohm's thesis that they reflected the practice of co-aration, but were inclined to distribute the emphasis within this interpretation somewhat differently. Thus, they attached more importance to the fact that the ploughs involved were of the *fixed* mouldboard type than the fact that they were pulled by two or more oxen. The use of a fixed mouldboard plough raised problems whose best solution lay in the strip or "land" as the unit of ploughing. Such a plough was drawn across each field on either side of each "land" throwing the soil inwards, thus forming the characteristics ridge or rig of the open fields, but avoiding the disorder that would be caused if such a plough was drawn back and forth along *adjacent* furrows throwing the soil in contrary directions all the time. The Orwins were also of the opinion that far from being a consequence of sub-divided fields, communally-regulated patterns of husbandry were, in part, a determinant of them. In their own words, they were "dictated by the common life of the community and by the manifestation of it in its daily work upon the land".[62] Lastly, like Bishop, they saw the progressive colonisation of new land by a community as a major contributory factor in the formation of sub-divided fields.[63] Whereas Seebohm depicted co-aration as a system capable of absorbing new land, new ploughs and new landholders without disruption, the Orwins went further and thought it was important in helping to fragment holdings that much more. It was, though, not a primary but a contributory cause in their view.[64]

The Orwins' attempt to explain the various cropping patterns associated with open-field systems had a very simple logic behind it. Like others before them, they took as the starting point the shifting cultivation of arable land as represented by Scottish outfields. For them, as for others, what made this seem credible was its consistency with the landholding system of runrig, a system conventionally defined as one in which landholders occupied their strips on a temporary, shifting basis, as they would under a scheme of outfield cultivation; the two seemed mutually supportive, the one helping to sustain the other. Indeed, the Orwins treat runrig and outfield as if they were merely different terms for the same system. Together, they suggested a primary system of landholding and cropping, a system from which other forms must have devolved. The crux of the Orwins' argument was in the way it explained the supposed evolution of this primary system to the two-field system. All it needed was a phase of population growth. The shifting system of outfield was thereby intensified until a point was reached at which half the land was under crop and the other half under fallow. If these two sectors were rotated on a yearly basis, then clearly, a two-field system had emerged.[65] But whilst applauding this as an ingenious idea, it was not original. Gray talked of outfield systems in Northumberland being intensified until, when a third was under crop, they resembled a three-field system.[66] The Orwins' contribution to this idea was to take a possible line of development in a particular locality and to give it a more substantive and central role in explaining the origin of the two- and three-field system generally. Of course, this comparison with Gray's treatment of the same idea conveniently highlights the main difficulty with it. Given that the three-field system is usually seen as an improvement from a two-field system, and given that Gray was appealing to the same logic as the Orwins, it follows that the latter's version would have us believe that outfield systems must have passed through a three-field phase of sorts on their way to becoming two-field systems, before then being *re*-improved back to a three-field system. In short, the very fact that the arguments of both Gray and the Orwins appear persuasive makes it less likely that either is right, for it would mean that a form of three-field system could have preceded a two-field one. The Orwins overlook this difficulty, as they do the problem of infield.

Reviews of the literature on the open fields usually move from the Orwins to the sudden renewal of interest in the problem by historians that began in the 1950s and has gained more and more momentum. However, this leap does some injustice to the work of G. C. Homans, the American sociologist. In his *English Villagers of the Thirteenth Century*[67], the extended discussion of field systems did not really offer any new interpretations of basic issues, but nevertheless, it undoubtedly had a certain freshness to it. This freshness sprang from the way he tried to stretch the problem out, asking questions about matters that had previously been glossed over. As regards the formation of sub-divided fields, he favoured an explanation rooted in shareholding rather than one based on co-aration. He did not neglect the latter. Indeed, his book affords one of the more weighty discussions of common ploughing, but when it came to its adoption as a form of husbandry, it was "a matter of indifference whether a villager had his land in a single parcel or in scattered strips".[68] In marked contrast to the evidence he was able to marshal for joint ploughing, he could offer little empirical support for shareholding as the vital determinant of sub-divided fields. "There are no words", he wrote, "which have come down to us in which an English villager of the Middle Ages expressed his sentiment that the strips of holdings ought to be distributed in this way".[69] Despite this lack of support, a deficiency which Vinogradoff had failed to solve, Homans pressed home his point that such villagers sought "an

equality of opportunity", to "share proportionately in the areas of the village
in which good and bad soils were found — not to speak of the matters of
exposure and drainage — and such sharing would necessarily mean that every
holding would consist of a number of parcels scattered over the fields".[70] He
recognised that in itself, this was not a complete explanation: it was based on
a premise. "The premise itself has yet to be explained".[71] He seemed unaware
of — or perhaps he did not agree with — Vinogradoff's attempt to explain it
through a form of tribal tenure.

His discussion had little to add on the question of how infield-outfield or
two-field farming systems came to be, but he had much of interest to say on
how the latter evolved into a three-field system, a transformation which he
tagged as "the direction of progress".[72] Nor was it a case of mere supposition.
He cited examples of two-field townships being re-organized into three-field
ones, such as with Marton in Dishforth (N. Riding).[73] Another means of
transformation from one to the other was by the straightforward addition of
an extra field by colonisation. In fact, he devoted much space to the process
of assarting, being especially concerned with how each bovater or virgater
could share in such expansion, with new land being apportioned according to
one's possession of land already in the township[74], though he hesitated from
joining with Bishop in seeing it as a prime cause of sub-division. In his
discussion, it remained merely a means by which cropping patterns could be
elaborated into larger, more complex forms.

An original contribution of Homans' discussion was the evidence he
published on how open fields may have been laid out as regards landholding.
If such fields possessed regularity, then it follows that some scheme may have
been employed to create this order. In fact, unlike Bishop, Homans believed
that all villages were initially laid out in an orderly fashion, replete with their
two-field systems, and that their differences by the thirteenth century
reflected the extent to which they had moved away from such neat, prescribed
layouts. Obviously, an allocation of strips in strict sequence as they were
ploughed was one method by which such layouts could have been devised, but
it is one that Homans ruled out. References to land or strips being measured
out, using a rod or rope, seemed contrary to it.[75] He thought that clues as to
the procedure adopted were provided by charters which referred to land lying
versus solem or *versus umbram* (against the sun or the shade). Drawing a
direct comparison with the practice of Scandinavian *solskifte*, he saw such
references as manifesting the use of a sun-division to set out each person's
holding in the open fields. By such a method, a person given his land towards
the sun had his strips in the east or south of each furlong, whilst a person with
his land towards the shade, had his strips in the west or north. Confronted
with similar references, other scholars, such as R. H. Hilton[76], were sceptical.
However, the use of a sun-division as a method of land division in England

was eventually settled by the Swedish geographer, S. Göransson. Bringing his familiarity with the Swedish *solskifte* to bear on English evidence, he effectively removed any remaining ambiguity over the latter. The use of a sun-division (and through it, the creation of orderly sub-divided field layouts) has to be accepted as a factor in the history of some, if not all, English villages.[77]

The rapid expansion of historical research over the 1950s and 60s inevitably brought with it further debate on field systems. Notable were the many fine regional studies, such as those of the north of England by R. A. Butlin[78] and A. Harris[79], or of Kent by A. R. H. Baker[80]. Much was gained from such work. The existence of cropping patterns like the two- or three-field system was extended away from the Midlands, to which Gray had tried to confine it, into areas like Northumberland; whilst the character of field systems in areas like Kent were given a much firmer definition. But such work did more than just refine our grasp of the geography of open fields; it also added to our knowledge of the processes involved in their formation. The work of Baker on Gillingham manor, for instance, provided us with a detailed and resourceful case-study of how partible inheritance and colonisation combined over the later medieval period to fragment and interject landholding.[81] At the same time, there was an increasing awareness that the ideal types identified by scholars like Gray were not as dominant as first thought. Indeed, the exceptions raised all sorts of new questions about how field systems developed. Typical in respect was Hilton's study of townships in the Feckenham Forest area of Worcestershire: these comprised compact nuclei of sub-divided fields surrounded by a generous fringe of small enclosures held in severalty even as early as the sixteenth century.[82] Clearly, such townships boasted a different history from the large two- or three-field systems that lay around them.

Predictably, this growing volume of local and regional studies generated new syntheses. That published by J. Thirsk in 1964 represented a major revision of received opinion on the subject.[83] Her paper began by systematizing the problem into four essential elements or sub-divided fields, rights of common grazing over arable (with their consequential controls over sowing and harvesting), common waste and disciplinary assemblies through which the entire system could be regulated, a task usually performed by the manorial court. The crux of her argument is that such systems could not have been born into a state of full maturity, possessed of all four elements. Rather it is more likely that common fields (as she prefers to call them throughout her paper) evolved, acquiring their different characteristics at different stages. Once this is accepted, then it follows that each characteristic must have a separate history and needs a separate explanation. We have to proceed from the one to the other, just as townships or villages must have done when piecing them together into fully-fledged common field systems.

Her interpretation of sub-divided fields relied on both the piecemeal colonisation of land and partible inheritance. The former acted as a general cause of fragmentation and intermixture in the sense that "as new land was taken into cultivation from the waste . . . the parcels of each cultivator became more and more scattered".[84] Partible inheritance, meanwhile, acted as an elaborative process that was capable of dividing such parcels up into intermixed strips.[85] To some extent, this was a similar argument to that advanced by Bishop, except that Bishop failed to stress that colonisation alone was capable of producing a fragmented pattern of landholding, thereby creating a framework within which partible inheritance could work to much greater effect in sub-dividing property further.

As cultivators became drawn more and more together by the progressive intermingling of their land, a point was reached when cooperation had to he forged and regulations introduced to make the most efficient use of resources. In short, village cooperation and regulations arose not from any innate social instinct that was always present, but from practical expediency or as the need arose. For Thirsk, a central issue in this new and growing dimension to the village economy was the rather mundane but critical practice of stubble grazing over the arable lands after harvest. As pasture resources became depleted with the expansion of the village, Thirsk envisaged a situation in which the grazing of harvest stubble could no longer be overlooked as it had hitherto been. "When once parceners and neighbours cooperated in cultivating their fields, *and* also recognized the need to graze the stubble, we may assume that in some places, at least, common grazing would suggest itself naturally".[86] However, there were consequences to having a system of common grazing over arable. To control grazing, one needed to also control cropping. Cultivators had to plough, sow and harvest in unison, otherwise the system would not function effectively; hence to adopt common grazing over the harvest stubble meant the adoption of controls over cropping as a concomitant. Such cropping controls, though, were unlikely to have involved totally new schemes. For Thirsk, it is quite likely that some individuals were already cropping their scattered parcels or strips with one or two years of grain, then fallow, before the translation of such a scheme to the fields of the village at large. Only at this point then, would the two- or three-field system have emerged as the prescribed cropping routine for such English villages. Of course, once this took place, it would have been imperative for cultivators to arrange their holdings between the two or three cropping sectors so as to always have land in crop. Somewhat cautiously, she avoided invoking a grand act of re-organisation as the only way this re-distribution of holdings could be achieved. Some villages may have worked their way towards such a layout by localized adjustments and agreements between neighbours.

Addressing herself to the contentious question of when rights of common grazing and two- or three-field cropping patterns were first instituted, Thirsk argued that concern over pasture and the general need for a more efficient use of resources probably arose during the rapid growth of population that occurred in England during the twelfth and thirteenth centuries. Needless to add, this was far later than anyone had previously imagined, but it was consistent with the chronology being established on the continent by German scholars for similar sorts of field systems: such comparisons played an important part in her argument. Of course, she fully acknowledged that sub-divided fields and less significant forms of cooperation had deeper roots. What was being maintained was that *fully-fledged* field systems — replete with rights of common grazing and communally prescribed systems of cropping — were late in appearance.

It hardly needs stating that there was more to the common fields than the two- or three-field system, though these were the basic theme of her paper. Setting them in their wider context, she asserted that their differences with other field systems, like infield-outfield, were in no way "fundamental" or culturally contrived. "The two systems coincide with, and arose out of, the distinction between arable and pasture farming types. The two- and three-field system characterized arable, that is mixed farming districts. Villages with more or fewer common fields were mainly pasture-farming communities".[87] In brief, their differences of field organization reflected resource availability and maturity of development, with pasture districts feeling the need for more efficient forms of resource use less acutely and more tardily than arable districts. But in essence, they were systems to be arranged along the same line of development or continuum rather than historically discrete systems born out of separate cultures.

Predictably, such a bold and exciting re-interpretation called forth replies, of which that by J. Z. Titow formed the most critical.[88] Broadly speaking, he considered her argument weakened through its insufficiency of documentary support, though this is a charge that could be levelled at all other interpretations. At the same time, he questioned its reliance on continental analogies in formulating the character and chronology of common field development. In a memorable phrase, he declaimed that whilst many an English battle had been fought on European soil, there was no need to fight this one. Others might beg to differ. The two- or three-field system was a European and not just a national or English institution. To establish the consistency or compatibility of an interpretation between the different parts of Europe where it prevailed will surely help in sorting out the valid from the invalid. The most specific criticisms were those directed at Thirsk's use of basic processes, like partible inheritance and holding re-organisation. Titow legitimately maintained that evidence or partible inheritance was most lacking in precisely those areas (such as the Midlands) where it was most required. Holding re-organisation, meanwhile, appeared to him as an unnecessary process to introduce. Could not order have been present from the very beginning, from the pioneering layout of townships? Further comment on Thirsk's ideas was published by Homans. As a sociologist, he found them too narrowly construed: they reduced the problem to an interplay of economic and environmental variables. His own work had suggested that (as Gray would have us believe) cultural variables discharged a bigger role than she allowed.[89] Nor was their influence felt solely in respect of field systems, but permeated the entire economic character of early rural communities. Given Thirsk's paper, and the re-statement of its main theme in her essay on the farming regions of England[90], he responded with a direct reply. He insisted that open or common fields were mediated through cultural filters in a way that was prejudicial to their character.[91] Such filters, Homans argued, were most easily detected in a comparison between areas like Kent or East Anglia and the Midlands.[92] But over and above such disagreement on the role of culture, he re-stated the belief that "communal systems of agriculture were very old institutions among the Germans, and that they could well have been brought to England by the Germanic invaders".[93]

On the credit side, Thirsk's argument has drawn support from scholars like H. S. A. Fox.[94] It had, Fox maintained, a logical impressiveness to it, relative to competing interpretations. He could not offer any substantially new evidence in support, but felt that there was every prospect of such evidence being found. What was important was that her paper directed attention to where, when, and in what form such evidence might be found. Prospectively, he saw it as an interpretation that was susceptible to proof, given more work on sources like manorial rolls, particularly in areas like the Welsh Borders or the west country, where the shift into organised cropping schemes like the two- or three-field system may have occurred late enough to be well-documented. More recently, he has re-emphasized his support, citing not only documented examples of such cropping changes, but tentatively suggesting that the resource problems experienced by such townships and inducing such changes might be linked with the longterm break-up of multiples estates and the inevitable narrowing of opportunities that this must have involved.[95]

Yet another major synthesis to capitalise on the growing wealth of local and regional studies, was that edited by A. R. H. Baker and R. A. Butlin.[96] This was a large, comprehensive volume that contributed to our understanding in two ways. First, it provided a series of regional perspectives covering most parts of the British Isles, the south-west being the only major omission; these brought Gray's geography of field systems up-to-date. In addition, they conveyed the structural and areal variety of field systems in a way that Gray's rather cramped and formal definitions of ideal types could not. Stated simply, distinctions were now recognized between regular sub-divided field systems and irregular ones; between those that involved only partial fragmentation as opposed to those displaying more comprehensive forms of fragmentation, and between those that juxtaposed open areas or strips with enclosed areas or parcels that were held in severalty. There also seemed to be a much greater variety of cropping pattern than earlier discussions had admitted, with some townships in parts of the Midlands having more than two- or three-cropping sectors. Such manifest variety raised many problems, not least over terminology. As Baker had pointed out in an earlier paper[97], it was now evidently clear that not all field systems could be described as open or common, in the sense of having no enclosed areas within them. Generic terms like "common fields" or "open fields", therefore, needed to be used more cautiously than in earlier discussions. Baker and Butlin's considered use of more neutral terms like "field system" or "sub-divided fields" has much to commend it.

The second type of contribution which Baker and Butlin's edited volume made to the debate was through the various interpretations which it contained. It hardly needs stating that the variety of local and regional condition revealed by the different essays must ultimately enhance our ability to understand how field systems developed, if only because they define the problem to be explained in more exact terms. Reviewing the evidence on how sub-divided fields came to be, they endorsed the efficacy of both piecemeal colonization and partible inheritance as causes. The validity of each had been demonstrated in relation to specific settlements. What is more, such a double-pronged interpretation had more power to explain how sub-divided fields could be formed in dis-similar sorts of area, such as Kent and the Midlands, two areas often contrasted in terms of their socio-economic character during the medieval period.[98] On the broad distinction between regular and irregular sub-divided field systems, they favour the view that it was a case of order replacing disorder, rather than vice versa. Although they accept that the two types could have been points on a continuum, with irregular systems slowly being re-worked into regular ones via mechanisms such as the partition of a family holding, they also concluded that the two types may have been separated by a more fundamental change, with irregular systems being cast overnight into a more planned form.[99] As regards cropping, they joined those who would have infield-outfield and the two- or three-field system placed on a evolutionary scale, the one preceding the other, technically and chronologically. Infield-outfield was proposed as "a primitive form of agrarian organisation" which "on *a priori* grounds and on the basis of surviving evidence" may have been "at some time practised throughout the British Isles".[100] However, in what they call the vales and plains of Lowland Britain, it was later replaced by more intensive systems like the two- or three-field system. In a direct reference to Boserup's idea that population growth induced agricultural improvement, they saw this shift into more intensive field systems as a function of population growth; they were more hesitant over when it took place. Confining their view to the historic period, they talked of the shift starting to occur "soon" in Lowland areas of "relatively high population pressure" but conceded that even here, "elements of the earlier system often survived into the Middle Ages".[101] The overall impression then, is that the two- or three-field system had started to replace infield-outfield during the *early* medieval period. It must be kept in mind that Baker and Butlin do not claim to speak for all contributors in reaching these tentative conclusions. Indeed, they freely acknowledge that when it comes to origins, "conjectures here outweigh conclusions"[102], and they were clearly aware that some of their contributors follow a different line of reasoning. This problem of reconciling viewpoints is well shown by what G. Whittington had to say on the infield-outfield systems of Scotland. Again speaking in terms of possibilities rather than probabilities, Whittington suggested that outfield may have preceded infield because it was the more primitive. The system expanded by creating an intensive cropping sector within it, or infield. The expansion of population over the twelfth and thirteenth centuries was seen as providing a possible incentive for this intensification.[103] Thus, as Thirsk would have us believe with the two- or three-field system, Whittington envisaged the possible emergence of fully-fledged infield-outfield systems only during the high population pressure and high farming era of the twelfth and thirteenth centuries. Baker and Butlin did not respond to this suggestion in their own discussion. Apart from cautioning readers over seeing infield-outfield as a "one-field" system, they pass no comment on which came first, infield or outfield. All they speculate about is how infield must have expanded until it precipitated the kind of resource crisis which they see as engendering a re-organisation into the more efficient two- or three-field system.[104]

The most recent chapter in the historiography of field systems has been written out for us by D. McCloskey: he approached the problem initially through an interest in enclosure. Trying to answer the problem of why open fields (or what others would prefer to call simply sub-divided fields) persisted in some areas but not others, he was forced to confront the issue of what advantages accrued to an open field community from having its fields or holdings laid out in the fashion of sub-divided fields. Reduced to essentials, his conclusion was that it represented an example of risk aversion, or an insurance against crop failure.[105] Ideas that sub-divided fields conferred a share of the good and bad land, or wet and dry, on landholders, have always been part of the debate over their origins. Both the shareholding and the partible inheritance interpretations appealed implicitly to such notions. In this sense, McCloskey's argument differed only in emphasis, not in kind.

To distinguish his interpretation from them becomes a matter of careful wording. Whereas others saw the attempt to assign different types of land to each holding as a function of the equality that was built-in to a share tenure or the division of land between co-heirs, he imputed a more practical purpose to it, or that of risk aversion.

This rather fine distinction between McCloskey's idea and previous interpretations is important when considering the way he tried to test its applicability. There can be no doubt that his detailed statistical analysis established that sub-divided fields could serve as an insurance against risk, but it is a different matter to assert that this was also cause and not just effect, or that it was a genuine case of behaviour against risk. We can only be assured of the latter if it is read from cause and not just effect, but his data does not allow him to do this. There is abundant evidence of McCloskey thinking his way back from pattern to process, but much less for peasants thinking along the same lines but in the reverse direction; and this is critical, because the uniqueness or distinction of his argument lies not in explaining the significance of the pattern — for other interpretations could have produced a pattern with a similar spread of risk — but in revealing the intent behind such a pattern. In his paper, this aspect is treated largely by assumption, particularly when one considers the need to distinguish it from other closely-related causes like shareholding.

As a recent contribution, McCloskey's argument is only just starting to attract replies. However, it is of interest that the two subsequent contributions which have devoted space to it both have reservations about whether it really stands alone. R. C. Hoffman, for example, saw risk aversion as part of the general or wider search for subsistence reliability by rural communities as growth exerted pressure on their resources, a cause of sub-divided fields which in no way contradicted his own stress on piecemeal colonisation and partible inheritance.[106] In another, more direct reply S. Fenoaltea likened it to shareholding, arguing that had "medieval agriculture really been so organized as to sacrifice productivity merely to stabilize individual shares in aggregate income, it would have been a monument of inefficiency — just as if aggregate output had been pointlessly sacrificed in order, say, to maintain equality".[107] He himself offered an explanation for sub-divided fields that was based on the transaction costs of purchasing or exchanging labour, because when "these are taken into account, diversification is seen to increase output by increasing the scope for useful self-employment and for economically small and stable teams of hired hands, and the open fields can be justified by the simple desire to maximise agricultural productivity".[108] Right or wrong, Fenoaltea provides the ideal foil to McCloskey in that he defines a contrary view that strikes at the heart of the problem, dealing — like McCloskey's argument — with the way peasants perceived the problem. Together, they demonstrate to any would-be discussant that ultimately the problem must be set in the context of why, and not just how, peasant communities came to adopt sub-divided fields as a form of holding layout.

The foregoing review of past work on field systems has tried to show that despite a long and distinguished historiography, there is still no agreement on any major aspect of their origins. To review the mass of questions and answers that make up their history, it is necessary to recapitulate a fairly extensive catalogue of opinion that stretches back to the pioneer contributions of Seebohm and Vinogradoff. Nor has the recent flurry of research shown any signs of overcoming this apparent impasse; a comparison between the ideas of Baker and Butlin with those of McCloskey or Fenoaltea emphasizes this continuing lack of concensus.

The present writer offers no excuse for adding still further to this abundance of viewpoint over the next five chapters: what will be argued is that a new formulation of the problem is needed. The basis of this re-formulation is straightforward: there has always been a tradition of looking to Celtic areas of Britain and Ireland for types of field system that added a revealing perspective to the problem. For some, they disclosed primitive forms against which English systems could be seen as more intensive and developed sequels. For others, they possessed predominantly pastoral systems of farming which, when contrasted with the arable systems of lowland Britain, afforded an explanation for their different types of field system. It will be argued here that ideas like these have taken too much for granted about the field systems of the north and west: this has led to false and misleading analogies being drawn with lowland Britain. What the closer analysis of field systems in areas like Scotland provides is simply a clearer definition of those factors which helped to give field systems their structure. Applied to lowland Britain, this re-definition of what was relevant yields fruitful results. It is my contention that the principal reason why past discussion has failed to advance the debate on origins significantly stems from its inadequate definition of the structural character of field systems rather than the more practical restraints of inadequate data.

Overall, it will be argued that far from being consciously-designed institutions — a constructive response to some innate need and desire for a communal system of farming — field systems were more makeshift in character and origin. The idea of a community of farmers sitting down and devising a field system that directly mapped their expectations of holding layout and husbandry has to be rejected. In its place, we need to see field systems as an amalgamation of responses to a number of influences, not all of which bore directly or exclusively on the question of field layout. Some were *extraneous* factors that cut across the decision-making path of farmers, deflecting their behaviour one way or another; but herein lies the value of field systems as an object of study. In reviewing their origins, we are forced to consider far more than the humble problem of field layout. Strands of argument have to be followed that run outwards into the wider history of rural communities. In addition, it will be suggested that the list of factors shaping the character of field systems was the same across the country, in lowland no less than highland areas. What produced the regional varieties of form was the way in which they were blended together or weighted in each regional situation. The notion of regional types, therefore, that were possessed of substantive differences, will be challenged. Field systems everywhere were structured in response to the same basic problems. When sorting out regional differences, it is the variety of response, not the variety of influences, that we need to focus upon.

References

[1] F. Seebohm, *The English Village Community*, London, 1st edition (1890).

[2] *Ibid.*, 4th edition, pp. 120-2.

[3] *Ibid.*, pp. 179-80 and 437-8.

[4] *Ibid.*, p. 78.

[5] *Ibid.*, pp. 409-10.

[6] *Ibid.*, p. 423.

[7] See T. H. Aston, "The Origins of the Manor in Britain", *Trans. of the Royal Historical Soc.*, 5th series, 8 (1958), pp. 7-8.

[8] Seebohm, *op. cit.* p. 411.

[9] *Ibid.*, p. 410.

[10] P. Vinogradoff, *Villainage in England*, Oxford (1892), p. 236.

[11] *Ibid.*, p. 400.

[12] P. Vinogradoff, *The Growth of the Manor*, London (1905), p. 150.

[13] *Ibid.*, p. 151.

[14] *Ibid.*, p. 152.

[15] Vinogradoff, *Villainage in England*, p. 235.

[16] *Ibid.*, pp. 236-7.

[17] Vinogradoff, *The Growth of the Manor*, p. 18 .

[18] *Ibid.*, pp. 18-9.

[19] *Ibid.*, p. 18.

[20] *Ibid.*, pp. 52-3.

[21] Vinogradoff, *Villainage in England*, p. 237.

[22] P. Vinogradoff, *Outline of Historical Jurisprudence*, Oxford (1920), vol. 1, p. 340.

[23] Vinogradoff, *Villainage in England*, p. 230.

[24] *Ibid.*, p. 162.

[25] H. S. Maine, *Village Communities in the East and West*, London, 4th edition (1881), pp. 65-99; G. L. Gomme, *The Village Community*, London (1890), pp. 191 and 201.

[26] *Ibid.*, p. 256.

[27] See for example, J. H. Romanes, "The Land System of the Scottish Burgh", *Juridical*

Review, 47(1935), pp. 103-19; F. D'Olivier Farran, "Run-rig and the English Open Fields", *Juridical Review*, 71(1959), pp. 134-49.

[28] F. W. Maitland, "The Survival of Archaic Communities", pp. 313-65 in H. A. L. Fisher (ed.), *The Collected Papers of Frederick William Maitland*, London (1911), vol. 11, p. 313.

[29] F. W. Maitland, *Township and Borough*, Cambridge (1898), p. 200.

[30] Maitland, "The Survival of Archaic Communities", p. 315.

[31] *Ibid.*, p. 316.

[32] *Ibid.*, p. 346.

[33] Sir Frederick Pollock and F. W. Maitland, *The History of English Law*, Cambridge (1968), 2nd edition, vol. 1, pp. 626-30. Further relevant discussion can also be found in F. W. Maitland, *Domesday Book and Beyond*, London (1960), Fontana edition, pp. 404-5.

[34] P. Vinogradoff, "An Illustration of the Continuity of the Openfield System", pp. 139-48 in *The Collected Papers of Paul Vinogradoff*, Oxford (1928), vol. 1.

[35] H. L. Gray, *English Field Systems*, Cambridge, Mass. (1915), pp. 324-5.

[36] *Ibid.*, p. 171.

[37] *Ibid.*, p. 162.

[38] *Ibid.*, p. 415.

[39] *Ibid.*, p. 418.

[40] *Ibid.*, p. 415.

[41] *Ibid.*, pp. 224-5 and 415.

[42] *Ibid.*, pp. 57-8 and 60.

[43] *Ibid.*, pp. 79-80.

[44] *Ibid.*, p. 415.

[45] *Ibid.*, pp. 415-6.

[46] *Ibid.*, p. 304.

[47] *Ibid.*, p. 296.

[48] *Ibid.*, pp. 349-54.

[49] *Ibid.*, p. 200.

[50] *Ibid.*, p. 201.

[51] *Ibid.*, p. 202.

[52] *Ibid.*, p. 199.

[53] *Ibid.*, p. 415.

[54] *Ibid.*, p. 198.

[55] T. A. M. Bishop, "Assarting and the Growth of the Open Fields", *Economic History Rev.*, VI(1935-6), pp. 26-40.

[56] *Ibid.*, p. 30-1.

[57] *Ibid.*, pp. 31-2.

[58] *Ibid.*, p. 35.

[59] *Ibid.*, p. 35.

[60] C. S. and C. S. Orwin, *The Open Fields*, Oxford (1938), pp. 23-4.

[61] *Ibid.*, p. 27.

[62] *Ibid.*, p. 39.

[63] *Ibid.*, p. 42.

[64] *Ibid.*, p. 42.

[65] *Ibid.*, pp. 38-9.

[66] Gray, *op. cit.*, p, 413.

[67] Cambridge, Mass., 1941.

[68] *Ibid.*, p. 81.

[69]*Ibid.*, p. 90.

[70]*Ibid.*, pp. 90-1.

[71]*Ibid.*, p. 91.

[72]*Ibid.*, p. 57.

[73]*Ibid.*, p. 57.

[74]*Ibid.*, pp. 83-5.

[75]*Ibid.*, pp. 69-70.

[76]R. H. Hilton, "Kibworth Harcourt", in W. G. Hoskins (ed.), *Studies in Leicestershire Agrarian History*, Leicester (1949), pp. 30-1.

[77]S. Göransson, "Regular Open-Field Pattern in England and Scandinavian Solskifte", *Geografiska Annaler*, XLIIIB (1961), pp. 80-101.

[78]R. A. Butlin, "Northumberland Field Systems", *Agricultural History Rev.*, XII (1964), pp. 99-120.

[79]A. Harris, *The Open Fields of East Yorkshire*, published in the East Yorks. Local History Series, IX (1959).

[80]A. R. H. Baker, "Field Systems in the Vale of Holmesdale", *Agricultural History Rev.*, XIV(1966), pp. 1-24; A. R. H. Baker, "Field Patterns in Seventeenth Century Kent", *Geography*, 50(1965), pp. 18-30.

[81] A. R. H. Baker, "Open Fields and Partible Inheritance on a Kent Manor", *Economic History Rev.*, 2nd ser., XVII(1964-5), pp. 1-22.

[82] R. H. Hilton, "Old Enclosure in the West Midlands: a Hypothesis about their Late Medieval Development", *Géographie et Histoire Annales de l'Est*, XXI(1959), pp. 272-83.

[83] J. Thirsk, "The Common Fields", *Past and Present*, 29(1964), pp. 3-29.

[84] *Ibid.*, p. 9.

[85] *Ibid.*, pp. 12-12.

[86] *Ibid.*, p. 16.

[87] *Ibid.*, p. 23.

[88] J. Z. Titow, "Medieval England and the Open-Field System", *Past and Present*, XXXII(1965), pp. 86-102.

[89] G. C. Homans, "The Rural Sociology of Medieval England", *Past and Present*, 4(1953), pp. 32-43.

[90]J. Thirsk, "The Farming Regions of England", in J. Thirsk (ed.), *The Agrarian History of England and Wales, vol. IV, 1500-1640*, Cambridge (1967), pp. 1-112.

[91]G. C. Homans, "The Explanation of English Regional Differences", *Past and Present*, 42(1969), pp. 18-34.

[92]*Ibid.*, p. 28.

[93]*Ibid.*, p. 33.

[94] H. S. A. Fox, "The Origins of the Two- and Three-Field System in England: Past Conjectures and Future Research", *Geographia Polonica*, 38(1978), pp. 109-18.

[95] H. S. A. Fox, "Origins of the two and three field system", in T. Rowley (ed.), *The Origins of Open Field Agriculture*, forthcoming, 1980.

[96] A. R. H. Baker and R. A. Butlin (eds.), *Studies of Field Systems in the British Isles*, Cambridge (1973).

[97] A. R. H. Baker, "Some Terminological Problems in Studies of British Field Systems", *Agricultural History Rev.*, 17(1969), pp. 136-40.

[98] A. R. H. Baker, and R. A. Butlin, "Conclusion: Problems and Perspectives", in Baker and Butlin (eds.), *op. cit.*, pp. 635-53.

[99] *Ibid.*, pp. 652-3.

[100] *Ibid.*, p. 656.

[101] *Ibid.*, p. 656.

[102] *Ibid.*, p. 655.

[103] G. Whittington, "Field Systems of Scotland" in Baker and Butlin (eds.), *op. cit.*, p. 573.

[104] *Ibid.*, p. 656.

[105] D. N. McCloskey, "English Open Fields as Behaviour Towards Risk", in P. Uselding (ed.), *Research in Economic History* vol. 1, Greenwich, Connecticut (1976), pp. 124-70.

[106] R. C. Hoffman, "Medieval Origins of the Common Fields", in W. N. Parker and E. L. Jones (eds.), *European Peasants and Their Markets*, Princeton (1975), p. 55.

[107] S. Fenoaltea, "Risk, Transaction Costs, and the Organization of Medieval Agriculture", *Explorations in Economic History*, 13(1976), p. 134.

[108] *Ibid.*, p. 149.

Chapter 2

The origin of sub-divided fields

The origin of sub-divided fields forms the logical starting point for any analysis. Not only were they the most distinctive attribute of field systems, but they were also the most fundamental. Other characteristics, such as rights of stubble grazing or the communal regulation of cropping, were consequential to them, though admittedly, they were not an automatic or immediate consequence. However, even this understates the significance of sub-divided fields, for contained within the problem of their origin is possibly a more seminal question about how the farming communities of old Europe emerged. As a network of intermixed property rights and communal patterns of behaviour, sub-divided fields embodied the very essence of the rural community as a social, economic and territorial unit. To ask how they developed must impinge on how the rural community itself developed. Of course, there are those who feel that the rural community provided the social context, the ethos of communalism out of which sub-divided fields were distilled. The one begat the other, and there was no confusing who was parent and who was child. But somewhat heretically, there are a few scholars who feel that the link between the two was quite the reverse with the growth of sub-divided fields fostering the emergence of rural communities as localized groups of common interests and action. Thus, on the simple question of how sub-divided fields developed may turn a still more fundamental one of how the rural community originated.

Sadly, having enobled the question, our answers are still rather mundane affairs, fraught with difficulties over data and definition. The following attempt to answer it is divided up into two sections. The first takes a critical overview of the different interpretations of sub-divided fields. Its purpose will be to demonstrate that the prime reason why no single interpretation has been agreed upon is because more than one appears valid. This naturally alters the problem. So long as we sought only to instate a single interpretation as more valid than others, then the discussion tended to conclude itself once the superior claims of that interpretation had been established. However, to offer a mix of interpretations — not from uncertainty but from the conviction that this is necessary — introduces new problems. In particular, it raises problems over how the interpretations that comprise this mix fitted together in the landscape, or how were they compatible. The second section takes up this theme of compatibility. It has a vital place in the discussion for to acknowledge the relevance of more than one invites dismissal as a facile way of over-coming the uncompromising disagreements which the discussion to date has engendered. It would make much more sense to interpret such an intricate and demanding form of field layout as developing from only one cause. As a reply, it will be argued that such a criticism loses its force when the different interpretations established as valid are considered in relation to each other. For what appear outwardly as separate interpretations can, on closer inspection, be linked together to form a *single compound interpretation*. Not only does this single compound interpretation explain the different forms of sub-divided field, but it also accommodates the variety of viewpoint with which their history has been surrounded.

Interpretations of sub-divided fields: a critical assessment

(a) Joint ploughing + fixed mouldboard plough = sub-divided fields
Despite its longstanding popularity, the practice of co-aration is the least convincing interpretation; its acceptance has always been founded on a misunderstanding. Put simply, the abundant evidence for co-aration occurring in association with sub-divided fields was taken as proof that the two were functionally linked. After all, there was a natural logic in assuming that the intertwined and shared relationships implicit in a system of cooperative ploughing was an appropriate context for the intertwined and shared relationships of a sub-divided field system. Reassuringly, the evidence for co-aration seemed as widespread as that for sub-divided fields. The manorial court rolls and extents of medieval England, such as those surveyed by Homans[1] and W. O. Ault[2], afford ample illustration of the harmonies and disharmonies of joint ploughing, but no more or less than barony court records or estate surveys for an area like Scotland. References to tenants being grouped into ploughs[3] or falling out of ageement over joint ploughing[4] can be found for Scotland to match those cited for England.

But to establish that joint ploughing was associated with sub-divided fields is not to establish that the two were in some way functionally related. To validate such a connection requires a more explicit analysis than has hitherto been accorded it. Generally speaking, those who have argued for such a connection have tended to simplify the whole business of land division, with vital stages in the process being conveniently glossed over. Considered hypothetically, three distinct problems can be identified. First, there is the cause or need for a division. Secondly, there are the principles which guided the division, or the reasons why a system of sub-divided fields rather than one of consolidated holdings was adopted. Thirdly, there was the more practical problem of laying out strips or holdings and allocating them to landholders. No interpretation of sub-divided fields can be regarded as effective or adequate if it does not address itself to the second of these problems, or the guiding principles behind the laying out of property. This is the critical gap to be bridged when linking cause to effect. Yet past discussions of joint ploughing have over-looked precisely this aspect. The extract from the Welsh Law Codes which Seebohm cited as conclusive proof of how joint ploughing led to sub-divided fields[5] only conclusively demonstrates that joint ploughing was as used as a method of allocating strips or holdings. It does not demonstrate conclusively that it was also the reason why such a division was necessary or why sub-divided rather than consolidated holdings were acceptable as an outcome. Subsequent work has not remedied this serious deficiency in the argument.

Just how serious it is can be gauged from situations in which the process of land division can be broken down into its different problems. An instructive example is provided by H. E. Hallam's work on reclamation in the Lincolnshire Fenland during the late medieval period. Altogether, he distinguished three levels of division. The first consisted of the division of new land between hundreds. The second of its division between villages. And the third, its division between lords and peasants. As regards its division between hundreds and villages, he was able to establish that it was accomplished by "twelve law-worthy men" using a "rod and cord". He goes on to suggest that this may also have been the method used to divide land within villages between lords and peasants for new land was often called *offaldfal*. The meaning of *offaldfal* was *terra mensurata* or "land measured out carefully with a rod and minutely surveyed".[6] But having laid bare the means by which new land was eventually apportioned between holdings, Hallam then overlays his evidence with the assumption that, initially, the apportionment was bound up with the act of ploughing such land, as Seebohm and the Orwins had suggested. The "twelve law-worthy men", it seems, merely followed in the footsteps of the joint plough-team, measuring and approving what the latter doled out to each landholder.[7] Yet since the case for joint ploughing as a cause of sub-divided fields in any situation remains unproven or inconclusive, this extra assumption only shifts his discussion from the secure to the insecure. Arguably, the value of his evidence on this aspect is that by showing "twelve law-worthy men" at work with a rod and cord, it makes any appeal to the role of joint-ploughing superfluous.

In fact, had Hallam looked at this problem elsewhere, he would have discovered many examples of landholding being laid out by small groups of "law-worthy men" using a rod and cord, without the aid of the common plough-team. Very fine examples are provided by the sixteenth- and seventeenth-century re-organization of Northumberland townships into smaller units, but units that were still cast in the form of sub-divided fields. Their re-creation as sub-divided field units allows the whole process to be viewed in some detail. In each case, it was the art of the surveyor not the ploughman that determined layout.[8] Equally explicit examples are available for townships north of the Border. Thus, at Caniglerich in Aberdeenshire, the four tenants who occupied the toun in 1636 and whose shares were laid out in the form of runrig were bound to "labour and manur thair pairts of the towne and lands of Caniglerich that was sighted, cawled, and laid by to them be the barlamen, and the oversight of the bailzie".[9] In Orkney, a division at Nierhouse in 1606 commenced with the words that "Malcome Yisbuster, bailye of Harray, with the XII chosin men abouvretin, according to the Shereiffis commissione, and conforme to ane former dicrete, was to pas to the ground with lyne and mett, to gif everie man hawand entres his just part of the landis of Nearhous".[10]

The evidence for property being measured out by law-worthy men and the like is only part of the problem. Once holdings or shares had been laid out — or even as they were being laid out — they had to be allocated to land-holders. This particular aspect of the problem spawned a whole family of procedures. The ease with which such procedures can be documented contrasts markedly with the extreme difficulty of finding instances of joint ploughing being used to the same effect. Two types of procedure can be recognized: the one assigning each landholder an order in each sequence of strip allocation and the other, laying out and identifying complete holdings which were then doled out. In the case of the former, a person's order in any sequence of allocation could be determined in a number of ways. The Welsh Law Codes detail one method by linking a person's order to the nature of his contribution to the common plough-team. Sun-division was another. In addition to the evidence published by Göransson for England, there is considerable documentation for its use to lay out sub-divided fields in Scotland. Quite apart from references to Scottish tenants having the sunny or shadow portion of a toun[11], there are valuable commentaries on the practice in early law texts. Sir Thomas Craig's *Jus Feudale* (first printed in 1655) talked of a widow's terce (her share of her deceased husband's estate) as representing a sunny or shadow third. The terms sunny or shadow, he explained, determined whether they "should begin from the east, which is called the sun side, or from the west, in thus designating this third or terce; and as the lot turns out, they will begin from the sunny part, that is with the rising sun, or from the shady part and the setting sun, and will number off the rigs, the first and second to the owner and the third to the widow".[12] A clearer definition of a sun-division in Britain will not be found. Its relevance to the laying out of sub-divided fields comes over from countless examples of its use in Scottish fermtouns, such as when land was divided between Melrose abbey and the lord of Haliburton at Haliburton (Berwickshire) in 1428, with one having the sunny portion and the other, the shadow.[13]

One of the problems with a sun-division is that it had limitations when faced with divisions that involved more than a few landholders. In Scotland, it is possible to find references to tenants or landholders who held holdings defined in terms like the sunny half of the shadow plough of a toun[14], but the limitations of such an approach are obvious. In England, where townships commonly had numerous landholders, these limitations were soon confronted. As Homans tried to show diagrammatically, when used in such townships, a sun-division could not locate strips exactly but only with regard to the sunny or shadow portions of each furlong.[15] In circumstances like this, landholders may have preferred alternative forms of holding designation. One used in Scotland was simply to give each landholder a numerical order, so that he held, say, the third or fifth rig throughout a particular toun.[16] Such a method can be aligned with a sun-division because it was one that often intruded into the way holdings or shares were designated when being conveyed or leased. Where it did not, then the landholders themselves had to decide in what order they were to receive their strips, and this was done by means of a lottery.

In those townships where land division involved the laying out of entire holdings or shares before their allocation took place, the use of a lottery to bring landholder and land together was virtually essential. It may say a great deal about the importance of this approach to the history of landholding that the tokens used to identify such holdings or shares had the same character as those used during the vital act of seisin which punctuated the exchange or transfer of property, namely, stones, earth, turf, sticks, and batons. Since both occurred at the same critical point in the transfer of land, or at the point when property could be truly possessed, the one could well have derived from the other,[17] but quite apart from this possible association with the ceremony of seisin, the importance of lotting to the allocation of land is beyond question. Its significance to the problem in hand is that it performs the very role which joint ploughing would have done. In doing so, it confirms that the latter was not prejudicial either to the cause or even the laying out of sub-divided fields. H. P. R. Finberg documented its relevance to landholding as early as the eleventh century, when two hides at Aston Somerville (Gloucestershire) were described as "sorte communes populari".[18] Later, it can be found being used to dole out assarted land, such as at East Maften (Northumberland) in the fifteenth century[19] or at Cowpen (Northumberland) in the sixteenth century.[20] It was also used to apportion entire holdings between landholders. Detailed sixteenth-century examples are available for the lands of the Cathedral Church of Durham, where tenants were said to have their "leases in lottery".[21] The Scottish evidence for lotting is particularly rich. It was used to divide land between proprietors, such as at Manerstoun and Westbyris (Peebles-shire) in 1438[22], or between tenants, such as on the Grange of Balbroggy (Angus) in 1468[23] or the toun of Bellnollo (Perthshire) in 1765.[24]

The purpose of the foregoing discussion has been the negative one of showing that joint ploughing cannot be instated as a convincing explanation for sub-divided fields. Its weakness is that it lacks explicit support in the form of well-documented case-studies that expose its formative influence at work. Nor can it be maintained that in default of this sort of evidence, its more persuasive logic can be used to uphold its case in comparison with alternative interpretations. Ample evidence exists for the laying out of sub-divided fields by means other than as part of the ploughing process, so that there is really no need to indulge in acts of faith on this matter. Until it can be placed on a firmer empirical basis, joint ploughing must be discounted as a credible cause.

(b) Shareholding

Despite Vinogradoff's elaborate formulation of shareholding as a cause of sub-divided fields, his line of argument has been neglected. Possibly the main reason for this neglect lay in his failure to demonstrate anything more than a rather vague and loose relationship between shareholding and the land tenure of English sub-divided field communities. In a sense, he chose to demonstrate his case in the wrong context; had he looked more to Celtic areas of Britain and to Ireland, he would have found it measurably easier to invest his argument with a substantive framework of support.

In fact, recent work on Scottish rentals and land charters for the period prior to 1750 has shown that the holding of townships in explicitly-stated shares (i.e. a half, quarter, or third) was commonplace.[25] In the case of rentals, tenants were either carefully assigned an aliquot portion of the township, a share of its rent or both. Where available, tacks for such townships confirm that tenants were each responsible for the management and rent of an aliquot portion, not a holding that was specifically fixed and defined on the ground. Equally unambiguous evidence for shareholding occurs at the proprietary level, with numerous instances available of townships shared between two or more heritors, each of whom had their holding described as a proportion of the whole, with no more exact specification given. Intermixed with these examples of explicitly-defined shares are other townships in which tenants held land in terms of so-many land units (i.e. oxgates, merklands or husbandlands) out of the total in the township. However, the essential point is that these two forms of share designation were merely two faces of the same basic tenure. The townships which appear in rental after rental as divided into quarters, thirds and the like, all had assessments in land units. The aliquot portions into which they were divided out between landholders, therefore, also had meaning as so-many land units. Indeed, on occasion, rentals, tacks and land charters go on to define the aliquot portions which they set or conveyed as comprising so-many land units out of the total in the township, the one being simply a form of the other.

The value of this early Scottish evidence lies not just in its documentation of how tenants and heritors could hold their land through a system of aliquot shares, but equally, in its elaboration of what those shares meant, tenurially. In theory, shares had no *exact* definition until they were laid out as holdings on the ground. Farmers could not begin farming until they had performed this vital task of reifying their shares, a task which involved closing the gap between their rights of tenure on the one hand and their actual pattern of landholding on the other. That this problem was a very real one for the Scottish peasant is amply revealed in a variety of sources. For instance, tacks and land charters sometimes highlight the open-endedness of shareholding as regards its layout on the ground by offering landholders a choice between having their shares divided into sub-divided fields (that is, runrig), or having them as consolidated holdings.[26] In other cases, the initial uncertainty implicit in a share tenure is starkly revealed by the way both tacks and charters of conveyance often describe the layout of a share as a matter to be decided by a lottery.[27] Of course, the evidence for the widespread use of formal methods of land division like sun-division is further proof of the gap that existed between tenure and landholding, since such methods were designed to close this gap in a systematic and orderly fashion. Nor did shares lose their distinction or meaning once they were laid out. If any landholders felt the prevailing division of shares was inequitable in any way, he was entitled to call for a re-division. Habakkuk-Bisset's *Rolment of Courtis* ruled that "if any portioner of landis, of twa thrie or ma partis fyndis theme greved and trubled, anent there landis, he guha thinkis him self interest or hurte in the occupation labouring or manuring of his pairt", then he had right to apply for a re-division.[28] Landholders were expected to keep "ane equalitie in the divisioun, for if the landis be unequitablie divyded, and any of the parties portioneris be hurte be the divisioun thereof the samin is of nane awaill".[29]

Local court records show that this right to a re-division was acted upon, such as at Petfurane (Fife) in 1437;[30] but it must not be concluded from this evidence that Scottish runrig townships were in a constant state of flux. In the Lowlands especially, it was a common practice for newly-leased shares to be linked to their previous occupant. In other words, no division was necessary; the existing layout of shares being allowed to stand.

The gap which existed between tenure and landholding under a shareholding system had a further consequence. It meant that because of its open-endedness, the laying-out of shares was a matter for interpretation. Some tacks and land charters lessen the doubt over the criteria being employed by describing shares as "just and equal", such as the tack of 1756 for the "just and equal third part of the whole Town and lands of Achlay" in Perthshire[31] or the charter for "the just and equal half of the lands of Over Auchintiber" in Ayrshire.[32] Of still greater interest are those sources which document the interpretation of shares more fully. For instance, a division at Corshill (Ayrshire) in 1685 required the birlawmen men of the toun 'to even and daill' its landholding shares.[33] A division of land at Buay in Shetland was required to lay out two merklands "als mekill in quantitie and qualitie" with other merklands.[34] An examination of runrig division proceedings available for townships in south-east Scotland that were shared between different heritors yielded similar evidence, with townships reportedly divided into runrig (or sub-divided fields) so as to equalise each share measure *in both extent and value*.[35] This stress on shares or land units being equal in both extent and value, is exactly the reasoning by which Vinogradoff linked shareholding to sub-divided fields.

A strong case for shareholding can also be constructed for other parts of Celtic Britain, as well as for Ireland. In Wales, later sources conceal the problem, with most lists of landholding, at either the proprietary or tenurial levels, dealing in tenements of a specified acreage by the seventeenth century, though some still assigned holdings of a land unit assessment.[36] However, earlier sources leave little doubt that many Welsh holdings had their origin in a shareholding system. Reviewing the very fine extents that exist for the thirteenth and fourteenth centuries, T. P. Ellis emphasized how land held by kin groups on the basis of *gwely* tenure was held by the different members of each *gwely* or *lecti* on a shareholding basis. In his own words, "the separation of interests in clan-land was expressed in fractional shares and not by metes and bounds".[37] In fact, he cites numerous examples of *gwely* land divided into aliquot portions amongst kinsmen.[38] The Welsh Law Codes shed light on what guided the allocation of rights within each *gwely*. Putting aside the question of how often *gwely* land could be divided and re-divided amongst kinsmen during the formative phases in the emergence of a new *gwely*, what matters for the present discussion is that the final partition, the so-called *gorffyn ran*, was meant to equalize shares between those who had a right of interest in it.[39] Interspersed with townships held by *gwely* land tenure, there existed townships and even parts of townships that were held by *tir cyfrif* or reckoned-land tenure. Unlike the former, townships held by reckoned-land tenure were shared out between the adult, male members of the community not between family groups, that is, on a *per capita* basis not *per stirpes*. As soon as each male came of age, he was entitled to a share of land. It was not a case of waiting to inherit from one's father, as under *gwely* land tenure. The Book of Iowerth stipulated that shares under reckoned-land tenure should be "as good as to each other".[40] Ellis talked of a person asserting his right in such a township by an action for equality or *hawl cyhyd*. However, at least one fragment of the Law Codes declared that "there was to be no joint possession in any place, except in a register treve; and, in such a treve, every one is to have as much as another, yet not of equal value".[41] This careful phrasing so as to avoid an equality of value, if not extent, is interesting given the substance of Vinogradoff's argument. On the face it suggests that caution may be needed when asking whether such a township, usually known as *tref gyfrif*, was invariably laid out as a sub-divided field system.

The Irish evidence is especially fruitful as regards shareholding. Survey after survey contains references to landholders possessing the aliquot part of a township. When combined with the widespread organization of townships or *ballybetaghs* into quarterlands, it produced a complex mesh of proportional property rights. For instance, the Civil Survey drawn up between 1654-56 for the County of Limerick listed proprietors holding "the 4th pte of 3d pte of one quarter of land" and "the 4th pte and the 8th pte of one quarter" of Cullinagh in the parish of Towgh.[42] Elsewhere, landholders shared ploughlands, as in the case of the proprietor who held "the third pte of halfe a plowland" in the parish of Ballynamonybegg.[43] Often shareholdings were spread across a number of different townships or quarterlands. A good illustration of this is provided by an Indenture of 1585 for the Barony of Moycullen in Ireconnaught, divided into two parts: *gnomore* and *gnobeg*. The former comprised 52 *townes* made up of 138 quarters, one "Moytie whereof is said to belong to Morogh O flahirties sept, and the other Moytie to Roryoge O flahirties sept", whilst the latter totalled a 138 quarters of which one half belonged to Gillduff O flahertie.[44]

As the foregoing examples show, shareholding was present in both Gaelic and Norman areas of Ireland, despite the fact that in other aspects of their tenure, these two areas were radically different. In a highly pertinent discussion of the former, K. Nicholls cited the example of two brothers of the O'Byrnes who held a 112th part of 26 townships scattered over part of Co. Wicklow.[45] He maintained that where kin or clan groups held land jointly, as with the O'Byrnes, the shares into which such land was divided between kinsmen remained notional shares of the total, rather than holdings actually laid out as described on the ground. In other words, the 112th share of these two brothers would not necessarily exist as a separately-demarcated holding in each of the 26 townships through which it was supposedly extended, but may well have been set down in a single location. To add weight to his point, Nicholls went on to argue that in many Gaelic areas, such shares were re-partitioned periodically between kinsmen so that holdings were unlikely to have been fixed or meaningful for any length of time. Thus, as late as the seventeenth century, the lands of the O'Kellys of Kyleawoga in Connaught were re-allocated annually at each May-day between the different kinsmen of the sept.[46] What mattered, what endured, it seems, was the notional share which each kinsmen had in the total pool of land held by the sept. However, we must keep in mind the analogy that can be drawn with the *gwelyau* of Wales. In the case of the latter, it has been argued that it was precisely because the shares into which each *gwely* was divided were represented by actual holdings, holdings that became more and more fragmented between townships as well as within them, that the joint tenure of the *gwely* eventually crumbled by the thirteenth and fourteenth centuries.[47] The same may have been true of similar tenures in Ireland. However, it cannot be assumed that townships shared between different proprietors or kinsmen were invariably laid out as sub-divided field systems. In some cases, shares appear to have been held as consolidated holdings. For example, a 1630 quitclaim to "the fourth part of the half quarter of Moegowna Knowen by the distinct name of Oullugort" in the Barony of Inchiquin hardly suggests that such a share was intermixed with other shares.[48] However, even where proprietary shares in a township or quarterland were disposed as consolidated holdings, the tenants sharing such holdings could still have reduced them to sub-divided fields. There is certainly no lack of rentals showing that tenants, as well as proprietors, could hold land on a shareholding basis.[49] Moreover, there are clues that shares were meant to be equally divided[50] and statements by early commentators which suggested that rundale, the term used in Ireland for sub-divided fields, was designed to maximise equality between holdings.[51] A circumstantial case for the potency of shareholding as a cause of sub-divided fields, therefore, could well be constructed using Irish data.

The case for English sub-divided field systems being connected with shareholding has already been reviewed by the writer in a paper published in 1975.[52] What follows is an attempt to summarize that argument. Without question, the most unambiguous evidence is that available for the north-east. It has long been appreciated that townships in Northumberland were formerly divided into *ancient farms* whose meaning differed significantly from the modern idea of a farm. In the words of one local observer, "in all the townships of all those parishes (in Northumberland) the word *farm* had been used to denote an aliquot part of an entire township, and that each township consisted of a recognized number of those ancient reported farms".[53] Thus, when we read of townships like North Middleton (Hartburn parish) or West Whelpington (West Whelpington parish) comprising 14 and 19 *ancient farms* respectively, it means simply that they comprised 14 and 19 equal share units. To complicate matters, landholders did not necessarily hold discrete *farms* but shares like 4/8ths or 15 5/8ths of a *farm*.[54] F. W. L. Dendy, who considered the problem back in 1894, was quick to perceive the difficulty of "how an equalization could have existed in spite of all the differences in the value of the soil in any one township".[55] An answer is provided by a group of well-documented township re-organizations which occurred over the sixteenth and seventeenth centuries. The purpose behind the re-organizations was to create smaller, more manageable townships, and their relevance to the present discussion stems from the fact their new layouts were cast in the form of sub-divided fields, just as they were before re-organization. In one or two cases, the logic behind such a layout surfaces in the discussion over re-organization. Thus, at Cowpen, holdings were laid out "so that some have not all the best ground and the other the worst, but that each have justice and right, having good consideration to the quantitie and also the qualitie of the partes so allotted, and wheare differences shalbe in goodness to be supplied in the advantage of measure of the worser".[56]

The value of the Northumberland evidence is that it links cause to effect in an unequivocal way. Elsewhere in England, the case for shareholding rests more on inference; the evidence is of two types. First, there are those documents which make reference to landholders having the aliquot portion of a piece of land; the circumstances vary. In some cases, it represents a fraction of a land unit like a carucate or oxgang, such as the three landholders who shared a moiety or half of 1½ carucates and an oxgang at Over Kellet in Lonsdale during the fourteenth century[57] or the tenants who held fourth shares of an oxgang in Thornton in Amounderness, again during the mid-fourteenth century.[58] Others held fractions of a township, such as the early thirteenth century landholder who possessed a "third part of the vill of Claughton" in Cumberland[59] or his contemporary who possessed the "fifth of a third of Grefholm and Driterum", likewise in Cumberland.[60] In a similar category were landholders who shared a manor in fractional shares. Examples of this sort are fairly easy to find, such as the twelfth-century landholders who held thirds or fourth-part shares of manors in Oxfordshire.[61] Blocks of waste could be partitioned on a fractional basis, as when the former vaccary of Saltonstall in Sowerbyshire was divided up into holdings during the early fourteenth century. A gloss on the division refers to the "division of the whole into sex equall partes, & everye parte was called a sextondole of Saltonstall".[62]

The second type of evidence concerns the interpretation of land unit assessments. As noted earlier (see pp. 34-5), there are sound reasons for believing that Scottish land units (such as ploughgates, oxgates and merklands) were aliquot portions of a township expressed in a different form but with no difference in meaning. Strictly speaking, both forms constituted shares in the whole, not holdings anchored to specific plots of land. Can this same assumption be extended to the use and meaning of land units in the context of the English medieval village? There can be no direct or conclusive answer to this question. However, a clearer grasp of the intrinsic nature of English land units may be approached through their changing specificity over the medieval period. Viewed during the late medieval period, many land units appear far from open-ended as measures or statements of landholding, being tied down by detailed lists of abuttals and furlong locations to very particular layouts. Seen solely through the terriers which afford such information, their possible origin in a shareholding system seems hardly worth a second thought. However, they were not always couched in such a detailed or restrictive form. Drawing on his work on the charters of the Danelaw, F. Stenton concluded that the earliest example of a charter which specified the selions or furlong location of a bovate, dated from c. 1200. It would be difficult, he wrote, to find earlier mention of "the component parts of an open field bovate . . . precision of this sort is rare . . . the earlier the charter the more concise will be its notes of identification".[63] Two tenth-century Anglo-Saxon charters examined by F. Seebohm for Kingston in Berkshire, cast the problem in a still more revealing light. Although they relate to different holdings, both had appended to them the same set of boundaries, boundaries that were those of the entire township.[64] Usually, this broad perceptible change in the specification of land units has been regarded as reflecting changes in the methods of the land surveyor and without tenurial significance; there is, however, a different way of interpreting it. It is the kind of evolution that can be expected of a shareholding system that slowly decayed, with holdings undergoing a change from shares in the total resources of the township to being bundles of scattered strips anchored to particular layouts. Such a change would have flowed naturally from any long-term stability in holding layout, a stability consistent with the kinds of tenures (i.e. copyhold) to be found in medieval England. By comparison, the shareholding basis of tenures in countries like Scotland or Ireland was constantly renewed by the periodic or occasional reallocation of property within townships. Whether such reallocation was linked to the joint tenure of land by kinsmen or, as the present writer has argued as regards Scotland[65], it is linked to the changes of occupancy inevitable under a system of short-term, non-hereditary tenures, it still meant that the relationship between an individual and his actual holding was being continually broken and re-forged. Under the circumstances, it is hardly surprising that landholders used terms like runrig and rundale to express the idea of their shares being converted into known property. In England, the replacement of shareholding by a particularist attitude towards holdings would not have fostered the *widespread* use of terms with this sort of meaning, though the Anglo-Saxon term *gedalland* (literally shared land) surely recommends itself as an early possibility.

(c) Sub-divided fields and partible inheritance

Our understanding of the extent to which partible inheritance was practised in medieval Britain and Ireland has been greatly revised since Gray's pioneer attempt to confine its role in the formation of sub-divided fields solely to Celtic areas. Admittedly, its prevalence as a custom in both Ireland and Wales remains beyond question.[66] However, the case for its widespread occurrence in medieval Scotland has still to be made out. By the time documentation became available, only the udal tenures of the Northern Isles permitted co-heirs to divide property between them as of right.[67] If Gray over-estimated its importance in Scotland, he made quite the opposite mistake as regards England. In recent years, its practice in England has attracted much attention, owing to a growing acknowledgement of its critical influence on the general history of landholding and on the family development cycle of peasant communities.[68] What has emerged clearly from this work is that its operation cannot be confined to discrete areas like Kent and East Anglia as Gray maintained, but was more widespread. In particular, the old-established generalization that property in areas of freemen or sokemen was partible whilst that in areas of villeinage was impartible, has lost its simplicity. Such a clear-cut dichotomy may still be applicable locally, as Hallam has shown for Lincolnshire[69], but it needs too much qualification when extended to the country at large. C. Howell especially, has stressed the importance of seeing its practice in relation not just to the problem of whether communities were free or otherwise, but equally in relation to the availability of land for additional colonization and in relation to the wider context of property, moveable as well as unmoveable.[70]

The ability of partible inheritance to fragment landholding has been noted in most of the aeas where it was practised. Thus, in Ireland, modern work has affirmed Gray's judgement of its potentially dramatic effects on the integrity of holdings.[71] Nor are examples lacking for Wales. The sixteenth-century observation made in regard to part of Radnorshire that "until the Statute of 27 Hen. VII the customary tenure of the l'p Lordship was such that in three or four descents a small tenement of 30 or 40 a. might be divided into thirty or forty parts, which greatly impoverished the inhabitants"[72] could quite easily be applied to many other parts of Wales. Roughly contemporary comments lament the excessive sub-division of property in the Northern Isles of Scotland, due again to partible inheritance. One relates that land is "equallie divyded among the children, be ane inquest founded upon a warrand of the superior, and now be oft divisione of air to air, yt many hath not one rig or two, and in some places one rig is divyded in foure".[73] Examples of its divisive influence on English landholding are provided by Hallam's work on Lincolnshire[74] and by F. R. H. Du Boulay's work on Kent.[75]

In so far as sub-divided fields are concerned, though, to simply establish that partible inheritance could divide property with great effect is insufficient: it has to be shown to create intermixed property in the process. A. R. H. Baker's study of how partible inheritance shaped the development of landholding in Gillingham manor was designed to illuminate precisely this point and it is, therefore, of crucial importance to the argument. By the careful analysis of land charters and family settlements, he was able to chart the growing dispersal and intermixture of holdings through the combined impact of partible inheritance and piecemeal colonization.[76] Baker himself outlined three ways in which a hypothetical family holding might be settled on two co-heirs. One solution was for one to be given the holding in its entirety and for the other to be allowed to carve a new holding out of the surrounding waste. Another solution was for the holding to be divided between them, but in the form of consolidated shares. Yet another solution was for it to be divided between them, but in the form of intermixed shares, thus forming a sub-divided field system.[77] Posing the problem in this way focusses on an aspect of the problem all too easily taken for granted. If co-heirs chose to divide inherited property into sub-divided fields in preference to any alternative form of layout, then it was because they chose to reason it out this way. Our understanding of how this created sub-divided fields must follow this reasoning through to be complete.

Where the basis of this sort of division is explained, it usually stresses that the shares devolved to heirs were meant to be equal, one with another. Bracton is informative on this aspect. Amongst the duties of those charged with making a division between co-heirs was the task of ensuring that each share or part was "equal in every respect to the other"[78] and that regard was had to both "extent and valuation" when deciding on what was equal.[79] Irish evidence for the settlement of land between co-heirs displays a similar stress on equality.[80] So, too, do the divisions of land between co-heirs traceable in court records for the Northern Isles, such as the "airff and divisioun" (as they were termed) of six merk lands at Gruting in the parish of Sandsting (Orkney) that was carried out in 1604 and which enacted that each heir was to have an equal share of good land "according to the use and consuetude of the countrie".[81] Where divisions between co-heirs can be located for the Scottish mainland, they also emphasize that shares were meant to be equal.[82] This stress on the equality of shares apportioned between co-heirs, a stress present wherever such divisions occurred, aligns it alongside shareholding. Where they both led to sub-divided fields, it was for the same reason, namely, an absolute stress on equality between aliquot portions of a holding or township. Seen in this way, partible inheritance appears as a particular cause of shareholding, rather than a truly independent explanation for sub-divided fields. Its effects on the latter operated through the mediating influence of a shareholding inter-pretation of property.

(d) Piecemeal colonization and sub-divided fields

Piecemeal colonization stands as a straightforward explanation for sub-divided fields. Its verification as a cause depends on processes and relationships that are familiar themes in the medieval township. So long as communities of landholders colonized land in a piecemeal fashion — a furlong here and a furlong there as each generation passed — and so long as landholders had a collective interest in the land so colonized, with each having right or access to a share at each stage, then the fragmentation of property rights would — given time — have resulted. That land was colonized in a piecemeal fashion is a fact beyond dispute. Recent work may have shifted the main weight of the process back beyond 1086, but few would challenge the statement that the cultivated land of most townships evolved through the cumulative efforts of successive generations of farmers. Posing more of a problem is the complementary question of whether landholders shared in each phase or enough phases of growth, so that their holdings grew not in a spatially-continuous fashion but in a leap-frogging manner from one area of colonization to another.

The simple answer is yes, but there was no uniformity or consistency to the relationships involved. In some townships, the relationship between new land and old was strictly defined, such that each holding received a share of newly-colonized land proportioned to how many bovates or virgates it contained. For example, in his work on land reclamation in the Lincolnshire Fens, Hallam refers throughout to what he calls the "land sharing function of the bovate", stressing that enclosers divided the new enclosure proportionately according to the amount of land they "defended", that is, according to the number of bovates they held.[83] J. A. Raftis has documented similar examples of waste being "apportioned strictly between tenements" for the lands of Ramsey abbey in Lincolnshire.[84] The *Black Book of Hexham Priory* contains an entry for the township of East Maften, dated 1479, which embodies this same measured relationship as a guiding principle of colonization. It stipulated that "if the present lord of Fenwick and lord of Maften wish to bring under the plough the waste land in the said common, then the said Prior and Convent shall receive their share for their portion in such plough land by lot; as they did before in the other arable land; namely, by the old intakes, in each place a third".[85] It occurs again in a sixteenth-century reference to the nearby township of Cowpen which laid down that "everie tenaunte was and is to have so much lande in everie new fields as everie of them layde forth in everie wasted or decayed corne felde".[86] As Hallam made clear in his work on Lincolnshire, where this sort of defined relationship existed, it was not even necessary for land to be colonized by the community for their collective interests to be asserted. Land colonized on the initiative of individuals could still be shared generally.[87]

However, it would be misleading to imply that all medieval communities followed this rule of apportioning newly-colonized land equitably. In some cases, it was a relationship firmly controlled and sanctioned by lords, and for that reason, it was one subjected to review at each phase of growth, so that we cannot assume it formed a constant, ongoing relationship. We need only consider detailed estate studies like that by E. Miller on the lands of Ely Abbey and bishopric, to realise the importance of lordly-decision-making in the matter. On the one hand, land assarted in the forest areas of Huntingdon and Hertfordshire before 1250 appeared as appendages to established tenements. On the other hand, assarted land in the Fen areas was incorporated as separate holdings.[88] Comparable work elsewhere show lords exercising an identical choice over how new land was treated from a landholding point of view.[89] Not only was the relationship between a community and its reserves of waste open to re-definition by lords, but equally important for the argument under review, is the fact that even where piece-meal colonization took place, it did not necessarily produce sub-divided fields. In his discussion of colonization in Midland forest areas like Feckenham over the thirteenth and fourteenth centuries, R. H. Hilton drew attention to the way it led to parcels of land and enclosures held in severalty.[90] Of course, Bishop's work on colonization in twelfth- and thirteenth-century Yorkshire also found that assarted land was initially held in the form of several parcels and furlongs by landholders; only later were these parcels and furlongs sub-divided and absorbed into the sub-divided field system of townships. However, the difference with Hilton's forest townships is that assarted land did not undergo this second stage of development, but remained as a girdle of several parcels and enclosures around the sub-divided field core of townships.

There are then, qualifications to be entered over the extent to which piecemeal colonization could have acted across the entire face of the country to produce sub-divided fields. But arguably, these qualifications are largely founded on the changes which came about during a period of growing land pressure that straddled the twelfth, thirteenth and fourteenth centuries, when lords probably supervised the processes of assarting and land allocation far more assiduously and, if money rents were involved, more selectively. Prior to this period, the rigidly-defined system of land allocation depicted for areas like the Lincolnshire Fens and Northumberland was probably **more** widespread. After all, it is fairly commonplace for scholars to typify the medieval holding or tenement as constituting not just a measured extent of arable, but a complex bundle of property- and use-rights. In his work on the west Midlands, Hilton described how "the holdings of the peasants were almost invariably expressed in yardlands, or in multiples or fractions of yardlands. This is a somewhat elusive thing to define, for it was more than a mere measurement of land, it also embodied a claim to common rights of meadow, pasture and access to woodland and so on".[91] A community's prior if by no means over-riding claim on their surrounding waste as a source of extra arable, fitted into this diffused notion of property- and use-rights, but in a feudal society, it would have been the first freedom (if that is not too strong a word for what was only a prior not an absolute claim) to disappear when abundance turned to scarcity.

Another qualification concerns how piecemeal colonization operated. It did not necessarily create a landholding pattern of intermixed strips. As Bishop tried to show in regard to twelfth- and thirteenth-century Yorkshire, piecemeal colonization led initially to blocks of land or parcels held in severalty. The shift into sub-divided fields occurred later, as a secondary stage of development. Such a conclusion appeared to shift the main focus of explanation away from piecemeal colonization, implying that other factors were responsible for the vital shift into sub-division. His paper, though, ignored the fact that what was important was that landholding became fragmented *at any scale*, whether in terms of strips or furlongs. Even if colonization led to intermixed furlongs, as one suspects Bishop's Yorkshire examples did, then the critical shift had been made. The principle was established of holdings having right to a variety of different land types at the expense of their spatial integrity. Other processes, like partible inheritance, could work more effectively once this principle was established. In other words, whilst it must be conceded that piecemeal colonization sometimes led in the first instance to a landholding pattern based on furlongs or large parcels rather than strips, such a conclusion does not preclude the possibility that the critical shift into fragmented or intermixed landholding has occurred through this process. Once this is appreciated, then the range of situations in which piecemeal colonization played a primary role in fostering the initial emergence of sub-divided field systems, increases.

(e) Sub-divided fields as behaviour against risk

The published arguments for and against sub-divided fields being a behaviour against risk have already been reviewed (see pp. 22-3). From that discussion, it was concluded that McCloskey's work offers conclusive support for sub-divided fields serving as an insurance against risk, but is less convincing on the more central issue of whether they were a case of behaviour against risk. To establish its validity as a cause and not just a consequence needs an investigation of the intent behind such field layouts.

To an extent, support of sorts can be found for this aspect. References like that of 1566 to the township of Chatton in Northumberland declaring that landholders "had their land allotted by rigg and rigg as is the custom in every husband towne, so that each should have land of like quality"[92] or the sixteenth-century tack for the township of Fortar in Angus which stipulated that the "land shall be equally divided in all its commodities between the said tenants as well in arable land as in pasture land"[93], like those cited earlier in the discussion of shareholding (see pp. 35-6), suggest an intent behind sub-divided fields not unlike that proposed by McCloskey; but herein lies the problem. When one considers what behaviour against risk meant as a justification for sub-divided fields, then it becomes difficult to separate it from shareholding. In fact, it could legitimately be argued that the distinction between risk aversion and shareholding may be a matter more of semantics than something easily read from real-world conditions. By this I mean that what farmers may have interpreted in one set of circumstances as a case of risk aversion may, in other circumstances or by those charged formally with the task of laying out sub-divided fields, have been expressed as an equality of both extent and value between the measures (i.e. bovates, virgates, etc.) out of which holdings were constructed. The whole idea of an equal spread of risk and profit can be accommodated within a shareholding interpretation as one dimension. McCloskey's analysis stopped short of the point at which the two ideas could be disentangled. Until they can be disentangled, risk aversion can only be admitted as a valid cause when buttressed by the wider ramifications of shareholding. On the evidence so far published it cannot stand alone.

Interpretations of sub-divided fields: a synthesis

The aim of the foregoing discussion has been to explore the different interpretations that have been advanced to explain sub-divided fields and to show that any reasonable assessment must conclude that more than one is valid. Recognition of this fact, though, poses an unavoidable dilemma. Sub-divided fields are not the most obvious way of laying out property. Some scholars have felt that having to devise even one interpretation capable of rationalising its purpose and design raised problems enough, without instating a number of independent causes as all proven. In consequence, where more than one seemed credible, they have asserted the claims of a supposedly stronger interpretation at the expense of those which they considered to be weaker. Such an individual institution had to be met with an equally individual explanation.

Yet arguably, any definitive interpretation of sub-divided fields needs the flexibility which a range of causes can offer. The reason for this is because an outstanding feature of sub-divided fields is that they occur under such widely differing circumstances and in such widely differing forms; their circumstances varied from fermtouns in Scotland held by tenants on short tacks to holdings shared between co-heirs in areas like Kent, or from Midland communities holding land by hereditary copyhold tenure or custom of the manor to those in the far north of Scotland holding land by udal tenure. Their range of forms was equally impressive; some were highly ordered systems, with methodically arrayed selions and each person's holding systematically scattered through the different parts of the township. The term *regular* is an appropriate description of these seemingly planned layouts (see Fig. 3).

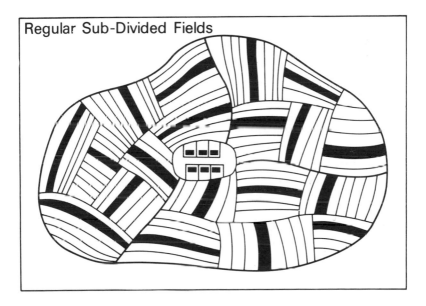

Regular Sub-Divided Fields

Fig. 3. Regular sub-divided fields

Others were quite the opposite. Landholding was disposed in blocks or strips of all shapes and sizes. Moreover, individual holdings show no sign of pattern but are randomly scattered or heaped in one sector at will. These were the *irregular* townships (see Fig. 4). In other townships, the degree of sub-division appears partial. Two types of partial systems can be identified: in the one, sub-division might be present in only a few scattered furlongs; in the other,

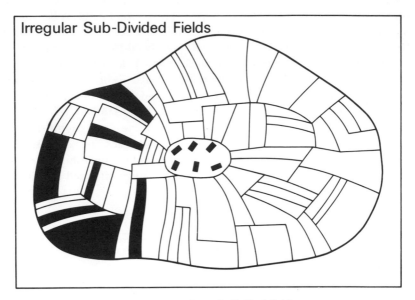

Fig. 4. Irregular sub-divided fields.

the inner core of the township appears laid out into sub-divided fields but not the parcels of landholding or enclosures that surrounded it. Such a variety of both circumstances and forms cannot have resulted from any single cause, or indeed, any simple cause.

But whilst supporting the few scholars, like Baker and Butlin[94], who have argued in favour of more than one cause being applicable, it need not be a case of having to invoke causes that were entirely independent of each other. As proposed at the start of this chapter, it is possible to structure those causes established as valid into a single, compound interpretation, compound because it highlights the very real links that existed between them without destroying their separateness as formative influences. Progress towards this end has already been made by the suggestions that partible inheritance operated only as a particular form of shareholding and that risk aversion, if of relevance, was probably part of the way shares were interpreted under such a system. If we exclude joint ploughing as a cause that has yet to be vouched for, this would leave two basic types of cause: piecemeal colonization and shareholding.

As the basis of a compound interpretation, these have the merit of being able to encompass all the different circumstances and forms of sub-divided fields. At the same time, they are causes that may have been related, in the sense that one may have created the conditions under which the other could develop, such a relationship being a perfectly feasible proposition; the main problem with it is deciding which came first: piecemeal colonization or share-holding. Given what has been written about them in past discussions, the strongest candidate as the first or primary cause would seem to be shareholding. According to Vinogradoff, shareholding was spawned during a tribal stage of society and for this reason, it can lay strong claims to having archaism on its side. However, Vinogradoff underpinned his argument with assumptions that are unconvincing. At the heart of his case was the idea that the shareholding basis of sub-divided fields represented a form of *communal* tenure, with differences from one region to the next manifesting stages in the progressive decay of this communal basis. The runrig system of areas like Scotland was portrayed by him as the archetypal example of shareholding's essentially tribal and communal nature, since its periodic re-arrangement of landholding served to continually re-assert the interests of the community above those of the individual.

His argument, though, is seriously flawed. In fact, there is a much stronger case for arguing that sub-divided fields in *most* areas had nothing to do with a communal tenure, whether in a pure or degraded form. They may have possessed rights of common grazing or communally-regulated systems of cropping, but their landholding was mostly based on a form of several tenure that was not only true of sub-divided fields in England[95], but also of the runrig system of Scotland. The very hallmark of runrig was that each tenant or landholder was assigned a *separate* share. This is evident from rentals carefully detailing each person's share of the township and/or its rent, and from the tacks which are freely available, setting individuals a specific share of the township. There can be no other conclusion except that such landholders were responsible only for their portion, and no more.[96] The frequent references to landholders in runrig townships being "kend to thair awn pairts" encapsulates in a phrase the essence of their tenure.[97]

However, it cannot be argued that sub-divided fields were based exclusively on tenures that were several in character. In a few areas, there almost certainly existed examples that were associated with a communal or, to use the preferred term, joint tenure. For instance, there were a significant number of Scottish townships held jointly by small groups of tenants and this can be inferred from both rentals and tacks[98], and from contemporary comments. Dr. Johnson, for instance, observed during his tour of the Highlands in 1773 that "land is sometimes leased to a small fellowship, who live in a cluster of huts, called a Tenants Town, and are bound jointly and separately for the payment of their rent".[99] This joint liability for the management and rent of the entire township and not just a portion of it makes it likely that such townships were farmed as a single unit, with the produce and not the land being divided. However the possibility cannot be ruled out that some were divided into separate holdings *on the ground* even if such an arrangement did not intrude directly into their tenure. More sharply delineated is the character of those townships in Wales and Ireland that were held jointly by kinsmen. Those held by *gwely*-land tenure in Wales appear to have been apportioned out into separate holdings on the ground — *but not separate tenures* — between those kinsmen who claimed an interest in them by the time they surface in thirteenth- and fourteenth-century documents.[100] Presumably, some were laid out into sub-divided fields, but so long as the integrity of such *gwelyau* was preserved, then so was their character as a joint possession. Some Irish townships held jointly by kinsmen may well have been in the same position by the late medieval period, that is, apportioned out into separate or several tenures and,[101] taken at their face value, such townships would lend support to Vinogradoff's argument. They suggest that whilst his belief that all sub-divided field systems were to a greater or lesser extent bound up with a communal tenure was questionable, his notion of a continuum along which field systems could be arranged was still plausible, but whereas Vinogradoff's continuum embraced only different stages in the decay, but not the disappearance, of communalism, it would now need to be revised to include a much greater preponderance of townships whose sub-divided field systems were wholly several in nature.

In place of this evolutionary scheme, it is suggested here that what these different types of sub-divided field system really show is that shareholding had nothing to do with a distinct stage or type of tenure. Its presence in such disparate circumstances as the Midland counties of England or the far north of Scotland can only mean that it was something that cut across what we would normally regard as constituting a separate tenure *sui generis*. The mistake is to see shareholding as a separate tenure in its own right; all it can be regarded as is a tenurial attribute, a single characteristic among the bundle of characteristics that usually give definition to a tenure. In short, it represented a way of defining the extent of a holding which had implications for the way it was laid out. It was an attribute that could be quite independent of whether the tenure was leasehold or allodial, hereditary or non-hereditary, devolved by primogeniture or partible inheritance. It is for this reason, that we find it present under such a diversity of conditions, and it is also the reason why sub-divided fields cannot be used to fashion an evolutionary sequence of tenure (predominantly communal-predominantly several) in the way that Vinogradoff proposed, but this is not to say that there is not a history of tenure to be read from sub-divided fields, only that it is not the history of change from one type to another. This sort of substantive history must be built up through other aspects of tenure, and once this is appreciated, then any assumption that shareholding was archaic because it was *ab origine* of a tribal character, breaks down. Moreover, shareholding becomes a much less obvious tenurial characteristic, one whose explanation is more problematical as a result.

For the discussion in hand, it also means that the choice between shareholding and piecemeal colonization as the basis of a compound interpretation of sub-divided fields cannot be taken for granted. The possibility that sub-divided fields sprang initially from piecemeal colonization has to be considered as well. To construe the problem in this way has three advantages. First, its preconditions make minimal demands on the nature of its tenurial context. All that it required was that groups of landholders competed for the same areas of waste, in the sense that the interests or rights of one family were set besides those of another, with no one having an exclusive or superior claim to any one section. If landholders colonized such waste step by step with each other or according to a strictly defined code of equal land allocation, then fragmentation would no doubt have been more complete and systematic; but even where it was a more casually-organized process, piecemeal colonization was still capable of generating an elementary form of holding fragmentation. Secondly, and a factor of critical importance, it was able to convert, via their growth and intermixing, a pattern of consolidated holdings into a more extensive one of intermixed holdings. Given the stress in recent work on early landholding being of a consolidated character[102], this alone is sufficient to shift the balance of argument in favour of piecemeal colonization being the basis of any compound interpretation for sub-divided fields. Thirdly, piecemeal colonization is better able than shareholding to cope with the varied forms of sub-divided fields, particularly the distinction between regular and irregular systems. The question of which of these two broad types of layout came first is of seminal importance for the history of sub-divided fields. To assume that regular systems denote their earliest form is to confront the antiquity of shareholding all over again, because only shareholding could conceivably have systematized the laying out of property in the manner of a regular system. To invert their order of development is to argue that regular systems resulted from the reorganization of irregular ones. The discontinuity in the history of sub-divided fields which this view necessarily invokes is not an insurmountable obstacle. Reorganizations of a kind have already been discussed in regard to the field layout of Scottish townships (see above, pp. 35-6). No matter how frequent or infrequent their occurrence was, they afforded an opportunity for altering the nature of field layouts from an irregular to a regular form. Also relevant are the growing number of English studies which have insisted on some form of reorganization to explain features of village settlement morphology. Thus, so-called regular villages of the north-east and Yorkshire are now considered to have acquired their regularity of settlement form not at the point of their foundation but by reorganization at some date during the period from the tenth to the fourteenth centuries.[103] Equally important work on East Anglia has likewise discovered that fundamental site changes, and consequent reorganization, were a vital part of village history.[104] Comparable work in Scandinavia, especially that on regular or "regulated" settlements, suggests that planned changes in village layout or morphology were usually accompanied by corresponding changes in field layout, with the sub-divided fields of such settlements being cast into a highly regular form.[105] With this in mind, the widespread references in the Midland counties and eastern England to procedures, like sun-division, that were specifically designed to create regular field layouts could well reflect the vital change-over in these areas from irregular to regular forms. Significantly, recent work on Holderness suggests that the planned character of villages there did embrace both settlement and fields, their reorganization along these lines occurring during the late eleventh or early twelfth century.[106]

The whole question of reorganization serving as a bridge between irregular and regular forms of sub-divided fields is critical for another reason. Put simply, it also provides a credible link between piecemeal colonization and shareholding as interpretations for these forms. Piecemeal colonization fragmented a person's holding or property rights over a variety of different land types. When the occasion arose for the township to be reorganized, it made sense for this diverse composition to be mapped back into the new layout and this could only be achieved by establishing it as a guiding principle of the new layout, something which holdings had a *de jure* and not merely a *de facto* right of claim to. Each holding, therefore, became a microcosm of the township at large, partaking in all it had to offer. Regular methods of land division discussed earlier (see pp. 32-4) were all used to implement such a principle. In other words, far from being archaic, shareholding was an attitude towards the definition of property that was conceived under quite different conditions. The motives that shaped it were not necessarily those of common welfare and brotherhood, but the understandable self-interest of families anxious to maintain the same blend of extent and value, the same advantages (such as risk aversion?), which they had *already* derived from their fragmented holdings. Where such reorganization recurred over time, such as in Scotland or Ireland, one would naturally expect shareholding to appear a more persistent and defined concept of landholding. In England, meanwhile, such a reorganization is likely to have been a rare, possibly individual event, so that shareholding was no more than a guiding principle seized upon at a single point in time to carry the farming community and its mesh of property rights through a fundamental reformation of layout.

It was stated above that the history of sub-divided fields is not the history of change from one tenure to another: its meaning lies in a different direction, a direction which did not escape Maitland. In response to Vinogradoff's march of tenure from communal to several forms, he argued that the broad trend of land law may have been "neither from communalism to individualism, nor yet from individualism to communalism, but from the vague to the definite":[107] in a phrase, it became more intense. To accept a compound interpretation of sub-divided fields is to establish a landholding context for precisely this sort of development. It was not an evolution of tenure in any holistic sense, but a change in the formulation of the link between tenure and landholding. The transition from a shareholding system to one in which holdings were regarded as bundles of specific strips and parcels is a change of this sort, a change towards greater definition, but in so far as shareholding may have derived from the fragmentation of holdings caused by piecemeal colonization, it is conceivable that a still cruder link beteen tenure and landholding may have preceded it. Holdings, or the land units of which they were composed, may have been regarded as shares in the total resources of the township long beforehand, but they need not have been regarded as absolutely equal in both extent and value. After all, in a world of relative abundance, it would not have been necessary to be so meticulous about the precise composition of shares. Sooner or later though, piecemeal colonization, as well as projecting property rights over a variety of different land types, would have served to reduce the amount of land available for colonization, so that landholders would have come under pressure to define their property rights more assiduously. Township reorganization would have focussed their anxieties. Perhaps the early use of land units which expressed capacity, capacity to sustain a family (i.e. hide or husbandland) or a plough team (i.e. ploughgate or oxgate), symbolizes this looser relationship between tenure and landholding that may once have prevailed, for they treat the extent of holdings, let alone their right to any particular plot of land, implicitly rather than explicitly.

References

[1] Homans, *English Villagers*, pp. 73-80.
[2] W. O. Ault, *Open-Field Farming in Medieval England. A Study of Village By-Laws*, London (1972), pp. 20-1.
[3] See, for example, "Rentaill of the Lordschipe of Huntlye alias Strauthbogye 1600" in *The Miscellany of the Spalding Club*, 4, Aberdeen (1849), pp. 261-319; J. Dunlop, "*Court Minutes of Balgair 1706-1736*", Scottish Record Society, Edinburgh (1957), p. 5; Scottish Record Office, John Macgregor Collection, GD50/159, Book of the proceedings held in the Baron Baile Courts of the Robertson of Lude 1621-1806, March 20th, 1766.
[4] J. M. Thomson (ed.), "The Forbes Baron Court Book 1659-1678" in *Miscellany of the Scottish History Society*, 2nd series XIX (1919), p. 318; Roxburgh MSS, Floors Castle, Act and Commission John Hood . . . Agt . . . Robert Davidson 1758).
[5] Seebohm, *op. cit.*, pp. 120-2.

[6] H. E. Hallam, *Settlement and Society: A Study of the Early Agrarian History of South Lincolnshire*, Cambridge (1965), p. 29.

[7] *Ibid.*, p. 29.

[8] See, for example, E. Bateson, *A History of Northumberland*, Newcastle (1895), vol. II, p. 367; M. Hope Dodds, *A History of Northumberland*, Newcastle (1935), vol. XII, pp. 109-11.

[9] "Court Book of the Barony of Leys 1636-1674" in *The Miscellany of the Spalding Club*, 5, Aberdeen (1852), p. 226.

[10] J. Storer Clouston (ed.), *Records of the Earldom of Orkney* 1299-1614, Scottish History Society, 2nd series, VII (1914), pp. 181-2. A discussion of further examples for Scotland can be found in R. A. Dodgshon, "Law and Landscape in Early Scotland: A Study of the Relationship Between Tenure and Landholding" in A. Harding (ed.), *Lawmakers and Lawmaking*, Proceedings of the Third British Legal History Conference, London (1979), pp. 127-45.

[11] A review of this evidence can be found in R. A. Dodgshon, "Scandinavian 'Solskifte' and the Sunwise Division of Land in Eastern Scotland", *Scottish Studies*, 19 (1975), pp. 1-14.

[12] Sir Thomas Craig, *Jus Feudale*, edited by J. Baillie Edinburgh, (1732) p. 425.

[13] *Liber Sancte Marie de Melros*, Bannatyne club, Edinburgh (1837), vol. 2, p. 521.

[14] See, for instance, J. H. Ramsay (ed.), *Bammf Charters A.D. 1232-1703*, Oxford (1915), p. 138 or D. Littlejohn (ed.), *Records of the Sheriff Court of Aberdeenshire vol. II: 1598-1649*, Aberdeen (1906), p. 77.

[15] Homans, *English Villagers*, p. 99.

[16] Examples can be found in *Liber de Scon*, Bannatyne club, Edinburgh (1843), appendix III, pp. 232-3; J. Storer Clouston, "The Orkney Townships", *Scottish Historical Review*, 17 (1920), p. 29.

[17] For further comment on this idea of a connection between early systems of land allocation and the ceremony of seisin, see Dodgshon, "Land and Tenure in Early Scotland", pp. 144-5.

[18] H. P. R. Finberg (ed.), *The Agrarian History of England and Wales I: ii AD43-1042*, Cambridge (1972), p. 495.

[19] J. Raine (ed.), *The Priory of Hexham*, vol. ii, Surtees society, XXXXVI (1865), p. 50.

[20] H. H. E. Craster, *A History of Northumberland*, vol. IX, Newcastle (1909), p. 324.

[21] J. Booth (ed.), *Halmota Prioratus Dunelmensis*, containing extracts from the Halmote Court or Manor Rolls of the Priory and Convent of Durham A.D. 1296-A.D. 1384, Surtees society, LXXXII (1886), pp. xlii-xliii and p. 189 et seq. A description of how the lotting was performed can be found on pp. xlii-xliii. For comparable examples for Warwickshire, see M. W. Beresford, "Lot Acres", *Economic History Rev.*, XIII (1943), pp. 74-9. According to Bracton, the division of land between co-heirs was also accomplished by the drawing of lots (Bracton, *On the Laws and Customs of England (De Legibus et Conseutudinibus Angliae)*, translation by S. E. Thorne of latin text edited by G. E. Woodbine, Cambridge, Mass. (1968), vol. ii, p. 20.

[22] Sir James Dalyell and J. Beveridge (eds.), *The Binns Papers 1320-1864*, Scottish Record Society (1938), pp. 2-3.

[23] C. Rogers (ed.), *Register of Coupar Abbey: Rental Book of the Cistercian Abbey of Cupar Angus*, London (1880), vol. I, p. 144.

[24] S. R. O. Abercairny MSS, GD24/I/32, Articles of Agreement between James Moray of Abercairny & Robert Maxtone in Bellnollo 1765-1773.

[25] Discussion of this work can be found in R. A. Dodgshon, "Towards an Understanding and Definition of Runrig: the Evidence for Roxburghshire and Berwickshire",

Transactions of the Institute of British Geographers, 64(1975), pp. 15-33; R. A. Dodgshon, "Runrig and the Communal Origins of Property in Land", *Juridical Review*, (1975), pp. 189-208.

[26] A good example of this is provided by a charter of 1578 which conveyed a sixth part of Knokorthe in the Barony of Abirchirdour in Banffshire, the landholder being given the choice of having it "per divisionem aut per lie rinrig", J. M. Thomson (ed.), *The Register of the Great Seal of Scotland 1546-1580*, Edinburgh (1886), p. 771.

[27] For instance, a 1586 charter for land in Kethik Barony, Angus, conveyed half a township, a half to be decided "per sortem et divisionem, incipiendo ad solem, per lie runrig", J. M. Thomson (ed.), *The Register of the Great Seal of Scotland 1580-1593*, Edinburgh (1888), p. 349. An example of a tack instructing a tenant that he was to decide on the layout of his share by means of a lottery with other tenants can be found in Scottish Record Office, Abercairny MSS, GD24/I/32, Articles of Agreement for third part of Bellnollo 1765-1773.

[28] Sir Philip J. Hamilton-Grierson (ed.), Habakkuk Bisset's *Rolment of Courtis*, Scottish Text Society, Edinburgh (1920), vol. I, p. 297.

[29] *Ibid.*, p. 298.

[30] *Registrum de Dunfermleyn*, Bannatyne club, Edinburgh (1842), p. 285 or at Balgair (Stirlingshire) in 1706; J. Dunlop (ed.), *Court Minutes of Balgair 1706-1736*, Scottish Record Society, Edinburgh (1957), pp. 10-11.

[31] Scottish Record Office, Abercairny MSS, GD24/I/32.

[32] *Archaeological and Historical Collections of Ayrshire and Galloway*, IX, Edinburgh (1885), pp. 212-3.

[33] "Corshill Baron Court Book", pp. 65-249 in *Archaeological and Historical Collections Relating to Ayrshire and Wigton* IV, Edinburgh (1884), p. 72.

[34] R. S. Barclay (ed.), *The Court Book of Orkney and Shetland 1612-1613*, Kirkwall, (1962), p. 18.

[35] Dodgshon, "Towards an Understanding and Definition of Runrig", pp. 28-9.

[36] See, for example, National Library of Wales, Calendar of Deeds and Documents, vol. II, F. Green (ed.), *The Crosswood Deeds*, Aberystwyth (1927); C. Baker and G. G. Francis (eds.), *Surveys of Gower and Kilvey and of Several Mesne Manors within that Seiniory*, Cambrian Archaeological Association, London (1864-70), vols. I-III.

[37] T. P. Ellis, *Welsh Tribal Law and Custom in the Middle Ages*, Oxford (1926), vol. I, p. 239.

[38] *Ibid.*, pp. 110-11 provides typical references. For original references, see. P. Vinogradoff and F. Morgan (eds.), *Survey of the Honour of Denbigh, 1334*, London (1914), pp. 45-6.

[39] A. Owen (ed.), *Ancient Laws and Institutes of Wales*, London (1841), p. 266; F. Seebohm, *The Tribal System in Wales*, 2nd edition, London (1904), pp. 73-4.

[40] G. R. J. Jones, "Post-Roman Wales", pp. 281-382 in H. P. R. Finberg (ed.), *The Agrarian History of England and Wales*, vol. I, part II, Cambridge (1972), p. 334.

[41] Owen, *op. cit.*, p. 536.

[42] R. C. Simington (ed.), *The Civil Survey A.D. 1654-1656 County of Limerick vol. IV*, Irish Manuscripts Commission, Dublin (1938), pp. 10-11.

[43] *Ibid.*, p. 111.

[44] *The Return of the Commissioners*, Irish Manuscripts Commission, Dublin pp. 54-5.

[45] K. Nicholls, *Gaelic and Gaelicised Ireland in the Middle Ages*, Dublin, (1972), p. 62.

[46] *Ibid.*, pp. 61-2.

[47] See, for example, W. Rees, *South Wales and the March 1284-1415*, Oxford (1924), p. 214.

[48] J. Ainsworth (d.), *The Inchiquin Manuscripts*, Irish Manuscripts Commission, Dublin (1961), p. 329.

[49] See, for instance, *ibid.*, pp. 546-8; M. J. Blake, "An Old Rental of Cong Abbey", *Jnl. Royal Society of Antiquaries of Ireland*, XXXV, Consecutive Series vol. XV, fifth Series (1905), pp. 130-8; P.K. Egan, *The Parish of Ballinasloe*, Dublin (1960), appendix I.

[50] Ainsworth (ed.), *op. cit.*, p. 503 is the sort of evidence the writer has in mind.

[51] Relevant comment can be found in R. H. Buchanan, "Field Systems in Ireland", pp. 58-618 in Baker and Butlin (eds.), *op. cit.*, p. 592; Gomme, *op. cit.*, p. 141.

[52] R. A. Dodgshon, "The Landholding Foundations of the Open Field System", *Past and Present*, 67(1975), pp. 3-29.

[53] This statement was made by a Mr. Woodman in a review of local tenures as part of his work as a solicitor. It is cited in F. W. L. Dendy, "The Ancient Farms of Northumberland", *Archaeologia Aeliana*, XVI (1894), p. 133.

[54] Dendy, *op. cit.*, p. 138. Further examples can be found in C. Creighton, "The Northumbrian Border", *The Archaeological Jnl.*, XLII (1885), pp. 59-61.

[55] Dendy, *op. cit.*, p. 137.

[56] H. H. E. Craster (ed.), *A History of Northumberland*, vol. IX, Newcastle (1909), p. 324.

[57] W. Farrer (ed.), *Lancashire Inquests, Extents, and Feudal Aids., part III. A.D. 1313-A.D.1355.*, The Record Society . . . Lancashire and Cheshire, LXX (1955), p. 147.

[58] *Ibid.*, p. 115.

[59] J. Brownhill (ed.), *The Coucher Book of Furness Abbey*, part I, Chetham Society, 74(1915), p. 273.

[60] *Ibid.*, p. 99.

[61] H. E. Slater (ed.), *The Boarstall Cartulary*, Oxford Historical Society, Oxford (1930); pp. 12, 29.

[62] W. P. Baildon (ed.), *Court Rolls of the Manor of Wakefield*, vol. II: 1297 to 1309, The Yorkshire Archaeological Society, Record Series, XXXVI (1906), p. xxx.

[63] F. M. Stenton (ed.), *Documents Illustrative of the Social and Economic History of the Danelaw*, Oxford, (1920), p. xlvii.

[64] Seebohm, *English Village Community*, p. 112.

[65] Dodgshon, "Runrig and the Communal Origins of Property in Land", pp. 196-8.

[66] In the case of Ireland, a fine recent discussion occurs in Nicholls, *op. cit.*, pp. 57-65. For Wales, the collection of papers reprinted in T. Jones Pierce, *Medieval Welsh Society* edited by J. Beverley Smith, Cardiff (1972) contains ample documentation of its practise, such as on p. 362. See also, G. R. J. Jones, "Field Systems of North Wales", in Baker and Butlin, *op. cit.*, pp. 446-57; R. Davies, *Lordship and Society in Medieval Wales, 1282-1400*, Oxford (1978), pp. 358-77.

[67] Evidence for this can be found in D. Balfour (ed.), *Oppressions of the Sixteenth Century in the Islands of Orkney and Shetland*, Maitland club, 75(1859), p. 58; J. S. Clouston, (ed.), *The Records of the Earldom of Orkney 1299-1614*, Scottish History Society, 2nd series, VII(1914), pp. xxxv-xliii; J. S. Clouston, "The Orkney Townships", *Scottish Historical Review*, 17(1920), pp. 37-8.

[68] See, for example, R. J. Faith, "Peasant Families and Inheritance Customs in Medieval England", *Agricultural History Review*, XIV(1966), pp. 77-95; C. Howell, "Peasant Inheritance Customs in the Midlands, 1280-1700", pp. 112-55 in J. Goody, J. Thirsk and E. P. Thompson (eds.), *Family and Inheritance: Rural Society in Western Europe*, Cambridge (1976), pp. 112-55; C. Howell, "Stability and Change 1300-1700. The Socio-Economic Context of the Self-Perpetuating Family Farm in England", *Jnl. of Peasant Studies*, VI(1975), pp. 469-82.

[69] H. E. Hallam, "Some thirteenth-century censuses", *Economic History Rev.*, 2nd series, X(1958), p. 368.

[70] C. Howell, "Peasant Inheritance Customs in the Midlands", p. 117.

[71] A review of the problem occurs in D. McCourt, "The Dynamic Quality of Irish Rural Settlement", pp. 126-62 in E. Jones and D. McCourt (eds.), *Man and His Habitat. Essays Presented in Estyn Evans*, London (1971), especially pp. 131-6.

[72] T. I. Jeffreys Jones (ed.), *Exchequer Proceedings Concerning Wales. In Tempore James I*, Cardiff (1955), p. 320.

[73] A. Peterkin, *Rentals of the Ancient Earldom and Bishoprick of Orkney*, Edinburgh (1820), section III, p. 20.

[74] Hallam, "Some thirteenth-century censuses", pp. 349-55.

[75] F. R. H. Du Boulay, *The Lordship of Canterbury*, London (1966), pp. 52-67.

[76] A. R. H. Baker, "Open Fields and Partible Inheritance on a Kent Manor", *Economic History Rev.*, 2nd series, XVII (1964-5), pp. 1-22.

[77] A. R. H. Baker, "Field Systems in Medieval England", in A. R. H. Baker and J. B. Harley (eds.), *Man Made the Land*, Newton Abbot (1973), p. 66.

[78] Bracton, *On the Laws and Customs of England (De Legibus et Consuetudinibus Angliae)*, translation by S. E. Thorne of latin text edited by G. E. Woodbine, Cambridge, Mass. (1968), vol. II, pp. 219-20.

[79] *Ibid.*, pp. 211-2.

[80] See, for example, E. Curtis (ed.), *Calendar of Ormond Deeds, vol. VI 1584-1603 A.D.*, Irish Manuscripts Commission, Dublin (1943), p. 74.

[81] A. Peterkin, *Notes on Orkney and Shetland*, Kirkwall (1820), pp. 39-40.

[82] A good example can be found in Mark Napier, *History of the Partition of Lennox*, Edinburgh and London (1835), p. 135 *et seq.*, the division being "in twa evenlie pertis as thai best ma be depertit and devidit".

[83] Hallam, *Settlement and Society*, p. 110.

[84] J. A. Raftis, *Tenure and Mobility*, Toronto (1964), p. 29.

[85] M. Hope Dodds (ed.), *A History of Northumberland*, vol. XII, Newcastle (1926), p. 366.

[86] Craster, *A History of Northumberland*, vol. IX, p. 324.

[87] Hallam, *Settlement and Society*, p. 110.

[88] E. Miller, *The Abbey and Bishopric of Ely*, Cambridge (1951), pp. 95-109.

[89] See, for instance, R. H. Hilton, *A Medieval Society: The West Midlands at the End of the Thirteenth Century*, London (1966), pp. 21-3; B. K. Roberts, "Medieval Colonization in the Forest of Arden", *Agricultural History Rev.*, XVI (1968), pp. 101-13.

[90] Hilton, *A Medieval Society*, pp. 21-3; R. H. Hilton, "Old Enclosure in the West Midlands: A Hypothesis about their Late Medieval Development"*Géographie et Histoire Agraires. Annales De L'Est*, 21 (1959), pp. 272-83.

[91] Hilton, *A Medieval Society*, p. 13.

[92] M. Hope Dodds (ed.), *A History of Northumberland*, vol. XIV, Newcastle (1935), p. 212.

[93] C. Rogers (ed.), *Rental Book of the Cistercian Abbey of Cupar Angus*, London (1880), vol. I, p. 157.

[94] Baker and Butlin (eds.), *op. cit.*, pp. 635-41.

[95] I have tried to argue a case for this statement in Dodgshon, "Landholding Foundations of the Open-Field System", pp. 14-26.

[96] The case for runrig being underpinned by a several tenure is argued in Dodgshon, "Runrig and the Communal Origins of Property in Land", pp. 189-208.

[97] Examples occur in Peterkin, *Notes on Orkney and Shetland*, pp. 40-1; *Habakkuk Bisset's Rolment of Courtis*, pp. 297-8.

[98] Examples are cited in Dodgshon, "Towards an Understanding and Definition of Runrig", pp. 16-7; Dodgshon, "Runrig and the Communal Origins of Property in Land", pp. 206-7.

[99] Samuel Johnson, *A Journey to the Western Islands of Scotland*, ed. by M. Lascelles, New Haven and London (1971), p. 89.

[100] Rees, *op. cit.*, p. 214.

[101] Some of the examples cited by Nicholls, *op. cit.*, pp. 61-2 seem to fall into this category.

[102] See, for example, Hoffman, *op. cit.*, p. 54.

[103] B. K. Roberts, "Village Plans in County Durham", *Medieval Archaeology*, XVI (1972), pp. 33-56; J. A. Sheppard, "Metrological Analysis of Regular Village Plans in Yorkshire", *Agricultural History Rev.*, XXII (1974), pp. 118-35; J. A. Sheppard, "Medieval Village Planning in Northern England: Some Evidence from Yorkshire", *Jnl. of Historical Geography*, 2 (1976), pp. 3-20; P. Allerston, "English Village Development: Findings from the Pickering District of Yorkshire", *Trans. of the Institute of British Geographers*, 51 (1970), pp. 95-109.

[104] P. Wade-Martins, "Rural Settlement in East Anglia", in P. J. Fowler (ed.), *Recent Work in Rural Archaeology*, Bradford-on-Avon (1975), pp. 137-57.

[105] See S. Göransson, "Field and Village on the Island of Oland: A Study of the Genetic Compound of an East Swedish Rural Landscape", *Geografiska Annaler*, 40 (1958), pp. 101-58; S. Göransson, "Regulated Villages in Medieval Scandinavia", *Geographia Polonica*, 38 (1978), pp. 131-7; S. Göransson, "Solskifte: A Confused Concept", in R. H. Buchanan, R. A. Butlin and D. McCourt (eds.), *Fields, Farms and Settlement in Europe*, Belfast (1976), pp. 22-37.

[106] M. Harvey, *The Morphological and Tenurial Structure of a Yorkshire Township: Preston in Holderness 1066-1750*, Occasional Paper no. 13, Department of Geography, Queen Mary College, University of London (1978), especially pp. 13-24.

[107] Maitland, "Survival of Archaic Communities", p. 363.

Chapter 3

Sub-divided fields and the farming community

By their nature, sub-divided fields drew landholders together into discrete groups. At the very least, the intertwined property interests of these groups must have imbued them with a shared sense of territorial association. However, in the majority of cases, they also formed the basis for differing degrees of common action or accord between them. In its most elementary form, their mutual involvement amounted to little more than agreements over access and the like. In its more developed form, it comprised elaborate schemes of joint or communal husbandry, the entire township or village farming as one. But whether elementary or elaborate, such agrarian associations constituted farming communities, communities that were articulated through the web of social relationships and interactions that overlay sub-divided fields.

Needless to add, there are those who see these farming communities as playing a decisive role in the formation of sub-divided fields; they were needed before sub-divided fields could develop. Any covering argument for the latter had to start from a position in which the existence of farming communities was taken as given. What mattered to the debate on field systems was reduced to the question of why they chose sub-divided fields as the preferred form of landholding. The wider question of how these communities had developed in the first place was construed as a separate issue. Where scholars did pursue this issue further, two types of explanation were offered to account them. First, there were those who saw them as reflecting the innate structure of early society. During a tribal stage of society, the cohesiveness of kin was assumed to have made clustered groups of landholders a logical unit of settlement. Sub-divided fields fitted neatly into this argument as a means by which the cohesiveness of the group could be developed further; they were a concrete expression of the social equalities and togetherness implicit in the social order. Vinogradoff's case for shareholding owed much to this sort of reasoning. Secondly, there have been those who explained the integral character of early farming communities as a consequence of their administrative function; they were the bases for the levying of tax or tribute and the focal points for the local exercise of law and order. The fact that so many farming communities were regulated through courts, such as the manorial courts of England and the barony or birlaw courts of Scotland, appeared to strengthen this belief. Especially noteworthy was the fact that such courts handled far more than agrarian matters. The entire legal superstructure of the township or village centered on them. Agrarian affairs were simply one dimension of their work. Such community courts and their jurisdictions seemed to impart territorial order to the countryside and its farming communities. Seen from this standpoint, the administrative shape and convenience of the farming community appeared to be a case well worth arguing.

An alternative to such views is to see the farming community as formed in response to purely agrarian matters: this too has had its supporters. Discussing the origin of the Germanic farming community in England, Maitland not only dispensed with its communal or administrative origins, but went on to stress that we "must not think of it as a closely knit body of men. The agrarian is almost the only tie that keeps it together".[1] Later in the same discussion, he re-affirmed his belief that "the village landowners formed a group of men whose economic affairs were inextricably intermixed, but this was almost the only principle that made them a unit, unless and until the state began to use the township as its organ for the maintenance of the peace and the collection of taxes".[2] The compound interpretation of sub-divided fields that was presented in Chapter 2 adds weight to this particular idea. If their formation at the outset took place in a gradual or piecemeal fashion, then it would be reasonable to infer that any sense of community or common involvement that was contingent upon them may have grown apace as a by-product of the same process and, if this were so, then it would effectively re-structure a basic sequence of argument. Instead of a situation in which the farming community existed from the beginning, modelled by social or political forces, and which, in the beginning, adopted sub-divided fields and the communal regulation of field husbandry as the only way it could think out these problems, we would now be faced with a new order of development: this new order would begin with the formation of sub-divided fields, lead on to a spirit of common interest and community and eventually culminate in the adoption of joint schemes of husbandry. In other words, the notion of a farming community becomes a social form interposed between sub-divided fields and the highly regulated systems of communal husbandry by which some were managed.

The aim of this chapter is to argue in favour of this second line of development. However, it is not suggested that sub-divided fields acted alone to produce farming communities. If sub-divided fields made out the case for co-operation between husbandmen, other factors contributed by helping to shape the form and scale of response. Put simply, these other factors represent the basic needs of feudalism, namely, its need to define the relationship between lord and tenant as regards land, its need to calculate or apportion liabilities and obligations and its need to provide a focus for the local exercise of law and order; but feudalism was not a stable or simple institution, either historically or geographically. Moreover, its variations were almost certainly manifest in its impact on the relationship between sub-divided fields and the emergence of communities imbued with a strong sense of corporateness. We are not yet in a position to give precision to when this impact first began to appear. Given recent work on the early history of multiple estates, the possibility cannot be ruled out that relationships of a feudal kind were present in Britain by the end of the Iron age.[3] Their presence and absence, therefore, cannot be used to structure the discussion without a great deal of difficulty owing to this uncertainty and instead, it is proposed to look at the relationship between sub-divided fields and farming communities through, firstly, archaeological evidence and, secondly, early documentation: this will lead on to a review in the third section of the institutions through which farming communities were ordered and regulated in respect of their farming activities.

Sub-divided fields and farming communities: the archaeological evidence

The most striking conclusion reached by recent work on prehistoric and Romano-British field systems is that they were far more extensive than had previously been anticipated. Not only were they virtually continuous in the downland areas of southern England but they are now recognized as forming a widespread underlay to modern field systems in low ground areas like the Vale of York, the Fens and Essex.[4] In their work on the Berkshire Downs area, R. Bradley and J. Richards distinguished between *aggregate* and *cohesive* field systems of Bronze or Iron age origin. The former appear natural or accretionary in their layout, with small cell-like fields clustered in a honeycomb fashion. The *cohesive* systems bore a strongly regular or planned appearance (see Fig. 5); indeed, Bradley and Richards see them as having been laid out in a grand act of land allocation and planning during the middle Bronze age.

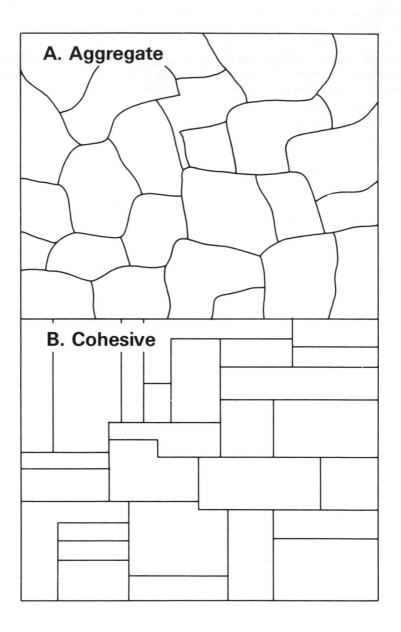

Fig. 5. Types of prehistoric field pattern (a) Aggregate and (b) Cohesive.

They frequently possess bold, straight-line axes that ran across the country-side for a mile or so. In between or appended to such axes were rectangular or square shaped fields.[5] This is a distinction that can be applied elsewhere. N. S. Higham and G. D. B. Jones have published examples of *aggregate* systems for Cumberland,[6] whilst splendid examples of *cohesive* systems, but probably dating from the Roman period, have been mapped for Essex.[7]

This broad contrast between *aggregate* and *cohesive* field systems poses a number of pertinent problems. For instance, given their character, did *aggregate* systems lead to the fragmentation of landholding during their formation? This is an almost unanswerable question in a purely prehistoric context, for it is virtually impossible to establish that landholding was fragmented just by looking at field structures on the ground for it is not something that would be legible in such evidence. Indeed, even in those parts of the country where prehistoric field systems display a strip-like pattern, such as in parts of Cornwall, Somerset and the east Midlands[8], it does not follow automatically that such fields or strips were the intermixed property of different landholders. Narrow strips without well-marked boundaries (i.e. walls, banks) could easily have been a by-product of the techniques of ploughing, without landholding significance. Broad strips that were bounded by walls may have represented separate holdings. These alternative explanations are not put forward in an effort to discount the possibility that some pre-medieval field patterns involved fragmented holdings, but only to underline that this would be an assumption and not a verified fact.

No matter how limited in scope, the foregoing review of late prehistoric and Romano-British field patterns forms an essential preliminary to any discussion of whether the countryside at this point was already peopled by farming communities in a medieval sense, that is, by groups of landholders practising some form of joint husbandry. Obviously, we cannot begin to read the network of social relationships and interactions that characterized such groups from landscape alone. Field patterns, though, can yield some clues on the matter. For instance, the small, *enclosed* nature of many of these early field patterns would hardly facilitate their use for a joint system of husbandry. What we might call the structural relationships between holdings is also of interest. In the case of so-called *aggregate* systems, some patterns hint at a definite focus of field layout around small, but clustered settlements.[9] However, the scale of such systems in terms of both landholders and hectares does not compare with the large complex communities of the typical medieval village, but such a comparison may be unrealistic, for many of the best preserved *aggregate* field patterns of pre-medieval date are to be found in those areas where even later settlements were small in terms of landholders and extent. By contrast, the so-called *cohesive* patterns, despite their description, lacked a definite focus, even though they had a definite overall plan. Considered solely as a pattern of farms and fields, they resemble the sort of layout produced by enclosure, with no sign of holdings being ordered around a single, large settlement.

The extent to which many early field patterns lacked the sort of focus we might expect if farming was managed through groups of landholders is also conveyed by the work of F. Cheyette.[10] Drawing on examples from continental Europe, and France in particular, Cheyette tried to decipher the different forms of early field layout and to fix them in their historical context. He distinguished between strongly regular field patterns that were seemingly centuriated and highly focussed or radial ones. In terms of chronology, the former were Roman in origin and the latter, early medieval or later and their relationship poses a problem that Cheyette, like others before him, saw as prejudicial to the history of settlement in Europe. The fact that some medieval field patterns incorporated earlier, centuriated elements, suggests that there was not necessarily a sharp discontinuity between the two, with one being swept aside to make way for the other. Cheyette himself preferred to construe the problem not as a discontinuity but as a drastic *thinning* of population at the end of the Roman period. As settlement re-expanded, it did so from foci that comprised clustered groups of landholders. In addition, its field pattern took on a pronounced radial pattern, the kind of pattern one might expect of a system that grew from its centre outwards along the footpaths and roads that led out of the settlement. There is no reason why the disused fields of an earlier, centuriated landscape should not have been absorbed or revived by such a growth process where it was appropriate.

There may be parallels here with the sequence of developments in England. The fundamental discontinuity between Romano-British and Saxon settlement proposed by an earlier generation of scholars has largely been abandoned, though there are still some who see discontinuity as the more acceptable thesis.[11] The nature of continuity needs to be specified exactly, for it could take different forms, ranging from continuity of site to continuity solely in the territorial structure of estates. Continuous use of particular fields forms only one dimension of the problem. The distinction between Celtic square fields and Saxon strips, whilst of some validity, is not the sharp distinction it used to be in the literature owing to the discovery of strip-like fields in a late prehistoric or Romano-British context. Even more challenging to stock assumptions has been the discovery that the banks and ditches that bordered the furlongs of some English sub-divided field systems could overlay Roman or Iron age boundaries;[12] again though, caution is needed when interpreting what this signifies. Since the intrinsic nature of sub-divided fields revolved around the sub-division of landholding within furlongs, apparent continuity in the overall layout of furlongs cannot — by itself — instruct us in the history of this aspect. Furthermore, it is not certain whether such an overlap between medieval furlongs and their pre-medieval antecedents implies the continuous use of such fields. Although the trend of modern opinion has been towards the continuity of estates, nevertheless, medieval archaeologists see the early Saxon period as marked by a sharp reduction in the population of England.[13] Thus, as Cheyette would have us believe for Europe generally, the pattern of development at this critical juncture may have been one of intense shrinkage followed by a long-term re-expansion. Such a view serves to marry two opposing arguments, since it explains why the countryside was so heavily settled during Romano-British times, yet appears predominantly English when we see it three or four centuries later. During the phase of re-expansion, communities may have devised whole new schemes of field layout, but as W. J. Ford has proposed, their decisions may have been guided by the abandoned pre-medieval fields that lay around them. He based this conclusion on his work in Warwickshire, where he found that "medieval surveyors, in setting out furlongs, were aware of, and used pre-existing landmarks and land divisions. Many of these alignments, which were legacies of the Roman and earlier periods, also appear to have influenced the orientation of plough-strips".[14]

Within the foregoing schemes of development, there exists the possibility of sub-divided field systems having different levels of structural order or disorder. The distinction between *aggregate* and *cohesive* patterns embodies a contrast with regard to prehistoric fields; where such patterns survived into, or were re-used during the medieval period, presumably as the basis for furlong layout, they must have imprinted their character on the broad framework within which sub-divided fields developed. But once formed, sub-divided field systems were not stable. As noted earlier (p. 51), it is likely that regular systems were created by the reorganization of irregular ones. By such reorganizations, what was re-shaped was the pattern of landholding — the sub-divided field pattern — *within furlongs*, and not necessarily the furlongs themselves. Cheyette also discussed reorganization, citing the way Italian settlement was altered from a dispersed to a nucleated pattern during the ninth and tenth centuries.[15] Although he questioned its wider significance, it is a transformation that has meaning for England. On the one hand, there has been a growing recognition of the abandonment of many small, hamlet-like settlements during the ninth and tenth centuries.[16] On the other hand, there has been a re-assessment of so-called regular or green villages showing that they probably date from the tenth century or later.[17] Combined, these two pieces of evidence suggest that prior to the late Saxon period, settlement in the English countryside probably consisted of loosely structured groups or even dispersed farmsteads, that were subsequently congregated into settlements of a much larger scale, some of which were laid out along regular lines. As J. G. Hurst has written, the "idea that the medieval village was planned at the time of its original settlement in Anglo-Saxon or early medieval times, and has simply grown, has been shown to be false".[18] Behind such a generalization lies all the new possibilities for settlement history now admitted by recent thought, possibilities that embrace the long term continuity of fields (furlongs?) and boundaries of prehistoric origin, the expansion and contraction of settlement, the reorganization of irregular fields and settlements into more regular forms, and the emergence of sub-divided fields out of a landholding pattern that was initially one of absolute severalty.

It was stressed at the outset of this section that the archaeological evidence for early field and settlement patterns was an imperfect basis for disentangling the roots of the farming community, for the latter drew its character from the joint actions and agreements of its constituent landholders and yet the relationship between the two is not devoid of meaning. The former can reflect the latter, even though it may only do so in a circumspect sort of way. To this extent, it is of interest that the field and settlement patterns of the later prehistoric and Romano-British periods manifest obvious differences when compared with those of the medieval period, differences as regards morphology and the extent to which both field and settlement patterns appear focussed around largescale groups or units. In addition, there is a growing body of evidence showing that whilst the history of field and settlement patterns from the late prehistoric onwards may have been one of continuous site occupation, there were other aspects in which it was far from being a smooth or continuous process. Break points can be identified at which the form of such patterns was subjected to reorganization. At other times, they were subjected to severe contraction, followed later by re-expansion, not necessarily along the same lines. Such changes say nothing direct or precise about *when* the farming community first developed. However, the value of the archaeological evidence is that it blurs the issue: it makes the case for an early origin appear much less clear-cut, placing a number of serious obstacles in the way of such an assumption. Indeed, if it can be shown that the documentary evidence favours a view of the farming community as an institution that was manufactured during the medieval period, rather than one that formed an innate part of the organic constitution of society, then there is nothing in the archaeological evidence that would contradict such a view.

Sub-divided fields and the farming community: the documentary evidence
It is the writer's contention that the formation of the farming community was greatly influenced by the distinction between freemen and bondmen. Put simply, the creation of defined groups of landholders centered on particular foci and overcast with a tightly drawn juridical net not only served the interests of feudalism, but provided the conditions under which co-operative

groups of farmers could *more easily* develop. For this reason, there is much to be learnt from the contrasts between areas of strong feudal lordship and areas where feudal lordship was either weak or absent and where groups of freemen formed the basis of rural society. There is nothing new in this suggestion, but it is one that needs greater specification than has hitherto been accorded it.

In looking more closely at areas where free communities prevailed, the following comments are not intended to apply to all free areas or groups at all times over the medieval period, but only to those who held their land allodially, that is, without a superior. Those holding land by *gwely* land tenure in Wales or the udallers of the Northern Isles fall into this category. Excluded are those landholders who were of free status and who held land by free tenure in the sense of having no service obligations, but who paid a money rent for their land. Broadly speaking, these were the free communities created during the spate of colonization that occurred in the lowland forest areas (i.e. Arden, Feckenham) and upland waste areas (i.e. the Pennines) of England during the twelfth and thirteenth centuries. A fuller review of how colonization produced such communities can be found on pp. 83-99. However, despite their freedom, they were still mostly tenants whose holdings and rights were rigidly defined by a superior.

Given free groups similar to those of early medieval Wales or of the Northern Isles, the growth of population, and the mapping of this growth back into landholding through partible inheritance, would have led over time to the formation of patrilocal groups. Patrilocal groups were groups of kin-related landholders clustered within a specific locality; they emerged through two complementary processes. Estates or large blocks of landholding would be sub-divided between co-heirs and, at the same time, added to by the projection of new offshoots into the surrounding waste. Needless to say, even when waste resources were depleted, ongoing partition between co-heirs could still add to the number of landholders and holdings within the group. What is important about such patrilocal groups is that they rarely led to the build-up of settlement at a single point, that is, in a village-like form. The process of their formation could sub-divide and intermix holdings, but it could not readily concentrate settlement at a single focus. Instead, settlement and its associated holdings tended to be dispersed over the territory which the group occupied and it displayed clustering only to the extent that garlands of settlement or holdings might be arrayed around particular pockets of arable land. Medieval Welsh examples of this sort of settlement pattern have been published by G. R. J. Jones. In his discussion of free *gwelyau*, he has continually stressed how their associated settlement tended to form a loose girdle of farmsteads around the periphery of arable sharelands or *rhandiroedd*.[19] J. Storer Clouston's work on Orkney settlement disclosed a similar pattern in those parishes where udal tenures predominated. The successive partition of family estates over a period of centuries did not necessarily lead to tightly compacted settlement groups, but often produced more loosely gathered settlement in which the isolation of each individual holding was emphasised through their possession of separate place-names.[20] Patrilocal local groups have been documented for parts of England, parts as widely separated as the northern Pennines and Kent.[21] Here too, the partition of hereditary holdings need not have led invariably to the growth of large compact settlements, but to a looser, more dispersed kind of pattern. Even in an area like Cornwall, where direct documentary evidence for partible inheritance is lacking, it may be possible to interpret the persistence of dispersed settlement patterns from the pre-medieval period as a sign of how population growth amongst an initially free (?) society served to create a denser network of landholding, but not necessarily to concentrate settlement within it.

The position with bond or servile communities differed in two respects. In the first place, their townships or settlements had much greater definition, a definition imposed from above. Care needs to be taken in distinguishing this problem from that of the holding definition raised in Chapter 2. What is being discussed here is the framework of settlements. The problem examined in Chapter 2 concerned the interpretation of shares or holdings within the bounds of this framework. It will be argued that the former had a much more defined structure to it than the latter, at least to start with, its close definition embracing both location and overall extent. The fixing of settlements to a particular location may seem a trite point to stress, and one easily taken for granted. However, its significance can best be measured alongside a tenure like, say, the *gwelyau* of early Wales, whose somewhat sprawling growth across a number of different sharelands or sites expresses a different set of checks and balances. Under *gwely* land tenure, an individual held land of the *gwely* (no matter how sprawled it might be) not of the township: this was the crucial difference between free tenures of an allodial character and bond or villein tenures. Looking at the problem of settlement location from another angle, an important feature of many large, compact settlements is the distinction made between the area allocated to dwellings or farmsteads and the arable fields around. In many settlements, it is a distinction embodied in what was *toft* and what was *townland* or *town fields*. These two sectors were quite different in status, the one the responsibility of the individual and the other, the responsibility of the entire township and their formal distinction was a widespread feature in medieval Britain.[22] Although prominent in areas of strong lordship, they were just as likely to be found in areas of free, allodial tenures.[23] As scholars like B. K. Roberts have emphasized, the toft alignment of a township formed the basis of any settlement plan that might exist.[24] Varieties of settlement plan were no more than varieties of toft alignment along regular or irregular axes. To talk of a township having a definite point of focus is really to say that its tofts or their equivalent had a definite point of focus; but there is more to the problem than this. In many settlements, the toft was deemed to be the very basis of landholding in the fields around.[25] Seen in this way, the regulation of large townships from a feudal point of view was greatly facilitated by the exercise of control over tofts, both as regards their careful distinction from the surrounding arable fields and their location. Yet in the exercise of this control, such townships must have acquired more coherence as communities from the side by side juxtaposition of tofts.

The control similarly exercised over the physical extent of townships held by bond or villein tenure was of the very essence to their feudal character. The careful computation of the township's overall area and the fixing of its boundaries on the ground provided the essential basis for the calibration of feudal dues and obligations: the one determined the other. But in stressing the *measured* or finite extent of such townships, it does not follow that their limits were unchangeable and all that is meant is that there was a calculation about their gross extent. Growth could and did take place, but it was always a measured growth, with a corresponding increase in the township's assessment and the level of its obligations or dues. The sense of the point being made is captured by the description of early bond tenures in Wales as *tir cyfrif*, that is, reckoned or assessed land, something that was of a calculated quantity. By comparison, *gwely* land tenure laid stress on the possession of land through a person's membership of a family group or stock. The calculation of how much land was held was something arrived at in a *de facto* and not a *de jure* sort of way. Only when such land passed to the Crown, when it ceased to be an allodial tenure, would the need to define its extent have arisen. Having a more questionable bearing on the discussion in hand is the distinction in Anglo-Saxon charters between folkland and bookland. Despite considerable and often involved debate, standard views tend to favour a fairly straight-forward meaning for these terms. Folkland is seen as land held by customary law or tenure (and presumably of an allodial rather than feudal character). Bookland is seen as land "held by the book".[26] Behind such a phrase possibly lies the recording of land tenure in a more precise way, not just as land held feudally of a superior, but as landholding that had a measure to it.

A deeper understanding of this issue can be gained from the situation in late medieval Scotland. Broadly speaking, two types of land assessment can be found north of the Border at this point. In the east and south-east of the country, land assessments were built up from units that measured land capacity, either its capacity to support a family (husbandlands) or a plough (oxgates, ploughgates). By contrast, those of the north and west appear to have more of a fiscal character (merklands, pennylands, ouncelands). Even the davach of the north and north-west may be of a similar type, given the now fashionable view that it was derived from a measure of grain paid as tribute by landholders; in fact, I have suggested elsewhere that all these land measures of the north and west can best be rationalised by seeing them as based on tribute payments of either money or grain that were formerly paid by freemen to their chief or king. As land tenure in these areas became more feudalised over the latter part of the medieval period, these tribute payments probably took on the meaning not just of rent but of land measures. Thus, to give a hypothetical example, the ounceland (gaelic = *tirunga*) may have begun life as a tribute payment by a family or lineage of one ounce of silver which, with the feudalization of tenure, became an equivalent in rent for one ounce-worth of land.[27] A critical aspect of this process was the transfer of tribute obligations from the person or family to the land. Such a transition almost certainly occurred in other parts of Britain where free groups likewise underwent a feudalization of tenure during the medieval period. A clear example has been documented for south-west Wales, where the payment of *gwestfa*, a tribute, took on the character of a territorial measure c. 1100.[28] T. Charles-Edwards' convincing case for the hide of Anglo-Saxon England starting out as a holding sufficient for a family hints at a similar, if not identical line of development, with its meaning as a land measure of fixed extent being of a secondary and adaptive nature.[29]

The importance of this proposed genealogy for certain land measures in early Britain is that it brings into focus the vital importance of feudalism as a force that served to concentrate landholders into the coherent, self-conscious groups that we recognise as the medieval farming community. It took tribute payments and dues that were incumbent on the person or kin groups and made them incumbent on land, thus giving the possession of land a calibrated scale of measurement. It did not achieve this transformation speedily. Early feudalism was equally interested in the obligations of the person or family, but it established this interest by fusing such obligations with the tenure of land. In doing so, it may well have initiated a change in attitude towards landholding, a change that spread step by step with feudalism. At the root of this change was the re-casting of landholding on a unitary basis, that is, as something doled out according to a definite scale of measures and imposed on the landscape as a geographically-structured grid of rights and responsibilities. Feudalism's need to clarify the balance of rights and responsibilities between estates, and then within them, using this devised scale of measure, must have contributed greatly to the growth of nucleated settlements. It demarcated units in the landscape (or townships) and ensured that landholders within these units held of them and not of the patrimony of family groups or lineages whose landholding may have been of a more geographically diffused kind. Under feudalism, landholders now saw themselves as belonging to a lord and a particular township, not to a joint family group. Herein lies its significance for the emergence of farming communities. As an overlay on those forces that promoted the sub-division and fragmentation of landholding, it helped add a new potential as regards the way landholders reacted to the organizational problems posed by sub-divided fields.

The second way in which bond or villein communities differed from those that were free was in their ability to govern themselves, an essential pre-condition for any farming community. This may seem to be a paradoxical statement, given that we are dealing here with groups that were legally unfree. However, whilst unfree communities did not have the freedom, the same degree of choice, over whether they should act as a single body on all matters, the impositions of lordship ensured that they were more likely to. Moreover, the feudal demands of lordship provided the means and, above all, the experience of the community acting together. Taking up these points in greater detail, few scholars have resisted the temptation of seeing the manor as providing the institutional framework within which the self-regulation of farming communities took place. In shaping the needs of lordship, the manor seemingly shaped the farming community. But such a simplistic view misleads; it misleads not least because our understanding of the manor admits so much variety to its form and composition, that it is difficult to believe that its relationship to the farming community could be so simple and straight-forward. The old idea of the village always equalling the manor is now recognized as only one of a number of possible relationships between the two, one largely confined to parts of the Midlands. In East Anglia, it was commonplace for the village to comprise a number of different manors. In parts of the east Midlands, the south-west, the far north of England and in Wales, their relationship was reversed with manors comprising groups of settlements: these, of course, were the so-called multiple estates. Such a variety could hardly have fostered a standardised relationship between the manor and the farming community. But a more serious criticism is that manorial courts were not the only courts by which farming communities in early Britain were administered. Despite a belief to the contrary in some discussions of field systems, Scotland had its equivalent in the court of Barony. Relatively few Scottish townships were not under the jurisdiction of one or another Barony court. Like the manor, their jurisdiction ranged from single settlements up to large clusters of touns,[30] but even outside the jurisdiction of the barony courts, there existed alternative instruments of juridical authority. Some townships, for instance, had what were called burlaw courts, whose status can best be described as that of a community court rather than a barony court.[31] In some localities, local administration was in the hands of a regality court, a court of higher status than that of a barony. Townships in the vicinity of Melrose (Roxburghshire) and Grant

(Banffshire), for example, were regulated through regality courts. Orkney and Shetland were administered through courts that bound their island groups together into a single jurisdiction, or the *Lawting*. Laws or enactments of the *Lawting* were applied at the local level by representatives known as the *foud*. Courts in Wales dealing with the ordinary affairs of the township show a similar variety. Many in south Wales were straightforward manorial courts, with a fairly close link with the townships they administered. However, along the border with England and in the north-east, there existed extensive territorial lordships within which the only court of jurisdiction was that of the lordship or honour itself.[32] However, the monolithic character of such juris-dictions was offset by the use of local *patria* or juries to establish and even enact local customs or rulings.[33]

All the forementioned courts had juridical authority over the affairs of the township. However, there were evident differences over how remote and comprehensive in effect this authority was. Some were clearly far removed from the day-to-day business of the ordinary farming community. In these instances, the effectiveness of the system's control over farming depended on how far the relationship between court and township was bridged by inter-mediating procedures and groups, like the use of local *patria* in the Marcher Lordships of Wales. The larger English manors solved the problem by employing a circuit system, meeting at different places at different times.[34] A similar solution was adopted in Orkney and Shetland, with the central court or the *Lawting* being supplemented by a series of provincial or local assemblies.[35] By comparison, there must have been many townships in the remoter corners of the western Highlands and Islands that had no such facility, with the barony court to which they were tied being distant both geographically and juridically. Many such townships possibly had a *constable* and recognized procedures for implementing decisions of their parent court[36], but their existence is not always apparent. Detailed court records often suggest that the burden of responsibility fell on the shoulders of the tacksman rather than all landholders, and that it had not the formality or the weight of responsibility to be found in those townships with a close link to a presiding court.[37] In all these cases, the social and physical distance between court and township must have left a great deal of the organisational problems of the latter to the initiative of the landholders involved. By comparison, where townships had a close relationship with a court, the latter probably served more as a community court in the sense that it could pay special attention to the needs of the individual community far more readily.

These differences can be apprehended through the different levels of interest actually shown by courts in the agrarian affairs of the ordinary township. Courts whose area of jurisdiction was geographically spread tended to be more specialized in the matters they dealt with. Their basic tasks centered on the lord's interests: his feudal impositions and dues, his labour service and rents, his forests and wastes. Beyond this distinctly feudal role, such courts handled criminal matters, debts, damages and broken contracts. What appears to be lacking are agreements over husbandry negotiated between landholders. The court rolls of Ruthin lordship, for example, are a record of precisely the matters just mentioned, with no reference to agreements designed to aid the smooth-working of farming communities.[38] H. S. A. Fox has highlighted an intriguing entry in the court rolls of the large, adjacent lordship of Denbigh which sanctioned the reorganization of a township on to a three-field basis, but such a condescension towards such mundane matters of husbandry are more usually lacking in the Denbigh court rolls, as well as in those for other marcher lordships.[39] The court records of Shetland and Orkney show they too were not a forum for deciding on the agrarian customs of individual townships, though varied *dis*agreements between husbandmen do surface in their records. However, the bulk of cases deal with divisions of land between co-heirs or family settlements, criminal actions, debts and damages.[40] It is, of course, probable that landholders themselves stepped into this breach when need arose, but where and when they did so, it would have lacked the element of coercion and force that a court act carried.

The failure of such courts to contribute to the agrarian organization of townships is most starkly revealed when they are compared with those that did. Generally speaking, these were courts with a close, more personalised relationship with townships, having one or, at most, a small handful under their control. Not only did they deal with a wide range of feudal dues and impositions, criminal offences, breaches of contract and the like, but they also enacted and upheld the by-laws which enabled the townships under their care to function as farming communities.[41] It is through this willingness to engage the mundane business of farming routine that courts of this nature had an impact on the growth of field systems. It would be wrong, though, to see the emergence of self-regulating communities of landholders as a direct and simple response to the more immediate ties which some townships had with their manorial or barony court. Usually — if not invariably — this sort of tie was most likely to be found in the more fertile areas, where population growth over time had led to fairly complex patterns of settlement and lordship: this was as true of English manors as of Scottish baronies.[42] For obvious reasons, these were the areas where labour services and demesne systems would have been most strongly developed during the medieval period.[43] Local court rolls contain regular references to both the nature and apportionment of labour services amongst customary tenants or villeins, such as those for the manor of Marydown (Hampshire)[44] or those documented by W. O. Ault[45] and Hilton[46]. Barony court records for Scotland are equally forthcoming. Details of the typical labour services performed by tenants can be found listed in court records for the Barony of Menzies in Perthshire[47] and for Balgair in Stirlingshire[48] as late as the early eighteenth century. By their very nature, labour services gave landholders the experience of work routines based on co-operative effort. The step from this to co-operative effort solely in their own interests was a short one. Indeed, this could well have been a critical factor in the emergence of farming communities. Certainly, when seen alongside the labour services owed to their lord, the by-laws regulating the farming routine of a township do not appear out of place, though the commonest form of entry in most surviving court rolls concerns the infringement rather than the enactment of by-laws.

The level at which these "local" courts dealt with the husbandry problems of individual townships is best understood through example. The court rolls of Acomb manor, near York, offer a rich source of illustration. In fact, so abundant is the matter dealing with the problems of the husbandman that one could be forgiven the temptation of seeing the court as designed specifically for him. Virtually every dimension of husbandry finds a mention, from the primary tasks of ploughing and harvesting, to more trivial matters, such as the act forbidding landholders "to thresh corn in their *laithes* by candle-light"[49], the burying of dead pigs[50] or the problems posed by a stray sheep and a lamb that stayed in the lordship for a year and a day.[51] As one might expect of a close community, there is even a record dealing with the case of a woman who stood "as an easinge droper at the wyndoo" of someone's house.[52] There are Scottish court records to match. The records of the Barony Court of Forbes (Aberdeenshire), for instance, allow a reconstruction to be made of the pattern of stock movements through the different parts of the township.[53] The court records for the Barony of Stitchill (Berwickshire) are especially informative on ploughing and cropping.[54]

It must be kept in mind that even where townships were closely supervised by manorial or barony court, they could still possess an assembly of landholders or panel of birlawmen to handle matters on the ground and to advise the court on what was accepted custom. Thus, in his discussion of communities in the west Midlands during the thirteenth century, an area where townships and courts were as intimately connected as anywhere, Hilton has written that "villagers" assemblies, however inadequately documented, must have been normal features of the village.[55] Most of the Scottish barony court records inspected by the writer suggest that there too, panels of birlawmen or landholders were interposed between the court and the day-to-day running of the township. Often their appointment and conditions of service are detailed.[56] The existence of such assemblies or panels of birlawmen has far-reaching significance for the so-called self-regulating character of farming communities. However, their effectiveness — and possibly even their existence — must have depended ultimately on the closeness of feudal supervision as expressed by the social (and geographical) distance between court and township. Where the territory of each was coterminuous — or nearly so — then feudalism is more likely to have been an active agent in drawing landholders together into farming communities, for it is mostly in these situations that manorial and barony courts went beyond their staple administrative and feudal functions and dealt constructively and directly with ordinary matters of husbandry: it is almost as if the more localised the jurisdiction of courts became, then the more localised and personalised were their matters of court. For this reason, it is under these circumstances that sub-divided field systems were more likely to have evolved further into farming communities, with the sub-division of holdings being used as the basis for co-operative systems of husbandry and enterprise.[57]

The farming community: an evolutionary perspective

In the final section of this chapter, it is proposed to review the different ways in which groups of landholders did co-operate and how this co-operation — the very essence of the farming community — helped shape the form and layout of field systems. Emphasis will be placed on the fact that differing degrees of co-operation can be identified and that only by distinguishing between these differing degrees of co-operation can the link between the farming community and field systems be fully comprehended. Behind this approach to the problem is the assumption that the farming community grew as a response to the logistical problems posed by the formation of sub-divided fields. Arguably, the agreements and common actions that gave character to the farming community emerged slowly rather than suddenly, a gradual adaptation to the fragmentation of landholding and the mixing of interests: if so, then some thought needs to be given to singling out those areas of a township's resource-complex that were "communalised" first and those that were "communalised" last.

Three phases of development are tentatively offered. The first probably concerned agreements over the use of common-property resources *outside* the land occupied as holdings in severalty or as sub-divided fields. The resources involved ranged from common grazings or waste to timber, from pannage to fisheries. Agreements over the level of their use were just as likely to be contracted between townships as within them. The second phase probably saw the spread of such agreements to the cultivation of localised areas of arable as holdings became more and more sub-divided and as pairs or groups of landholders tried — between themselves — to offset the increasing dis-economy of working their scattered blocks or strips as separate units of husbandry. The third, and final phase, probably saw the elevation of these localised agreements to the entire arable of the community. As Thirsk reasoned, the most critical of those adopted by the community at large were the common grazing of the harvest stubble and, as a consequence of this, the establishment on all available arable of a single, communally-regulated cropping system. Such changes clearly formed a vital threshold in the history of a community or township, for it was the point at which sub-divided fields, having induced co-operative systems of husbandry, were now re-shaped through the same spirit of co-operation into more efficient layouts for the purposes of cropping: cause and effect were thereby reversed.

The earliest sign of an agreement between landholders is provided by the reference in the seventh-century laws of Ine to the fencing of common meadow and other shareland. The full extract declares that if "ceorls have common meadow (gaerstun haebben gemaenne) or other shareland (gedalland) to hedge and some have hedged their share and some have not, and cattle eat their common land or grass, let those who are responsible for the gap give compensation to those who have hedged their share for the injury which may have been done". Faced with this extract, the verdict of some scholars has been that if "this is not open-field farming, it is hard to know what it can be".[58] There is some ambiguity, though, so that a measure of caution is needed.[59] It cannot be taken as proof that fully-matured field systems, replete with rights of common grazing over arable, existed at this early date; at most, it only establishes for us the existence of common grazing rights over meadow and rules governing how such land should be hedged when in use. It represents an agreement over a common-property resource that is still compatible with a system of several holdings. As early patterns of landholding unfolded, such agreements must have proliferated rapidly as landholders, or groups of landholders, negotiated with each other over their rights of common pasture, waste, timber, etc., the more so where such resources threatened to become scarce. Concern over such rights was not contingent on the existence of sub-divided fields, but there is another reason why agreements of this sort recommend themselves as the earliest forms of co-operation between landholders. The fundamental process of assarting impinged on the whole question of what an individual's rights were in respect of common-property resources. No matter how abundant was the reservoir of waste, access to such a vital resource would soon have acquired a framework of regulations ensuring that landholders were equally endowed by the process.

Less certainty surrounds the origin of agreements affecting arable land and its husbandry. According to Thirsk, it is likely that agreements over the sharing of harvest stubble, ploughing and harvesting began with the co-operation of small groups or neighbours within a community: this is an attractive hypothesis, but it has to be conceded that evidence for such piecemeal co-operation as a stage preparatory to the adoption of such agreements by the entire community is still largely circumstantial, though Thirsk has published some examples.[60] In theory, we can expect townships in areas like the south-west, the north-west and along the Welsh Border which possessed sub-divided fields without regular cropping patterns to be the most promising for future investigation, since they appear frozen at a stage which evidently falls short of the full, communal regulation of husbandry.

But by their very nature, agreements between small groups or pairs of landholders will be difficult to find. Yet their existence and role in the making of fully-fledged farming communities has a persuasive logic to it, simply because it is fairly easy to envisage ways in which these localised agreements could develop. For instance, co-parceners may have wanted to preserve the established working structure of a family holding after it had been divided between them. Perhaps the problems of dividing farm equipment and working cattle may also have induced co-operation in husbandry. Of course, ultimately, successive fragmentation of family patrimony may have reduced shares to a size at which they could no longer sustain a plough without co-operation. Taking a quite different view of the problem, the discharge of labour services on the lord's demesne would have given landholders the experience of working together at the tasks of husbandry. As noted in the previous section, this would have meant that as holdings became more and more fragmented and intermixed, landholders would have had sufficient foreknowledge of how best to overcome the grosser handicaps of their predicament. More to the point, where demesne and tenant land were intermixed — as in many south-eastern townships — their obligation to share with each other in ploughing and harvesting demesne must have been almost inextricably fused with the management of their own holdings: the habits of one would sooner or later have overflowed on to the other; but to construe the issue in this way underplays a vital point. For landholders to co-operate in small groups to overcome the problems of sub-divided fields must have been a logical step, one that placed minimal demands on the neighbourliness of adjacent landholders. The real hurdle was the adoption of joint agreements over stubble grazing and cropping at the community level. Given the ease of the one when compared with the difficulty of the other, we can hardly be surprised if small groups of landholders acted on their own behalf in advance of the community at large.

If there was a point in the history of field systems at which the presence of strong lordship or feudalism mattered more than at any other time, then it was in facilitating this translation of local agreements over stubble grazing and cropping up to the level of the township or village *in toto*. The reason why was because it demanded not just group decision, but some degree of physical re-planning. For Thirsk, this re-planning was confined to the notional grouping of arable furlongs into two or three large sectors for the purposes of cropping, a move made necessary by the introduction of rights of common grazing over arable. The roughly equal dispersal of each landholder's strips between these two or three sectors — an essential adjustment if they were to avoid having all their land under fallow during a single cropping season — was seen by her as achieved by a series of private agreements or exchanges. However, since she put forward these ideas, far more evidence has been forthcoming for the radical re-structuring of both settlements and their fields at different points in their history. To invoke a re-arrangement of landholding when they adopted communal cropping schemes, therefore, seems less of an unfounded assumption. With so much involved, though, only communities organised for collective action were likely to make such a step, and this was most likely to be found where lordship was strong and where local courts were available to strengthen the hand of the village assembly. In fact, communally-regulated cropping systems were invariably confined to such areas. Conversely, areas where no such cropping system prevailed and where landholders were permitted to enclose their individual strips, such as in south-west England and Pembrokeshire[61], tended to be areas where the hand of lordship — whilst present — rested only lightly on the rural community. But the difference between the two broad types of field system being contrasted here runs deeper. Only where husbandry was framed within a communally-regulated system can it be said that the medieval farming community had fully developed; a community bound together not just by an overlap of interests but by common action in all the main aspects of its field economy. Only by setting such fully developed farming communities beside those which failed to achieve this degree of collective action can it be appreciated why the seemingly timeless character of farming communities must not be taken for granted. It needs to be argued out as something that grew in response to the fragmentation and intermixture of holdings, a contrived arrangement born out of expediency rather than the innate corporateness or communalism of early society.

References

[1] F. W. Maitland, *Domesday Book and Beyond*, Fontana edition, London (1960), p. 407.
[2] *Ibid.*, p. 408.
[3] See G. R. J. Jones, "The Tribal System in Wales: A Reassessment in the Light of Settlement Studies", *Welsh History Review*, I (1961), pp. 111-32; G. R. J. Jones, "Multiple Estates and Early Settlement", pp. 15-40 in P. H. Sawyer (ed.), *Medieval Settlement*, London (1976), pp. 15-40.

[4] A general survey of recent work can be found in H. C. Bowen and P. J. Fowler (eds.), *Early Land Allottment in the British Isles*, British Archaeological Reports no. 48, Oxford (1978), pp. 1-199. More comprehensive discussions can be found in P. Salway, S. J. Hallam and J. I'A. Bromwich, *The Fenlands in Roman Times*, Royal Society Research Series, V (1970), pp. 40-48; Fowler (ed.), *Recent Work in Rural Archaeology*, esp. chapters 6, 7 and 8.

[5] R. Bradley and J. Richards, "Prehistoric Fields and Boundaries on the Berkshire Downs", in Bowen and Fowler (eds.), *Early Land Allotment in the British Isles*, pp. 53-60, especially p. 56. In a more general discussion of this contrast between small, irregular or curvilinear prehistoric fields and those of rectangular form, C. C. Taylor has ascribed a roughly similar date (2000-1500 BC) to this shift from one to another, at least in the more settled parts of lowland England. He too, was in no doubt that rectangular field systems were planned or laid out *en bloc*, writing that there "is a clear indication of long, often straight, parallel and continuous boundaries forming huge land units of several hundred hectares, within which the actual fields are fitted". C. C. Taylor, *Fields in the English Landscape*, London (1975), p. 38.

[6] See N. S. Higham and G. D. B. Jones, "Frontiers, Forts and Farmers", *Archaeological Jnl.*, 132 (1975), p. 39.

[7] See W. Rodwell, "Relict Landscapes in Essex", pp. 89-98 in Bowen and Fowler (eds.), *Early Land Allotment in the British Isles*, p. 92.

[8] Plans of such systems are reproduced in C. Thomas, "Types and Distributions of Pre-Norman Fields in Cornwall and Scilly", pp. 7-15 in *ibid.*, p. 11; P. J. Fowler, "Pre-Medieval Fields in the Bristol Region", pp. 29-47 in *ibid.*, p. 47; D. N. Riley, "An Early System of Land Division in South Yorkshire and North Nottinghamshire", pp. 103-8 in *ibid.*, p. 108.

[9] Good instances can be found in Fowler, "Pre-Medieval Fields in the Bristol Region", p. 47; N. J. Higham, "Early Field Survival in North Cumbria", in Bowen and Fowler (eds.), *op. cit.*, pp. 121 and 125; G. D. B. Jones, "The North-Western Interface", pp. 93-106 in Fowler (ed.), *Recent Work in Rural Archaeology*, pp. 96-7.

[10] F. Cheyette, "The Origins of European Villages and the First European Expansion", *Jnl. of Economic History*, XXXVII (1977), pp. 182-206.

[11] See, for instance, H. C. Darby, "Anglo-Scandinavian Foundations", in H. C. Darby (ed.), *A New Historical Geography of England*, Cambridge (1973), p. 1; M. M. Postan, *The Medieval Economy and Society*, London (1972), p. 1.

[12] C. Taylor and P. Fowler, "Roman Fields into Medieval Furlongs?", pp. 159-62 in Bowen and Fowler (eds.), *op. cit.*, pp. 159-62; M. W. Beresford and J. G. Hurst, "Wharram Percy: a Case Study in Microtopography", pp. 114-44 in P. H. Sawyer (ed.), *Medieval Settlement*, London (1976), pp. 141-44.

[13] See, for instance, P. Fowler's suggestion that the archaeological evidence for settlement fits J. C. Russell's calculation of a drop from around 2 million to less than one in P. J. Fowler, "Agriculture and Rural Settlement", pp. 23-48 in D. M. Wilson (ed.), *The Archaeology of Anglo-Saxon England*, London (1976), pp. 43-4. In fact, more recently, Fowler had postulated a much greater reduction at this point, proposing a population of around 4-5 million for the late Roman-British period and a fall to under one for the early Saxon period. See P. J. Fowler, "Lowland Landscapes: culture, time and Personality", in S. Limbrey and J. G. Evans (eds.), *The Effect of Man on the Landscape: the Lowland Zone*, C. B. A. Research Report no. 21, London (1978), pp. 6-7; P. J. Fowler, "The Gwithian Fields and the Evidence for Early Ploughs: A Review" in T. R. Rowley (ed.), *The Origin of Open Field Agriculture*, London (1980), forthcoming.

[14] W. J. Ford, "Some Settlement Patterns in the Central Region of the Warwickshire Avon", pp. 274-94 in Sawyer (ed.), *op. cit.*, p. 294.

[15] Cheyette, *op. cit.*, pp. 199-200.

[16] See the summary of work in C. C. Taylor, "Aspects of village mobility in medieval and later times", in Limbrey and Evans (eds.), *op. cit.*, pp. 126-34. Relevant discussion can also be found in P. Wade-Martins, "The origins of rural settlement in East Anglia", in Fowler (ed.), *Recent Work in Rural Archaeology*, pp. 136-57.

[17] B. K. Roberts, "Village plans in County Durham: a preliminary statement", *Medieval Archaeology*, 16 (1972), pp. 33-56; J, Sheppard, "Medieval village planning in Northern England", *Jnl. of Historical Geography*, 2 (1976), pp. 3-20.

[18] J. G. Hurst, "The Changing Medieval Village in England", pp. 531-40 in P. J. Ucko, R. Tringham and G. W. Dimbleby (eds.), *Man, Settlement and Urbanism*, London (1972), p. 540.

[19] See G. R. J. Jones, "The Tribal System in Wales: A Reassessment in the Light of Settlement Studies", *Welsh History Rev.*, 1 (1961), p. 1; Jones "Post-Roman Wales", p. 331.

[20] J. Storer Clouston, "The Orkney Townships", *Scottish Historical Rev.*, 17 (1920), pp. 37-42.

[21] J. A. Tuck, "Northumbrian Society in the Fourteenth Century", *Northern History*, VI (1971), p. 28; Du Boulay, *op. cit.*, pp. 136 and 146-7.

[22] The best review of the problem is to be found in B. K. Roberts, *Rural Settlement in Britain*, Folkestone (1977), pp. 139-44.

[23] See, for example, the very fine summary of Orkney township plans in Storer Clouston, "The Orkney Townships", especially pp. 20-1. Discussion of an individual township can be found in W. P. L. Thomson, "Funzie, Fetlar: A Shetland Run-rig Township in the Nineteenth Century", *Scottish Geographical Magazine*, 86 (1970), pp. 174-81.

[24] Roberts, *Rural Settlement in Britain*, pp. 139-44. On p. 144, for example, he declares that "the importance of tofts cannot be overstressed: together with the buildings, they were the basic stuff of the village".

[25] *Ibid.*, p. 142.

[26] H. R. Loyn, *Anglo-Saxon England and the Norman Conquest*, London, (1962), p. 171.

[27] For further discussion, see Dodgshon, "Law and Landscape in Early Scotland", pp. 127-45.

[28] Jones Pierce, *Medieval Welsh Society*, p. 322. See also, R. A. Dodgshon, "Society and Economy 400-1100", in E. G. Bowen (ed.), *A History of Cardiganshire*, vol. I, forthcoming.

[29] T. Charles-Edwards, "Kinship, Status and the Origins of the Hide", *Past and Present*, 56 (1972), pp. 3-33.

[30] A general discussion of barony courts can be found in P. Mc.Intyre, "The Franchise Courts", pp. 374-83 in *An Introduction to Scottish Legal History*, Stair Society, Edinburgh (1958), pp. 374-83.

[31] The burlaw court at Chirnside in Berwickshire appears to fall into this category, see R. A. Dodgshon, "Farming in Roxburghshire and Berwickshire on the Eve of Improvement", *Scottish Historical Rev.*, LIV (1975), p. 153. A similar court functioned at Fintry in Stirlingshire, carrying out all the duties of a barony court but without being officially of that status, see J. Dunlop (ed.), *Court Minutes of Balgair 1706-1736*, Scottish Record Society, Edinburgh (1957), especially p. 5.

[32] A review of the administration of these areas can be found in T. B. Pugh (ed.), *The Marcher Lordships of South Wales 1415-1536*, Cardiff (1963), pp. 3-48; R. R. Davies, "The Law of the March", *Welsh History Rev.*, 5 (1970), pp. 1-30.

[33] *Ibid.*, p. 8.

[34] The manor of Wakefield is one that adopted this solution to its size problem, see W. P. Baildon (ed.), *Court Rolls of the Manor of Wakefield, vol. II: 1297 to 1309*, Yorkshire Archaeological Society, Record Series, vol. XXXVI (1906).

[35] G. Donaldson, *Shetland Life Under Earl Patrick*, Edinburgh (1962), pp. 1-6.

[36] See, for example, W. F. Skene, *Celtic Scotland*, vol. III Edinburgh (1976), p. 390.

[37] The role of the tacksmen in the juridical processes affecting Highland townships comes over strongly from the barony courts of Strathavon (Banffshire) and Menzies (Perthshire), both courts with geographically dispersed areas of responsibilities. See V. Gaffney (ed.), *The Lordship of Strathavon*, Third Spalding Club, Aberdeen (1952), appendix I, pp. 208-11; SRO, GD50, John Macgregor Collection, no. 156, List of Inhabitants in Rannoch 1676 *et al.*

[38] R. A. Roberts (ed.), *Ruthin Court Rolls (Temp. King Edward I)*, Cymmrodorion Record Series, London (1894), pp. 1-37.

[39] H. S. A. Fox, "The Chronology of Enclosure and Economic Development in Medieval Devon", p. 202. The original entry can be found in P. Vinogradoff and F. Morgan, (eds.), *Survey of the Honour of Denbigh, 1334*, London (1914).

[40] See, Storer Clouston, *Records of the Earldom of Orkney, 1299-1614*, p. 1 *et seq.*; Donaldson, *Shetland Life Under Earl Patrick*, especially introduction and chapter on the law; G. Donaldson (ed.), *The Court Book of Shetland 1602-1604*, Scottish Record Society, Edinburgh (1958), p. 1 *et seq.*

[41] The range of matters dealt with by this sort of court is reviewed at length in Hilton, *A Medieval Society*, especially chapters 5, 6 and 8.

[42] Jolliffe's suggestion that the large, extensive shires (= multiple estates) of Northumbria probably reflected the way a lack of arable could inhibit the normal development of the typical or "Midland-type" manor is relevant here, see J. E. A. Jolliffe, "Northumbrian Institutions", *English Historical Rev.*, XLI (1926), p. 2.

[43] Local or regional studies have tended to confirm that demesnes and the labour services that went with them were more widespread in the older-settled and more fertile districts of England, see, for example, D. Roden, "Demesne Farming in the Chilterns Hills", *Agricultural History Rev.*, XVII (1969), p. 11; R. H. Hilton, *The English Peasantry in the Later Middle Ages*, Oxford (1975), especially chapter on "Gloucester Abbey Leases and of the Thirteenth Century", pp. 139-55 and "Lord and Peasant in Staffordshire", pp. 215-43. Access to markets is also recognised as a critical factor.

[44] G. W. Kitchin (ed.), *The Manor of Marydown*, Hampshire Record Society (1895), pp. 143-59.

[45] W. O. Ault, *Open-Field Farming in Medieval England*, London (1972), pp. 167-72.

[46] Hilton, *A Medieval Society*, pp. 136-7.

[47] SRO, GD50/135, May 20th, 1706.

[48] Dunlop, *op. cit.*, pp. 6-7.

[49] H. Richardson (ed.), *Court Rolls of the Manor of Acomb, vol. 1*, Yorkshire Archaeological Society, Record Series, CXXXI (1969), p. 70.

[50] *Ibid.*, p. 10.

[51] *Ibid.*, p. 19.

[52] *Ibid.*, p. 76.

[53] J. M. Thomson (ed.), "The Forbes Baron Court Book, 1659-1678" in *Miscellany of the Scottish History Society*, 2nd series, XIX (1919), pp. 267, 299, 307 and 318.

[54] C. B. Gunn (ed.), *Records of the Baron Court of Stitchill 1655-1807*, Scottish History Society, 50 (1950), pp. 2, 110, 131 and 146.

[55] Hilton, *A Medieval Society*, p. 154.

[56] See, for example, Dunlop, *op. cit.*, p. 5; "Corshill Baron Court Book", pp. 65-249 in *Archaeological and Historical Collections Relating to the Counties of Ayr and Wigton*, IV, Edinburgh (1884), p. 72.

[57] Since this section was written, C. Dyer has likewise suggested that the closer the link between settlements and the manor, then the more effective was the latter in regulating the affairs of such settlements. See C. Dyer, "Landholding Units During the Later Middle Ages in the Eastern Midlands", *Landscape History*, I(1979), in press.

[58] Loyn, *op. cit.*, p. 157.

[59] See, for instance, the comments of Thirsk, "The Common Fields", pp. 4-5.

[60] *Ibid.*, pp. 16-7.

[61] Fox, "The Chronology of Enclosure and Economic development in Medieval Devon", pp. 189-90; B. Howells, "Open Fields and Farmsteads in Pembrokeshire", *The Pembrokeshire Historian*, 3 (1971), pp. 14-5.

Chapter 4

Infield-outfield and the territorial expansion of early townships

Mention has already been made of how feudal tenure imposed a strict definition on landholding through its concern for calibrating the amount of land to be held in return for military and/or labour services. This definition gave townships a framework of land assessment made up of units like virgates, bovates, ploughgates, husbandlands and pennylands. In the process, it gave them a territorial sense, a sense of what was with*in* and with*out* the township. This chapter looks at the significance of this territoriality for the development of field systems. It will be argued that its prime significance was in forming the basis for the growth of infield-outfield. However, this was not its only by-product as far as field systems were concerned. In addition to infield-outfield, it can be seen as providing the basis for a diverse family of other, less distinctly labelled field contrasts.

Land assessments and lordship: a chronology

Before evaluating their impact on the growth of field patterns, there are two aspects of early land assessments that need to be clarified. The first concerns their boundedness or physical demarcation on the ground. The second concerns the extent to which this notion of boundedness needs to be set in a definite chronological context.

The boundedness of early land assessments can be inferred from evidence for their acreage-equivalence and from the customs and practices built up around their formal perambulation. I have explored both these aspects in relation to Scottish evidence elsewhere.[1] Only a summary of the main points need be given here. On the question of the acreage-equivalence of early assessments, there exist fairly numerous references in both official or Crown documents and estate papers declaring a particular land unit to equal a particular acreage. For instance, the oxgate and ploughgate are commonly referred to as equalling 13 and 104 acres respectively.[2] It does not necessarily follow that these fixed acreages were attached to land units from their very inception, nor does it preclude their interpretation as being equal in value as well as extent. The very fact that the Scottish Parliament saw fit to attach acreages to them suggests there was some ambiguity about their precise extent. In all probability, these efforts to fix an official definition represent a concerted attempt to standardise their meaning as measures between townships, to provide a more objective yardstick in the face of local custom.

However, whether sustained by local custom or official definition, a land unit framework only had meaning if it conferred a fixed amount of land on a township. No more emphatic proof of this can be found than early charters which detail the perambulation of a township, or the setting and fixing of its boundaries on the ground. Looked at through late medieval or early modern sources, though, Scottish townships appear to possess two boundaries: the reason why hinges around the intrinsic nature of land assessments. If defined strictly, they constitute an assessment solely of arable land not pasture. Pasture was conveyed only as a set of appendent rights allowing the landholder either to graze a set number of stock or *soums* or to graze as many stock as could be maintained by his holding over winter. A few early foundation charters do, in fact, show the laying out of assessed land, or the land embraced by the land unit framework of a township,[3] but outnumbering this sort of perambulation in early sources are those which set the bounds of assessed land plus pasture. The Abbeys, in particular, were understandably anxious as stock farmers to exert a more private control over their grazing resources; their cartularies are rich in perambulations which, in effect, were divisions of pasture rights or waste between adjacent townships.[4] Unlike the perambulation of assessed land, these outer boundaries embracing pasture were usually determined by circumstance. Charters for townships in the north-east, for instance, talk of boundaries fixed "where wind and water shears".[5] The outcome of this widespread effort to create or establish more exclusive control over a township's pasture rights was that townships acquired two boundaries: an inner one around its assessed or arable land and an outer one around its arable plus pasture. Broadly speaking, the further back in time, the more important was the inner boundary, or that around assessed land.

Although there are differences of detail, the same basic principles of township layout can be applied south of the Border. In the first place, there can be no doubt that the land units out of which English townships were constructed equalled — at least within each settlement — a definite amount, thus imposing a fixed measure on the total settlement.[6] Amongst recent literature, that dealing with so-called regular villages in northern England has devoted a great deal of substantive discussion to the way the land unit framework of settlements prescribed its extent.[7] There is also little doubt that land units prescribed the arable area of a township. Pasture was provided by appended rights of common grazing in the surrounding waste.[8] Arable and pasture, therefore, were of quite different status. As in Scotland, the laying out or perambulation of early landholding concerned itself with assessed land, and no more. What lay outside, or was non-assessed, represented common waste (or forest land). But as townships overflowed the bounds of their assessed land, new bounds were eventually established that included a share of the surrounding waste as well as assessed land.

The main difference compared with Scotland was that far more of the English countryside was drawn into the assessed area of townships. Only in livestock-woodland or upland pasture districts did one find a situation comparable to that in Scotland, with scattered pockets of assessed land surrounded by vast expanses of waste, "an island in an ocean of unreclaimed barrenness" to use a phrase of R. H. Tawney.[9] Elsewhere, the balance between assessed and non-assessed land was much more heavily weighted in favour of the former (Fig. 6). Seeing the problem through Domesday Book, R. Lennard maintained that "Anglo-Saxon farmers were not nibbling the edges of a wilderness that was still unsubdued. The villages were small, and we may well believe that the village fields were in many cases severed from those of neighbouring villages by a thin belt of land that remained in a wild state".[10] Already, "England was an old and settled country at the time of the Norman Conquest . . . The wilderness had been subdued and mostly reduced within narrow limits".[11] This stress on how much had been accomplished by way of colonization by the time of Domesday is now very much the fashionable view, a view most succinctly put by M. M. Postan in his phrase that Domesday Book "is more an epitome of past performance, than an announcement of things to come".[12] Given that the land occupied by 1086 would invariably have been assessed in the land units of the time[13], it follows that we can hardly expect non-assessed land to have been substantial, at least in those regions which had borne the brunt of early colonization, but whether the balance between assessed and non-assessed land was tilted one way or the other, there was clearly scope for townships to occupy land *without* as well as within their framework of land assessment.

But the whole question of why some land should have an assessment in land units like the virgate or husbandland and other parts should not cannot be divorced from its chronological context, for much depended on when land was settled or colonized. Land or tenemental units like the virgate or husbandland were inextricably bound up with feudal tenure and formed customary holdings held in return for labour services of one kind or another. Feudal tenure, though, was not static. As circumstances changed, so did the conditions of tenure. A major change — in both England and Scotland — appears to have taken place over the thirteenth and fourteenth centuries. Put simply, newly colonized land was no longer incorporated into a land unit framework or the assessed area of townships; rather was it treated as something distinct, something outside the traditional or customary area of the township and its bounds. It is this sudden freezing of land assessments *before the colonizing process had played itself out* that led to this fundamental distinction in the way occupied land was described. Obviously, at the point when this freeze on land units took effect — or during the thirteenth and fourteenth centuries — the different regions of Britain were at different stages of colonization. Arable areas like eastern Scotland still boasted sizeable amounts of unoccupied non-assessed land, whilst parts of the Midlands or southern England were more completely absorbed into the assessed bounds of one township or another; but whether a vast encircling waste or a narrow fringe, non-assessed land stood out everywhere as something apart, even when occupied (see Fig. 6).

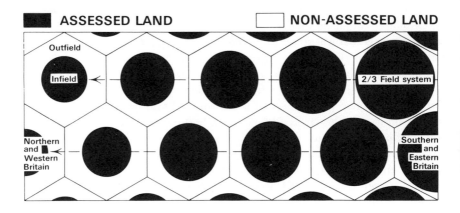

Fig. 6. Diagram showing how the balance between assessed and non-assessed land alters from Lowland to Highland Britain and how their designation alters accordingly.

Given the greater volume of work on English medieval colonization, the overflow of townships into non-assessed land is documented more fully for England. A range of work can be used to buttress this basic point. J. Z. Titow, for instance, in an overview of the country generally, stated that there "are numerous instances in twelfth and early thirteenth century surveys of standard customary holdings of explicitly assart or demesne origin and it would seem that in the past newly created holdings were looked upon as customary land, unlike the later practice when assarts and land from the demesne were held as just so many acres".[14] In his work on the Sussex manors of Laughton and Stockingham, J. S. Moore reached a similar conclusion but set a slightly earlier chronology for the changeover. He found "that land on which tenemental units are found was colonized before 1086, whilst assart land, properly so called, represents colonization after that date".[15] This was a conclusion which he felt had general application.[16] Others would favour a later date *terminus ante quem* for the creation of tenemental units. For example, P. T. Brandon, working on the Sussex manors of Rotherfield and Ramfield suggested that the terminal date for the incorporation of new land as customary holdings measured in *ferlings* was circa 1200. Holdings endowed after this point were non-customary and measured in acres.[17] A particularly explicit illustration of how non-assessed land accumulated outside the rigidly-defined bounds of a township, is afforded by R. Hilton's study of Stoneleigh manor in Warwickshire. The monk who compiled the Stoneleigh Leger Book in the fourteenth century, looking back over the expansion of settlements from the mid-twelfth century onwards, observed that in "each hamlet in the manor of Stoneleigh there are eight yardlands, and no more. Whatever they have further, they have by the improvement and assarting of the wastes".[18] An equally rich source of example is Hallam's work on the Lincolnshire Fens. In village after village, it is made clear that twelfth and thirteenth century colonization did not induce any corresponding change in their bovate assessment. New land was added to the bovate framework of villages as *terra mensurata* or *offaldfal*.[19] Further north, comparable examples from Yorkshire have been published by Homans. Highlighting their wider implications, he stressed that a feature "to be noticed was that no new oxgangs or yardlands would be formed by assarting. The old tenement would simply grow in size".[20] A term widely used in Yorkshire, as well as in other parts of the north and even the Midlands, to capture the essential meaning of land colonized beyond the assessed framework of townships, was that of *forland*: it meant literally the land outside.[21]

Why did lords alter the basis on which the extent of townships was measured? The answer to this question is prejudicial to any consideration of what effect this change might have on landholding and husbandry. The logical assumption would be that *prior* to the twelfth and thirteenth centuries, growth was absorbed by the creation of new land units. The land unit framework of townships, therefore, would be something elastic or expandable rather than fixed in character. In fact, a number of studies have documented the creation of land units *de novo* during the early middle ages, 950-1300.[22] This would suggest that the shift from tenemental units to acres was linked to circumstances that developed over the twelfth and thirteenth centuries. In view of the association between tenemental units and feudal tenure, an obvious approach would be to seek an explanation in changes that were affecting the nature of feudalism at this point. By the end of the thirteenth century, not only was free tenure spreading rapidly in some areas[23], but demesne farming was experiencing contraction, a contraction which — unlike earlier fluctuations — was to prove irreversible.[24] Both these trends would help make sense of the switch from one kind of land reckoning to the other. In short, they would explain the latter as a manifestation of fundamental changes in tenure that had been set in train by the thirteenth century and which gathered momentum after the Black Death. This is an appealing interpretation, not least because it was the colonization of non-assessed land under new or distinct tenures that fostered its contrasts of landholding and husbandry *vis à vis* assessed land. It was the underlying difference between the two types of land from which other differences flowed.

Although this is the view that the writer favours, other points of view cannot be ignored. In particular, some consideration must be given to Moore's suggestion that all land or tenemental units like the virgate were in existence by 1086.[25] The studies referred to earlier that demonstrate conclusively the formation of land or tenemental units after 1086, make it impossible to accept his suggestion in any simple or raw form. However, if the basis of his point is accepted in a qualified form, with those tenemental units created after 1086 being very much the exception rather than the rule, then the explanation of why new land colonized from the thirteenth century onwards was assessed in acres is far from closed. It could be that the land unit framework of townships seen in post-Domesday documents were fixed deep in the early medieval period, and that only with the sustained population growth of the twelfth and thirteenth centuries was there sufficient pressure for their bounds to be breached. Pertinent to the discussion here is the growing belief amongst medieval archaeologists that the population of the English countryside underwent a severe contraction during the early Anglo-Saxon period and that it was not until after 1086 that it recovered to anything like its former levels. Needless to say, if this perspective on early English population was combined with the view that the land unit framework of most townships was archaic and unchanging, it would certainly lend credence to the idea that not until the twelfth and thirteenth centuries did the need to overflow the assessed bounds of townships arise. If the problem is construed in this way it would mean that the contrast between assessed and non-assessed land was not the product of changes that only came into operation during the twelfth and thirteenth centuries, but may well represent the delayed impact of changes initially concealed because there was still slack or room for growth *within* the framework of assessed land. Only when the need eventually arose to take in part of the surrounding waste, may scope have been provided for the application of fresh ways of reckoning land, ways which would have been applied much earlier had the need arisen and which therefore cannot necessarily be tied to changes over the twelfth and thirteenth centuries. I do not subscribe to this interpretation, but it is the sort of alternative view which must be kept in mind.

Although outwardly signified by the difference between land held in terms of land units and that held in terms of mere acreage, it is crucial to what I propose to say about the wider implications of the contrast between assessed and non-assessed land to grasp that it was underpinned, above all else, by differences in tenure. It is precisely for this reason that their differences were further elaborated through differences not just in the method of land reckoning, but also in landholding and husbandry. Hence, the relevance of the contrast to the problem of field systems. It formed a break-point in the territorial order of the township. This was appreciated by R. H. Tawney. After referring to "the manorial population overflowing the boundaries of the customary land" into the surrounding waste, he went on to describe how it "was new land which did not come into the original scheme of manorial finance and organisation". It was, therefore, "the point from which new relationships could spring".[26]

Non assessed land and the growth of infield-outfield

Discussions of field systems have always linked infield-outfield very closely with Scotland. Not only was it widely practised throughout Scotland, but it is from there that we have the most explicit descriptions of how it operated. It is also through Scottish evidence that the association between infield-outfield and assessed and non-assessed land can most easily be pieced together.

In the extreme south-east of Scotland, there existed a number of large runrig townships that involved the intermixture of land belonging to different heritors or landowners. Involving complex hereditary rights, such townships were ultimately divided under the authority of the 1695 Act anent lands lying runrig, largely during the eighteenth century.[27] Their division proceedings in the local sheriff courts yield an abundance of information on the details of their organization. In each case, the land unit framework of the township played a prominent part in the proceedings, since it not only gave definition to the township, but also formed the basis for the allocation of each landholder's rights. However, close inspection of this land unit framework reveals a feature of enormous significance: it is that whilst there are phrases in their division proceedings linking the land unit framework of townships to the total area of the township, both infield and outfield, such crude statements can mislead. Where more detail is given, such as for townships like Gattonside and Newstead, it is evident that their land unit framework refers only to infield.[28] Each landholder's share is listed as comprising so-many husband-lands, merklands or "Computed Acres" of infield plus so-many acres of outfield. When the number of land units or "Computed Acres" of infield are grossed, they equal the total number supposedly in the total township. In effect, they alone formed the assessed area of the township and refer to outfield only in the sense that the latter was an appendent property held through possession of, and in proportion to, infield.

Guided by such evidence, support for this relationship between infield and assessed land has been uncovered in other parts of Scotland. In some cases, the evidence consists of passing references in land charters. Thus, a sixteenth-century document for the two Orkney touns of Feaye and Moir leaves little doubt that tenants were set the "inlands" *sensu stricto* and that which was called the "ut tylling" was something extra.[29] An Aberdeenshire decreet of adjudication dated 1725 mentions the "just and equal half of the Lands of Coults, Extending the eight oxgates of Land comprehending there intill".[30] Eighteenth-century tacks for the Monymusk estate in Aberdeenshire refer to intoun and outfield, the intoun presumably being that which was within the toun proper.[31] Support is also forthcoming from early land surveys which allow a comparison between the infield acreage of townships and their land unit assessment. Given the potential variety of interpretation between town-ships as regards supposedly similar land units, and given that some townships were starting to add outfield to their infield by the time eighteenth-century land surveys become available, it would be unreasonable to expect infields to display an *exact* accordance with the acreage-equivalence of their land unit framework. But once these problems are allowed for, a comparison between their infield acreage and land unit framework yields a more realistic measure per land unit than a similar comparison between the total acreage of a township (infield/outfield/pasture) and its land unit framework. An analysis of such data for the Breadalbane estate in Perthshire, based on a survey of 1769, can be seen in Fig. 7. The comparison between infield acreages and merkland assessments provides a much tidier correlation, with a tendency for merkland size to cluster around eight acres: this, in fact, is the acreage per merkland disclosed by similar calculations for the extreme south-east.[32]

Especially revealing of the in-built rigidity of land unit assessments are the references in early Scottish land charters to outsets: the term means literally the land outside what was set. It is the Scottish equivalent to forland. Early definitions of it define it as land "newly win without the dykis".[33] If a comprehensive source of charters like the *Register of the Great Seal* is examined, mentions of outsets appear at the close of the fifteenth century and become fairly common over the first half of the sixteenth century. By con-trast, whilst there is an isolated reference to outfield in the late fifteenth century

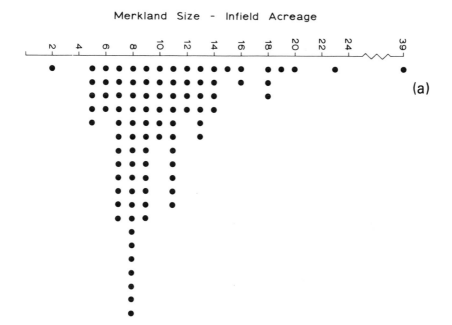

Merkland Size - Infield Acreage

(a)

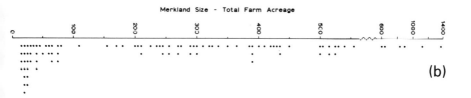

Merkland Size - Total Farm Acreage

(b)

Fig. 7. *Average acreage per merkland on the Lochtayside Estate (Perthshire).*
(a) Calculated in relation to infield only (b) Calculated in relation to the total acreage
of infield, outfield and grazings. Based on M. McArthur (ed.), 'Survey of Lochtayside'
1769, Scottish History Society, 3rd series, 27 (1936).

and a few scattered references over the first half of the sixteenth century, it is only during the second half that mentions become easy to find.[34] Outsets and outfield not only shared the same meaning as land occupied outside the assessed framework of townships, but the former seems to have taken over from the latter as the preferred term. Together, they shed light on when this overflow into non-assessed land may have taken place in Scotland. From uncertain beginnings in the fifteenth century, its invasion became general and formalised in the sixteenth. Only at this late stage in the colonization of the Scottish countryside did infield-outfield take shape. Naturally, as the assessed area of townships, infield would have long pre-dated this period, but it is only with the emergence of an outfield that, the whole sense of land within and without the township would have impressed itself on field organization.

A variety of English evidence can be marshalled to demonstrate a similar link between assessed and non-assessed land and infield-outfield. The existence of infield-outfield in East Anglia has been an established fact since the study by H. C. Darby and J. Saltmarsh of West Wretham in the 1930s.[35] Unfortunately, trying to link its infield-outfield system to the land assessment of the township is complicated by the fact that the region lacks a definite nomenclature for tenements smaller in size than a carucate. Peasant holdings were arranged into regular-sized tenements corresponding to accepted notions of what a peasant holding should extend to, but they were not overtly labelled in the same fashion as, say, virgates or bovates. In other words, in seeking to validate an extension of the argument to East Anglia, it is not a case of looking for a conspicuously-marked contrast between an area of virgated or bovated land and one of acres, but for a much more muted contrast between an area of regular-sized tenemental units and an area where no such regularity prevailed or where holdings were regular but of a different order of size. This is far from being an easy task in an area where peasant land transactions led to the progressive break-up of holdings throughout the twelfth and thirteenth centuries. In the words of B. Dodwell, the "integrity of holdings both old and newly established, was constantly being assailed".[36]

Despite this difficulty, studies by a number of scholars have shown that many villages in East Anglia once possessed a nucleus of ancient tenements whose external shape was maintained in spite of the physical disintegration of individual tenements and the further expansion of the settlement into the surrounding waste. For example, in a discussion of the Newton extent in the thirteenth-century Register of the Bishop of Norwich, D. C. Douglas wrote that it "contains no reference to a virgate or any unit which is similar to it. Instead, the Survey begins with a very detailed description of a series of holdings, each usually held by more than one person. These tenements which are given such prominence in the extent contain 13 acres of arable land and

1 acre of meadow. They are carefully distinguished from any additional land that may have been acquired by their tenants, and their fundamental integrity is alike shown in their collective character and in the fact that, even when they have been broken up, their essential unity seems to be recognized".[37] Documented case-studies of settlements maintaining the individual and collective identity of their ancient tenements, despite the pressures of internal fragmentation and external accretion, have been published by H. L. Gray[38], W. Hudson[39] and by Maitland. The latter's overall conclusions speak for them all. According to an extent of 1221, the manor of Wilburton near Cambridge, consisted of "fifteen and a half full lands", a total reaffirmed in 1385. From "1221 down to the very end of the Middle Ages", wrote Maitland, "the manor seems to have kept with wonderful conservatism what we may call its external shape".[40]

The resilience of this inner core of tenements raises the possibility that where infield-outfield existed in East Anglia, it was developed around this rigidity in the territorial layout of townships. Converting this possibility into hard fact is the evidence for West Wretham published by Darby and Saltmarsh. They found that tenements at West Wretham consisted of 14 acre units and that these units "consisted of a homestead containing an acre and a half, and 12½ acres scattered by strips in the furlongs": these furlongs comprised the infield. Furthermore, "concerning these furlongs of infield we must point out one final singularity. The figures given for each in the terrier of 1612 — though confessedly approximate — seem likewise to tend to a norm", a norm of about 14 acres. This "coincidence", as they call it, with the "normal arable holding of a peasant is too striking to be passed over" but they themselves hesitated "to say what significance, if any, should be attached to it".[41] Its significance is surely that the infield at West Wretham derived its meaning from the fact it formed the original nucleus of its tenements, with outfield being the land outside.

The problem of infield-outfield in the south-west needs a cautious approach. H. P. R. Finberg, in particular, referred often to the south-western evidence for infield-outfield dating from as early as the tenth century onwards, and made it quite clear that he saw its origin as rooted in a much earlier period.[42] However, his very early references are no more than signs of waste being casually cropped which he had interpreted as outfield cultivation. A more recent critical analysis of the problem has been published by Fox. Basing his ideas on Kenton Manor in Devon, Fox has argued that whilst a form of outfield cropping was practised in the south-west, its character as a cropping system was different from that in Scotland. ". . . outfield cultivation in the south-west", he suggested, "far from being an integral part of a community's system of managing its land from year to year, took place infrequently at intervals of perhaps a decade, two decades or even of a whole generation".[43] This conclusion, though, does not rule out the possibility that outfield in the south-west drew its separateness as a system from the fact it was developed on what was regarded as non-assessed land. Finberg, for example, discussing Tavistock abbey, treats local assessments as fiscal in character, as having lost their initial character as field or land units, because they had "failed to keep pace with expanding cultivation".[44] More direct support is afforded by material for the manor of Taunton. "In this manor", it was reported, "there are two sorts of land, bondland and overland. The bondland is that whereon there have been, and commonly are, ancient dwelling tenements, and is held by a customary fine and rent certain, paying heriots, and doing other suits and services to the same belonging. The overland is that whereon, in ancient time, there were no dwellings, and is held by a fine and rent certain and fealty; but the tenants thereof pay no heriots, and do no other customs, suit or services for the same".[45] The full bearing of this extract on the discussion becomes apparent only when it is appreciated that "overland" is W. C. Hazlitt's translation of "fortirs", a term which equates with forland as indicating land held outside that which was customary.

Although H. L. Gray argued for the widespread existence of infield-outfield in areas like the north-east, more recent work has qualified its importance to the region.[46] Indeed, even its close similarity with infield-outfield in Scotland has been questioned;[47] this is mainly because in a number of townships, infield or ingrounds were cropped as a two- or three-field system. Arguably, such doubt over their similarity with the infields of Scotland is allayed if the term is seen as conveying the idea of land which lay within the traditional bounds of a township, with outfield or outgrounds being the land without. In fact, some townships give expression to this vital distinction in status between infield and outfield by labelling them as "Townfields" and "Common Pasture or Moor".[48] Really substantive support is most likely to be gained by the detailed examination of individual townships. At Embleton (Northumberland), the township was assessed as 27 2/3 *farms* or *farmholds*. During its division in 1730, it was said that these *farms* "made up the ingrounds". Outside, lay the "moor or common".[49] At Gunnerton (Northumberland), it was reported in 1714 that the township was "held on the ancient system of undivided infield or townfields and a common pasture in the outfield or fell, cultivated only by the tenants who resided in the village in houses".[50] Not only does this bring out the character of outfield as land occupied outside the township proper, but it also underlines its dependent nature as a tenure. A document of 1296 refers to all "the land of Byres near Hexham, and common of pasture without the bounds of the said town".[51] What seems clear from later evidence is that even when such "common of pasture" was cultivated as outfield, it neither lost its status as common land[52] nor as a possession "without the bounds of the said town". At the root of the whole problem was the simple fact that by the end of the middle ages, assessed land or customary tenements could not reproduce themselves by colonization. New land taken in from the common waste was strictly apportioned between tenements, but only as an appendage. An early reference to the cultivation of waste at Cowpen (Northumberland) embodies this gulf between old and new in a way that sums up the problem: it refers to land "in mora etiam cum arabilur, sive ad opus domini sive ad communem divisionem quam inter homines fiat, partem habeant canonici quarter ad dimidiam carucatam pertinent".[53]

On the western side of the Pennines, infield-outfield is mentioned in charters as early as the thirteenth century.[54] When these skeletal references can be fleshed out with greater detail, they confirm that here too, infield-outfield coincided with the distinction between assessed and non-assessed land. G. E. Elliott, for example, established that in townships like Holme Cultram (Cumberland), outfield has the status of "common waste"[55], and that townships drew a "clear distinction between the anciently cultivated areas (Oxgangs) and newly reclaimed areas (rodeland)".[56] Further south, G. H. Tupling's work on Rossendale uncovered a slight variant. Infield-outfield systems were absent, but a number of townships distinguished between *in*pasture, or stubble grazing on the township fields, and *out*pasture, or that afforded by common pasture.[57] Indeed, local townships seem to have been imbued with a very strong sense of territory. Typical of this sense of territory is the extract quoted by Tupling from the court rolls of the manor of Worston. The extract, dated 1583, records "yt is agreed That no men shall take or surcharge the Common with any kynde of Cattale sheep or geese But what he or they shall Keapp in Wynter within the saif Towne or townshippe of Worstone and that withoute helpe of any outlandes".[58]

Assessed and non-assessed land: their tenurial differences

The foregoing section has tried to illustrate how infield-outfield was structured around the distinction between assessed and non-assessed land: this, it is suggested, forms the basic meaning of infield-outfield. Without this institutional rigidity in the territorial organization of townships, infield-outfield would not have developed. Once this is appreciated, infield-outfield can be set in its true and proper context, a context that integrates differences in tenure, landholding and farming.

Tenurial differences between assessed and non-assessed land are implicit in their very description, as well as in the way they were measured, the one in land units or tenements and the other in acres. However, tenure can express itself in different ways. An important dimension to it is how it was compounded.

Assessed land was largely held by customary tenure. In other words, it was held in return for services and a range of dues and fines. The colonization of land outside the framework of assessed land over the thirteenth century or later provided an opportunity for breaking with customary tenures. With remarkable uniformity, non-assessed land throughout Britain was compounded for a money rent and given the status of freehold. Nor was Britain alone in this trend. The relationship between assarted land and freehold was, as Hilton put it, "a commonplace in Western European agrarian history".[59]

The emergence of rent-paying freeholds on non-assessed land in England is a theme well-served by case-studies, both local and national. Where writers have commented on the disposition of such land, the impression given is that of a belt of freehold stretching in an outfield-like fashion around the edge of customary tenements. Thus, in his work on the land belonging to Ely abbey, E. Miller talked of a "rapidly expanding periphery of lands held by rent-paying tenants" in the twelfth and thirteenth centuries.[60] Writing over 20 years later, he set the matter in a broader perspective with the comment that "manorial surveys of the late twelfth and early thirteenth centuries carry an implication that population had been growing . . . and very often the nucleus of standard tenements was surrounded by cottages and small holdings seemingly far more numerous than they had been in Domesday times".[61] Tawney in his day was also aware of this growth and he recorded it with the comment that "at an early date, a fringe of leasehold land forms itself around the manor in addition to the ordinary customary tenements".[62] Perhaps the most specific references to the spatial disposition of new freeholds are those published by E. A. Kosminsky. Basing his observations on the hundred rolls of 1279, he suggested that freeholds were "far more than a narrow fringe around the typical elements of the manor, the demesne and villein land".[63] Over the entire area covered by the rolls, they accounted for as much as 28% of all arable land, yet the rolls only partially covered those countries where freehold is known to have been important. As Kosminsky himself stated, the "percentage of freeholdings is undoubtedly higher than this in the northern and eastern counties".[64] Of special interest are those attempts to map the distribution of freehold. P. T. Brandon has done this for the Sussex manors of Rotherfield and Ramfield and the pattern revealed makes for any easy comparison with infield-outfield in Scotland with extensive areas of freehold or assart encircling or infilling between the nuclei of demesne and customary land.[65] Maps compiled for the nearby manors of Laughton and Stockingham show a similar arrangement.[66]

Even in Scotland, non-assessed land, or outfield as it was invariably termed, was held by a separately defined tenure. Not only was it a dependent tenure, held through possession of infield, but it allowed changes to be made in the nature of tenure. Compared with England, the change is more concealed. Usually, it is manifest only through a careful inspection of rentals, especially those for the sixteenth, seventeenth and eighteenth centuries. Rentals for this period reveal that many Scottish townships still paid their rent in kind; such payments were composed of grain, livestock, fowls, cheese, wool and the like; their amount was fixed by tradition and, more important, it was linked to the assessed area of the township, the stability of the former being a measure of the stability of the latter. Straightforward comparisons between township assessments and their rent-liability in terms of grain, such as those provided by sources like the *1627 Report on the State of Certain Parishes in Scotland*[67] or the 1610 rental for the Lordship of Huntly in the north-east[68], bear this out. Where townships breached the bounds of their assessed land with outfield cropping systems, then rent could be augmented. Such augmentations can be discerned in rentals by the fact they were not absorbed into whatever maill payments were made by a township, but stood apart as payments additional to customary rent forms.[69] There are no shortage of reasons why such augmentations were being widely levied over this period, but the projection of townships beyond their traditional bounds — and the area covered by their customary rent — was likely to have been a prime reason.

Assessed and non-assessed land: their differences in landholding

In townships where infield-outfield farming was practised, then outfield or non-assessed land is likely to have been held on a sub divided field basis during the phases when it was being cropped. Its temporary and partial occupation apart, outfield would not have differed from infield in respect of landholding. In fact, given that outfield was held through infield, even the balance of landholding between the two would have been similar.

Not all townships shared these similarities between assessed and non assessed land. Many English townships, as well as some in south Wales, displayed quite sharp differences of landholding between the two sectors. The most conspicuous contrast to emerge was in those settlements whose assessed land was disposed in the form of sub-divided fields, but whose non-assessed land was occupied in the form of enclosures held in severalty (see Fig. 8). J. Sheppard's work on Wheldrake (Yorkshire) provided a detailed reconstruction of this kind of response, with the bovated core of the township being ringed by enclosures held in severalty.[70] Hilton has published equally fine examples for the Arden district of Warwickshire. Just like Wheldrake, settlements in the Arden district of Warwickshire as they developed over the latter part of the medieval period comprised an "old established core" of open field, surrounded by a broad belt of assart land held in severalty. Inspected

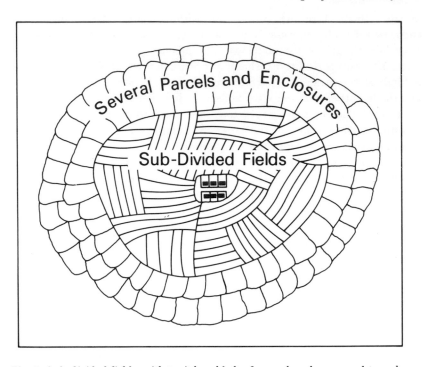

Fig. 8. Sub-divided fields, with peripheral belt of several enclosures and parcels.

closely, this landholding contrast can be seen to coincide with that between assessed and non-assessed land. In Hilton's words, the "yardlands were the holdings of traditional layout, intermixed and common. The assarts were held in severalty, often enclosed, varying in size between peasant crofts of one or two acres and those as large as the 193 acres from the waste granted to the Templers of Fletchamstead out of the woodland of Westwood".[71] A graphic illustration of his conclusion is given by a 1591 map of Feckenham. The plan "shows that beyond a small core of open fields with intermixed strips around the village itself (an old settlement) there is a considerable outer ring of small hedged fields".[72] Although the evidence is less explicit as to their underlying associations with assessed and non-assessed land, similarly arranged settlements are documented for Durham[73] and East Anglia[74]. There are strong hints that landholding contrasts between assessed and non-assessed land developed in south Wales. On the one hand, townships existed that comprised an inner core of sub-divided fields and an outer periphery of enclosures.[75] On the other hand, analysis of extents and surveys for the thirteenth and fourteenth centuries has shown that rent-paying freeholds were being created out of demesne land and "in outlying hamlets or on the waste".[76]

Monmouth manor exemplifies how these two patterns may have been intimately connected. After discussing demesne and customary lands, W. Rees went on to say that a "class of freemen, generally limited in numbers, holders of a few acres or many acres, had usually been present among the tenantry of the manor in the medieval days, their holdings fringing the open-field arrangements but not an essential part of it".[77]

The situation that developed at Monmouth Manor introduces yet another source of variation. In infield-outfield townships, outfield was related to possession of infield, with the one being the basis of right in the other. In most parts of England and in the Normanised parts of Wales, such an automatic association between new land and old had ceased to exist by the thirteenth century. New land was asserted only with the lord's permission and this introduced greater variety. At one extreme, it could produce a relationship little different from that in an infield-outfield township, with tenements having so-many acres of assart appended to them. This sort of link between old and new is commonplace in extents of the thirteenth, fourteenth and fifteenth centuries.[78] At the other extreme, it led to the creation of *entirely independent* holdings on new land. As in the case of Monmouth manor, the size of these independent holdings ranged from a few acres up to units measured in hundreds of acres. Miller's work on the lands of Ely abbey and other estates provides ample proof of smallholdings and cottages being created by the asserting of non-assessed land.[79] Pembrokeshire examples of large holdings and even small hamlets being funded by the asserting of waste around the older core of manors have been cited by B. E. Howells.[80] But overall, it is the colonization of forest areas like Arden (Warwickshire) in the centuries immediately after 1086 that offer the most convenient source for documenting the varied relationship between old land and new. Thanks to the work of Roberts, we can find here all the different possibilities outlined for us. After an initial stage of colonization, dated by Roberts to the pre-twelfth century, when asserting spawned tenements that were probably laid out in the form of sub-divided fields, subsequent colonization took on a different character, with non-assessed land being appended to old-established tenements, used to create separate smallholdings and cottages or to endow large, extensive holdings.[81]

Assessed and non-assessed land: their differences in farming

The aim of the foregoing discussion has been to put infield-outfield farming in its proper place. Far from being a farming system and no more, infield-outfield farming formed only one aspect of a diverse range of patterns moulded around the distinction between assessed and non-assessed land.

Without this fundamental break in the tenurial geography of townships, it would simply not have existed. Moreover, any attempt to understand its development and character as a farming system, particularly why it combined intensive and extensive cropping patterns, must be set firmly in this context.

To start with, the distinction between assessed and non-assessed land offers a clear chronology for the development of infield-outfield. Put simply, fully-matured systems of infield-outfield farming could only have taken shape with the overflow of townships into non-assessed land; this began to occur in England at least over the twelfth and thirteenth centuries. From this point onwards, infield-outfield farming systems could develop, though the writer would argue that most English examples, like their Scottish counterparts, probably did not take shape (or did not acquire an outfield sector) until as late as the fifteenth and sixteenth centuries. Exactly when depended on the point at which townships reached saturation in terms of the occupation of their assessed land; exactly where depended on whether lords allowed communities to decide collectively on how their available waste should be cultivated.

Such a chronology dispels completely any suggestion that infield-outfield combined the two most primitive farming techniques: constant and shifting cultivation. Infield was the more intensive sector simply because, as assessed land, it was the longer-established and more fertile nucleus of the township. Only when pressure on assessed land warranted it would attempts have been made to cultivate non-assessed land. The intensive cultivation of infield was, in effect, the precondition for the growth of outfield. However, beyond saying it was the relatively more intensive sector, infield cropping had nothing distinctive or exclusive about it, and this is a point of some significance. In Scotland, infield cropping possessed a fair degree of variety, with some townships in the far north and west cropped with oats and barley alter- natively,[82] but townships in the more fertile south-east employing four- or five-course rotations, including a fallow break, by the early eighteenth century.[83] Making the point at issue more emphatically are those townships in the north-east of England which had two or three field systems laid out on their infields or ingrounds (see Fig. 9). These townships were the main reason why Butlin felt that the infields or ingrounds of the north-east were not to be compared directly with their namesakes north of the Border.[84] What matters above all else, though, is that these two or three field systems were developed on assessed land: this alone was the prime meaning of infield; the details of its cropping were secondary.

The implications of this primary meaning can be developed still further. Broadly speaking, English townships subjected to a communally-regulated cropping scheme can be classed into three types as regards the balance between assessed and non-assessed land. First, there were those whose assessed

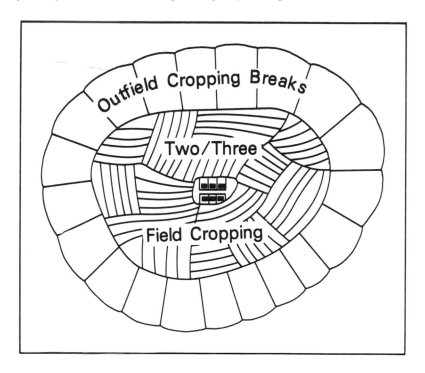

Fig. 9. Sub-divided fields and two/three field cropping system, with peripheral outfield cropping system.

land occupied virtually all available land. Having no non-assessed land of any consequence, the cropping pattern on their assessed land (i.e. two- or three-field cropping) would have predominated. Secondly, there were those townships that had a more equal balance between the two. However, if non-assessed land was divorced from assessed land in terms of landholding — with the one sub-divided fields and the other several enclosures — then the only communally-regulated cropping system would again have been that on assessed land. As in the case of examples like Wheldrake (Yorkshire) and Feckenham (Warwickshire), the cropping of assessed land in these townships was often on a two- or three-field basis. Thirdly, there were those townships in which the balance between the two sectors was again equal, but in which *both* were subjected to communally-regulated schemes of cropping, the one infield and the other, outfield. As Butlin's Northumberland examples demonstrate, the assessed land or infield of even these townships could be cropped on a two- or three-field basis. The point being made is that in each case, assessed land was associated with a distinct or separate cropping pattern and, to this extent, it technically amounted to an infield in each case. However, only where it was contrasted with a communally-regulated cropping pattern on non-assessed land, would the terms infield and outfield have been used to capture the distinction between the two; this essential similarity between Scottish infields and so-called two- or three-field systems in areas like the English Midlands is perhaps most sharply focussed by those examples of the former which made use of a three-break system, one of which was a fallow. What is more, just as some west Midland examples of the two- or three-field system were elaborated over the sixteenth and seventeenth centuries into systems based on four, five or more breaks or *quarters*, similar trends affected Scottish infields.

Turning to those townships which practised outfield cropping on their non-assessed land, the key problem is how such cropping acquired its character as a partial and temporary cultivation of waste. It is this feature, more than any other, which has caused scholars to denigrate infield-outfield as a primitive farming system. The answer possibly lies in reconstructing the resource-framework of townships at the point when the cultivation of their non-assessed land as outfield was first contemplated (see Fig. 10). Assessed land or infield would have been the only cropped area, an area cropped intensively and maintained at this level by receiving all available manure, notably that

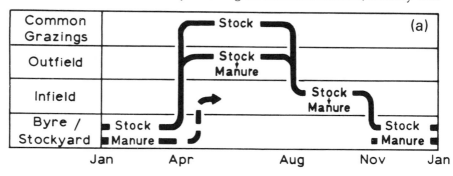

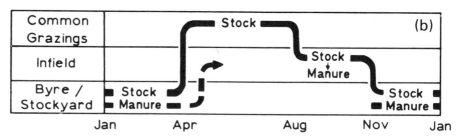

Fig. 10 (a) Stock movements in an infield-outfield system and (b) an infield only system.

afforded by the grazing of harvest stubble. In seeking to supplement their infield arable, husbandmen would have been acutely conscious of the unutilized manure produced by stock when they were on the common grazings during summer. In a system of farming heavily committed to manurial inputs, this summer waste of manure would surely have been the weak link. Any considered attempt to crop non-assessed land would have been designed to make more effective use of this wasted resource. Detailed descriptions of outfield cultivation in Scotland show this choice may well have been seized upon by communities faced with this particular problem for they show that outfield cropping was invariably preceded by the tathing or folding of stock during summer on that part scheduled for cultivation the following spring. Each night, stock were herded together in temporary folds or pens, where they dunged the ground with their droppings.[85] Less evidence has been published for tathing or folding in the context of English outfield systems, though a great deal of generalised information has been collated in respect of the East Anglian foldcourse system which, in infield-outfield townships, probably extended to outfield.[86] A seventeenth century description of outfield cropping in Pembrokeshire by the antiquary, George Owen, contains a good description of its use in a Welsh context. Farmers, he wrote, built temporary folds on "some peece of grounde wheare they meane to till the next yeare, and therein drive their cattell everie night from mydd *Marche* till mydd *November*", after which they plough it and crop it for as much as seven to ten years "till the lande growe so weake & baren" that it is put down to pasture again.[87]

The importance of tathing or folding to the character of outfield cropping is that once a piece of waste had been tathed over summer and brought into cultivation the following spring, it was automatically removed from any further tathing whilst under crop. A new tathfold had to be prepared. As a result of this annual removal of the tathfold, a cycle of partial and temporary cropping was set in motion. Outfield's supposedly primitive character then, reflected the constraints of tathing as a source of manure.

Conclusion

Infield-outfield has always discharged a vital role in the explanation of field systems, either as the starting point for evolutionary schemes or as the Highland equivalent of more productive Lowland varieties. The purpose of this chapter has been to cast its role in totally different terms. Infield-outfield stands uncomfortably as a distinct or substantive *type* of field system, one to be arranged alongside the two- or three-field system. The error of this view is starkly underlined by the knowledge that two- or three-field systems of a kind could exist *within* the framework of infield! Instead, the lesson of infield-outfield is that it serves to emphasise the importance of changes in tenure to the growth of townships, and especially the radical shift from assessed land and customary tenures to non-assessed land and freehold. This was a territorial divide scarred deeply and enduringly on the face of most townships. However, to focus solely on those townships that developed infield-outfield farming systems around this divide, is to exclude from view a whole family of tenurial, landholding and cropping patterns which shared or displayed similar affiliations. Infield-outfield as a farming system may have been of restricted importance and distribution outside of Scotland, but if the terms infield-outfield are used loosely to capture the underlying similarities of structure which these other patterns shared with them, then it was far more widespread. Only then can we join Sir John Clapham and others in concluding about infield-outfield that "if we knew medieval England completely, we should no doubt meet plenty of it".[88]

References

[1] Dodgshon, 'Tenure and Landholding in Early Scotland", pp. 127-45.

[2] See, for example, *Acts of the Parliaments of Scotland, I (1124-1424)*, appendix V, p. 387; SRO, RHP 2487 and 2488.

[3] G. W. S. Barrow (ed.), *The Acts of William I 1165-1214. Regesta Regum Scotorum II*, Edinburgh (1970), pp. 241-2.

[4] See, for example, *Liber S. Thome de Aberbrothoc*, Bannatyne Club Edinburgh, (1848), p. 310. It is worth noting here that Habakkuk Bisset, *op. cit.*, p. 315 refers to the process of perambulation as "worne out of use".

[5] J. G. Mitchie (d.), *The Records of Invercauld 1547-1828*, Spalding Club, Aberdeen (1901), p. 128.

[6] One of the most informed discussions of land units and their acreage equivalences in England is still that by Maitland in *Domesday Book and Beyond*, chapter on "Measures and Fields", pp. 422-62.

[7] See, Roberts, "Village Plans in County Durham", pp. 33-56; J. Sheppard, "Pre-Enclosure Field and Settlement Patterns in an English Township", *Geografiska Annaler*, 48B (1966), pp. 59-77; J. Sheppard, "Metrological Analysis of Regular Village Plans", *Agricultural History Rev.*, 22 (1974), pp. 118-35; Harvey, *The Morphological and Tenurial Structure of a Yorkshire Township*, pp. 13-21; M. Harvey, "The development of open field agriculture with particular reference to Holderness, Yorkshire", in Rowley (ed.), *The Origins of Open Field Agriculture*, in press.

[8] Hilton, *A Medieval Society*, p. 113.

[9] R. H. Tawney, *The Agrarian Problem in the Sixteenth Century*, London (1912), p. 88.

[10] R. Lennard, *Rural England 1086-1135*, Oxford (1959), p. 3.

[11] *Ibid.*, p. 9.

[12] M. M. Postan, *Medieval Economy and Society*, p. 16 and "Medieval Agrarian Society in its Prime: England", in M. M. Postan (ed.), *The Cambridge Economic History of Europe*, vol. 11, p. 550.

[13] Compare J. S. Moore's suggestion that mapping medieval "tenemental units will enable the cultivated area of Domesday England to be precisely located" in J. S. Moore, "The Domesday Teamland: A Reconsideration", *Trans. Royal Historical Soc.*, 5th series, 14 (1964), p. 129.

[14] Titow, "Medieval England and the Open Field System", p. 101.

[15] J. S. Moore, *Laughton: A Study in the Evolution of the Wealden Landscape*, Leicester University Dept. of English Local History, Occasional Paper no. 19 (1965), p. 28.

[16] Moore, "The Domesday teamland", p. 129.

[17] P. T. Brandon, "Medieval Clearances in the east Sussex Weald", *Transactions of the Institute of British Geographers*, 48 (1969), pp. 136-49.

[18] Hilton, *A Medieval Society*, pp. 22-3.

[19] Hallam, *Settlement and Society*, pp. 9-14, 20, 62, 110 and 159-61.

[20] Homans, *English Villagers of the Thirteenth Century*, p. 84.

[21] Sheppard, "Pre-Enclosure and Settlement Patterns in an English Township", p. 171; A. B. Hinds (ed.), *A History of Northumberland*, vol. III, part I, Newcastle (1896), p. 68; Tawney, *op. cit.*, p. 94; I. Kershaw (ed.), *Bolton Priory Rentals and Ministers' Accounts, 1473-1539*, Yorkshire Archaeological Society, Record Series, CXXXII (1970), pp. 1, 4-5 and 9; Farrer (ed.), *Lancashire Inquests . . . A.D. 1313-A.D.1355*, pp. 194-5; R. R. Darlington (ed.), *The Cartulary of Worcester Cathedral Priory (Register I)*, Pipe Roll Society, LXXVI, New Series, XXXVIII (1968), pp. 234 and 253.

[22] M. M. Postan, "Glastonbury Abbey in the Twelfth Century", pp. 248-77 in M. M. Postan, *Essays on Medieval Agriculture and General Problems of the Medieval Economy*, Cambridge, p. 258; Barrow, *The Acts of William I 1165-1214*, pp. 241-2; G. W. S. Barrow (ed.), *The Acts of Malcolm IV 1153-1165*, Regesta Regum Scottorum I, Edinburgh (1960), p. 278.

[23] R. H. Hilton, *The Decline of Serfdom in Medieval England*, London (1969), especially pp. 17-24.

[24] Postan, "Medieval Agrarian Society in its Prime: England", p. 587.

[25] Moore, "The Domesday Teamland", p. 129.

[26] Tawney, *The Agrarian Problem in the Sixteenth Century*, p. 141.

[27] Fuller discussion of their division can be found in R. A. Dodgshon, "The Removal of Runrig in Roxburghshire and Berwickshire, 1680-1766", *Scottish Studies*, 16 (1972), pp. 127-33.

[28] A summary of this evidence is presented in R. A. Dodgshon, "The Nature and Development of Infield-Outfield in Scotland", *Transactions of the Institute of British Geographers*, 59 (1973), pp. 3-5.

[29] Clouston, *Records of the Earldom of Orkney 1299-1614*, pp. 373-4.

[30] J. G. Mitchie (ed.), *The Records of Invercauld MDXLVII-MDCCCXXVIII*, Spalding Club, Aberdeen (1901), p. 472.

[31] H. Hamilton (ed.), *Selections from the Monymusk Papers (1713-1755)*, Scottish History Society, 3rd series, XXXIX (1945), pp. 43-6.

[32] Dodgshon, "Infield-Outfield", p. 8. An average of eight acres per merkland when infield is compared with the total assessment of merkland has also been discovered at Chirnside, see Berwickshire County Library, Decreet of Division of the Runrig Lands of Chirnside, 1740.

[33] Peterkin, *Rentals of the Ancient Earldom and Bishoprick of Orkney*, part II, p. 2.

[34] Dodgshon, "Infield-Outfield", pp. 15-6.

[35] H. C. Darby and J. Saltmarsh, "The Infield-Outfield System on a Norfolk Manor", *Economic History*, III (1935), pp. 30-44.

[36] B. Dodwell, "Holdings and Inheritance in Medieval East Anglia", *Economic History Rev.*, XX (1967), p. 59.

[37] D. C. Douglas, *The Social Structure of Medieval East Anglia*, Oxford Studies in Social and Legal History, IX, Oxford, (1927), p. 41.

[38] Gray, *English Field Systems*, pp. 333-7.

[39] W. Hudson, "Traces of Primitive Agricultural Organization as Suggested by the Manor of Martham Norfolk 1101-1292", *Transactions of the Royal Historical Society*, 4th series, I (1918), pp. 28-58.

[40] F. W. Maitland, "The History of a Cambridgeshire Manor", pp. 16-40 in H. M. Cam (ed.), *Selected Historical Essays of F. W. Maitland*, Cambridge (1957), p. 18.

[41] Darby and Saltmarsh, *op. cit.*, pp. 39-41.

[42] Finberg, *The Agrarian History of England and Wales*, I, part ii, pp. 494-5.

[43] H. S. A. Fox, "Outfield Cultivation in Devon and Cornwall: A Reinterpretation", pp. 19-38 in M. Havinden (ed.), *Husbandry and Marketing in the South-West 1500-1800*, Exeter Papers in Economic History, no. 8 (1973), p. 32.

[44] H. P. R. Finberg, *Tavistock Abbey*, Newton Abbott (1969 edition), p. 40.

[45] W. C. Hazlitt, *Tenures of Land and Customs of Manors*, London (1874), p. 308.

[46] R. A. Butlin, "Northumberland Field Systems", *Agricultural History Rev.*, XII (1964), p. 114.

[47] *Ibid.*, p. 115.

[48] R. A. Butlin, "Field Systems of Northumberland and Durham", pp. 93-144 in Baker and Butlin (eds.), *op. cit.*, pp. 108, 110 and 137.

[49] E. Bateson, *A History of Northumberland*, vol. II, Newcastle (1895), p. 45.

[50] J. C. Hodgson (ed.), *A History of Northumberland*, vol. IV, part II, Newcastle (1897), p. 328.

[51] Hinds (ed.), *op. cit.*, p. 139.

[52] Compare, for example, the divisions of the outfield or common land at Wall in Hodgson (ed.), *op. cit.*, p. 171 and that of Glanton in Dodds (ed.), *op. cit.*, p. 543.

[53] Craster (ed.), *op. cit.*, p. 314.

[54] J. Wilson (ed.), *Register of the Priory of St Bees*, Surtees Soc., CXXVI (1915), p. 400.

[55] G. E. Elliott, "The System of Cultivation and Evidence of Enclosure in the Cumberland Open Fields in the Sixteenth Century", *Géographie et Histoire Agraires Annales de L'Est*, XXI (1959), pp. 123 and 127-9.

[56] G. E. Elliott, "Field Systems in Northwest England", pp. 41-92 in Baker and Butlin (eds.), *op. cit.*, p. 45.

[57] G. H. Tupling, *The Economic History of Rossendale*, Manchester (1927), pp. 103-4.

[58] *Ibid.*, p. 111. See also the similar reference for Haslingden on the same page.

[59] Hilton, *The Decline of Serfdom in Medieval England*, p. 17.

[60] E. Miller, *The Abbey and Bishopric of Ely*, Cambridge (1951), p. 120.

[61] E. Miller, "England in the Twelfth and Thirteenth Centuries: An Economic Contrast", *Economic History Rev.*, XXIV (1971), p. 5.

[62] Tawney, *op. cit.*, p. 144.

[63] E. A. Kosminsky, *Studies in the Agrarian History of England in the Thirteenth Century*, Oxford (1956), p. 131.

[64] *Ibid.*, p. 204.

[65] P. T. Brandon, "Medieval Clearance in the East Sussex Weald", *Transactions of the Institute of British Geographers*, 48 (1969), pp. 145 and 148.

[66] Moore, *Laughton*, p. 35.

[67] *Reports on the State of Certain Parishes in Scotland 1627*, Maitland Club, Edinburgh (1835), pp. 36-99 contains many examples. The basic equation appears to be that "Everie husband land payes fourtene bollis victuall beir aitis and quheit", p. 56.

[68] SRO, GD44/51/747. This rental suggests that rents were standardised at £5. 6s. 8d.

per davach for maill and four bolls of multure or grain per davach. See also, A. Macpherson, *Glimpses of Church and Social Life in the Highlands in Olden Times*, Edinburgh (1893), pp. 503-15 which provides a 1603 rental for Badenoch on the same estate and a brief discussion of *silver maill* and *ferm vitual*.

[69] Examples are provided by *Reports on the State of Certain Parishes*, pp. 46, 79-80 and 95; *Collectanea De Rebus Albanicis*, edited by the Iona Club, Edinburgh (1847), printed with the Transactions of the Club, I (1839), pp. 172-9.

[70] Sheppard, "Pre-Enclosure Field and Settlement Patterns in an English Township", p. 65.

[71] Hilton, *A Medieval Society*, pp. 22-3.

[72] Hilton, *A Medieval Society*, p. 21. Further discussion of Feckenham and similar settlements in the district can be found in Hilton, "Old Enclosure in the West Midlands", pp. 272-83, the theme of which is precisely this contrast between old open field areas and newer enclosed areas.

[73] E. Hughes, *North Country Life in the Eighteenth Century: the North East 1700-1750*, Oxford (1952), p. 133.

[74] W. J. Corbett, "Elizabethan Village Surveys", *Transactions of the Royal Historical Soc.*, XI (1897), pp. 81-2.

[75] M. Davies, "Field Systems of South Wales", pp. 480-529 in Baker and Butlin (eds.), *op. cit.*, pp. 494 and 501.

[76] Rees, *South Wales and the March 1284-1415*, pp. 144 and 148-9.

[77] W. Rees (ed.), *A Survey of the Duchy of Lancaster Lordships in Wales 1609-1613*, Board of Celtic Studies, University of Wales History and Law Series, no. 12, Cardiff (1953), p. xxxi.

[78] Farrer (ed.), *Lancashire Inquests . . . A.D. 1313-A.D. 1355*, pp. 194-5; Kershaw (ed.), *Bolton Abbey Rentals*, pp. 4, 5 and 9; J. Z. Titow, *English Rural Society 1200-1350*, London (1969), p. 140.

[79] Miller, *The Abbey and Bishopric of Ely*, p. 120; Miller, "England in the Twelfth and Thirteenth Centuries", p. 5.

[80] B. E. Howells, "Open Fields and Farmsteads", *The Pembrokeshire Historian*, 3 (1971), p. 16.

[81] B. K. Roberts, "A Study of Medieval Colonization in the Forest of Arden, Warwickshire", *Agricultural History Rev.*, 16 (1968), pp. 101-13.

[82] See, for example, J. Macdonald, *General View of the Agriculture of the Hebrides or Western Isles of Scotland*, Edinburgh (1811), p. 22, H. Marwick, *The Place Names of Birsay*, Aberdeen (1970), p. 115.

[83] Examples are cited in R. A. Dodgshon, "Farming in Roxburghshire and Berwickshire on the Eve of Improvement", *Scottish Historical Rev.*, LIV (1975), pp. 141-2.

[84] Butlin, "Northumberland Fields Systems", p. 114; Butlin, "Field Systems of Northumberland and Durham" in Baker and Butlin (eds.), *op. cit.*, pp. 136 and 144.

[85] A sample of these descriptions of tathing can be found in Dodgshon, "Farming in Roxburghshire and Berwickshire on the Eve of Improvement", pp. 145-7.

[86] A. Simpson, "The East Anglian Foldcourse: Some Queries", *Agricultural History Rev.*, IV (1958), pp. 87-90; M. R. Postgate, "Field Systems of East Anglia", pp. 281-324 in Baker and Butlin, *op. cit.*, pp. 313-22.

[87] H. Owen (ed.), *The Description of Pembrokeshire by George Owen of Henllys*, part I, London (1892), p. 62.

[88] Sir John Clapham, *A Concise Economic History of Britain: From Earliest Times to 1750*, Cambridge (1949), p. 48.

Chapter 5

The splitting of townships
in medieval Britain

In recent years, it has become fashionable for archaeologists to characterize the history of medieval settlement as one of flux rather than stability, both as regards site and morphology. As a backcloth to the study of field systems, this revised history of settlement holds out many possibilities. Vital features of early field systems, such as regular sub-divided field layouts or communally regulated cropping patterns, demand reorganization as part of their explanation. This chapter seeks to isolate certain kinds of settlement change that occurred generally over the medieval period. It will be suggested that they were symptomatic of basic changes in the organization of townships precipitated by the splitting of individual townships into two or more *sub*-townships. By exploring the connection between township splitting and settlement change, the ground can be prepared for a more specific under-standing of how and why many field systems were comprehensively replanned over the medieval period.

Township splitting: the English evidence

Pride of place in any discussion of township splitting in England must be given to Maitland, for it was he who first directed attention to the problem.[1] Typically, he approached it from a broad standpoint, seeking to answer through it the question of why the early village community lacked a court of its own, a village court *sui generis*. His answer sought to link the juridical framework of such communities with the ancient hundred, via a complex process of successive fissioning. "In all the Anglo-Saxon dooms there seems no trace of the court of the township. The hundred is the lowest unit that has a tribunal; the 'township moot', if it exists, is not a tribunal. But it is very hard to conceive a 'village community' worthy of the name which has no court of its own".[2] The idea of a farming community whose land had once been co-extensive with the hundred, but which had become smaller through progressive fission, offered a route out of this dilemma.

The basis for his assumption that the hundred and territory of the farming community had initially been one and the same thing, rested on a familiar element in the landscape. When the latter is surveyed, "very often we find two or more contiguous townships bearing the same name and distinguished from each other only by what are called their surnames. Cases in which there are two such townships are in some parts of England so extremely common as to be the rule rather than the exception".[3] The settlements he had in mind were those pairs or groups that shared a place-name together, but which were distinguished from each other by prefixes like East, West, Great or Little (as with East and West Barnby in Yorkshire or Great and Little Dunmow in Essex) or by prefixes of a more personalised nature (such as Charlton Mackrell and Charlton Adam in Somerset or Dalton Norris, Dalton Travers and Dalton Gayles in Yorkshire).

Maitland's interpretation of their origin was built around two propositions. First, he suggested that whilst some were pre-Domesday in origin, the majority date from after 1086. "In general", he wrote, "where two neighbouring modern villages have the same name, Domesday does not treat them as two".[4] Amongst those examples already formed by the time of Domesday Book, some have a distinctly fresh appearance, like *Emingforde* and *Emingforde Alia* (or the "other" Hemingford) in Hunts. For Maitland, "this clumsy nomenclature forcibly suggests that the two Hemingfords were already two, but had not long before been one".[5] Secondly, he construed such related groups of villages as the by-product of fission, with single settlements being split into two or more separate villages. At one point, he spoke of the need to see some villages of the late middle ages not as direct survivors of ancient settlement, but "as one of several co-heirs among whom the lands of the ancestor have been partitioned".[6] In short, the settlement pattern of the middle ages was born as much of the forces of involution as of evolution, with settlements sub-dividing themselves, cell-like, into new ones.

It is remarkable that Maitland's paper prompted little interest in the subject of split settlements, despite their overwhelming importance to the history of the countryside. No scholar has thought it worthwhile to consider their origin in depth. However, a number have touched on the problem indirectly. M. Gelling, for example, has recently underlined the role played by the sub-division of early estates in the formation of new place names.[7]

In some cases, the conclusions reached run counter to those of Maitland. Thus, Postan was inclined to explain split settlements as formed by the packing of filial settlements around the edge of a primary or parent settlement.[8] In other cases, the chronology of their formation has been pushed much further back than that proposed by Maitland. For instance, in his work on early boundaries in southern England, D. J. Bonney concluded that parish boundaries, as well as internal township boundaries, were probably established before the end of the Anglo-Saxon pagan period. For the present discussion, it is the suggestion that township boundaries *within* parishes were formed by the seventh century, that is of greatest interest, since some of those he cites were connected with split settlements. As with parish boundaries, his conclusion was based on their association with pagan burials. Writing specifically of Hampshire examples, he argued that if this association is accepted, "then it would appear that some small units òr estates, of considerably less than parish dimensions, were recognizable entities in pagan Saxon times, e.g. those based on Aughton, Shaw, Choulston and West Chisenbury. There is no reason to regard these as exceptional either on account of their size or in any other way. Each unit comprises land associated with a single settlement or community which farmed and obtained a livelihood from it; and certainly from the later Saxon period onwards there is abundant evidence that these were the basic units of settlement and land utilisation over much of England, especially the more densely settled parts of the lowland zone".[9] Equally fine-scaled work on Dorset boundaries by C. Taylor reached similar conclusions, with not only the layout of parishes, but their internal sub-division into townships and hamlets being seen as established by the late Saxon period.[10] Two aspects of this work on early boundaries stand out. First, neither Bonney nor Taylor focus on the particular character of split settlements, even though they form a prominent part of the patterns they were seeking to comprehend. Secondly, both push the laying out of parishes and townships back before 1086, with little allowance for any subsequent modification in the number or disposition of townships and hamlets. Taylor, in particular, was very explicit on this point, stressing throughout the pre-Domesday completeness of the Dorset settlement pattern.

Contrary to these shifts of viewpoint and emphasis in recent discussions of settlement history, it is claimed here that a strong case can still be marshalled in favour of Maitland's interpretation of split settlements. Comprehensive data sets like Domesday Book, the Hundred Rolls or the *Nomina Villarum* form an obvious source of support. Although the support they afford is of a circumstantial nature, comparison between them provides a broad perspective on the extent and chronology of splitting. A convenient illustration of this comparative or serial approach can be derived from R. Skaife's edited transcripts of Yorkshire vill names in the so-called Kirkby's Inquest of the late thirteenth century, the Inquisitions of Knight's Fees of roughly similar dating and the *Nomina Villarum* of the early fourteenth century, and his comparison of them with both Domesday Book and the modern map. Altogether, just over 80 split township groups (comprising up to four settlements in each) occur. Approximately one-fourth existed in 1086, and a further two-thirds appear to have taken shape between 1086 and the early fourteenth century; the rest appear to post-date the early fourteenth century.[11]

The main criticism with this sort of approach is that it relies on sources like the Domesday Book, that are notoriously unreliable as a record of settlement. No less an authority than H. C. Darby preferred to tread cautiously when using the Domesday Book to examine split settlements. The view which he and his co-authors of the Domesday geographies upheld is summarized by Darby himself in a discussion of Dorset settlement. He stated that "when two or more adjoining villages bear the same name, it is not always clear whether more than one existed in the eleventh century. There is no indication in the Domesday text that, say, the East Lulworth and West Lulworth of today existed as separate villages: the Domesday information about them is entered under only one name (Loloworde), though they may well have been separate in the eleventh century as they certainly were by the end of the thirteenth".[12] Others have insisted on the need for a still greater degree of caution when using the Domesday Book. Consistent with his view that the settlement pattern of Dorset was complete by 1086, Taylor seems to take the view that the Domesday Book is more likely to deceive than inform when it treats as one those settlements which appear later as split, as in the case of Lulworth. Its "Inadequate picture of settlement" was, he maintained, "Domesday Book's greatest weakness".[13] Amongst the instances of its shortcomings which he cited was that of Piddletrenthide. Held by only a single landholder, it was entered in the Domesday Book simply as Piddletrenthide and assessed at 30 hides. Yet Taylor's own work on early boundaries and charters showed that its division into an Upper, Middle and Lower Tithing, each a discretely defined estate with its own settlement focus, must have been finalised by 1086.[14]

However, there is a danger here that two quite separate issues are being confused. I have no dispute with the general assertion that as a record ostensibly of landholding, Domesday Book omits to mention numerous rural settlements of its day; but it is vital to be clear under what circumstances it does gloss over settlement. Domesday Book's basic deficiency flows from its strict concern with who held what land. If a manor — *one embracing a number of quite distinct vills* — was held *in toto* by a single landholder or tenant-in-chief, then the Domesday commissioners found it sufficient to record only the manor, not its constituent vills. In other words, the one entry or place name could conceal a number of different settlements. When dealing with a large manor, the error in taking Domesday Book's listing of settlement at its face value is obvious enough and requires no special pleading. The difficulties arise when we are confronted with a smallish manor, in which the headquarters or main settlement may or may not be the only settlement and where no clues are offered to enable us to resolve the matter. It is under these circumstances that Domesday Book misleads, as a long and distinguished line of scholars have explained.[15]

It is tempting to see split settlements, or rather the lack of them, in Domesday Book in the same terms. Given the tendency in some quarters to see split settlements as signifying a parent-daughter relationship, there is a logic in seeing such groups as entered under the heading solely of their parent settlement, without mention of the offspring. After all, the great Book dealt with manors in this way, specifying their caput or headquarters but not their constituent members. There is an important point of difference, though, which cannot be overlooked; the majority, if not all split settlements c.1086, involved different landholders. In these circumstances, the question becomes one of asking whether the Domesday Book would fail to distinguish between the different parts of a split settlement group, *even when they constituted different estates*. In fact, there are many occasions when it records two or three different estates within a manor or vill, but not the two or three settlements into which such manors or vills *later* appear divided. Some might argue that such estates probably formed different or discrete settlements in 1086 and that here is yet further proof of Domesday Book inadequacy as a source of information about settlement. Such a view is rejected here because it ignores the fundamental fact that we are dealing with a quite different question to that considered in the previous paragraph. To group vills or settlements together under a single manor when the latter was held by a single tenant-in-chief is explicable as a convenient form of shorthand in a survey designed specifically to list and locate landholding; but to group settlements or vills held as separate estates by different landholders under a single locational entry would surely have confused the Domesday Book's contemporaries as much as it would confuse us. If caution is to be exercised in these circumstances, then we must suppose that such settlements had not yet been split by 1086 not that they were. To establish that a manor or vill was shared between two or three landholders is only to establish the preconditions of splitting, not the event itself. It is perhaps only because they have glossed the process involved — the splitting of one settlement into two or three physically separate settlements — that some scholars have tended to gloss the evidence relating to it, assuming far too easily that the split settlements of later documents were matched on the ground by the tenurial units recorded in the Domesday Book.

There is, however, a further, more technical reason for taking sources like the Domesday Book more at their face value on this matter and it is that the establishment of a new vill was not a casual or informal affair. As Maitland and Sir Frederick Pollock put it, "the boundaries of the vills are matters of public law, not to be abolished by the lord of the soil, for in doing so he would disarrange the fiscal, administrative, and justiciary scheme of the hundred, the county, the kingdom, and might aggravate the burdens incumbent on their neighbours. The powers of making new vills without licence from above must cease as the centralization of government and justice becomes more perfect":[16] this has a direct bearing on the discussion. Splitting led to either the creation of two hamlets within a single vill (= two Demi-vills or a vill *cum membris suis*) or to the creation of two separate vills. Where it led to the latter and, where, on a straight reading of the evidence, it appears to have done so after 1086, we cannot so easily reverse this conclusion by presuming that the vill had been split in 1086 but that the Domesday Book had ignored the fact, for too much hinged around the status of a vill for it to be so lightly overlooked. Similar reasoning can be applied to other comprehensive data sets like the Hundred Rolls. What is at stake here is the question of what sufficed as a definition of landholding in early surveys once splitting had taken place. For example, once Hackney became Over and Nether Hackney, was it necessary for land charters to specify which Hackney they dealt with for them to be correct? There are grounds for believing that the answer is yes and that failure to specify which portion of a split settlement group a claim or process applied to, weakened its case.[17]

Strengthening this confidence in data sets like the Domesday Book even further, are those sources of a more localised character which, when examined, confirm that many split settlements appear to have taken shape during the two or three centuries after 1086. For example, P. H. Reaney's work on the place-names of Essex — a country rich in split settlement groups — employed a diversity of sources. Together, they endorse Maitland's conclusion that the twelfth and thirteenth centuries saw the formation of many split settlements, provided, that is, one is prepared to take charter references to settlement at their face value. Examples like Great and Little Wigborough, Great and Little Bentley, Great and Little Bromley, Great and Little Clacton, Great and Little Wakering, East and West Horndon, and East and West Ham all make their first charter appearances as split settlements at this point.[18] Cartularies are productive sources of example, gathering together in a convenient form a sequence of charter references to particular townships. For instance, the Register of St Bees Priory in Cumberland, suggests that the vill of Stirkland began the thirteenth century in a singular form but ended it as Great and Little Stirkland[19], whilst the *villa de Gillecruce* of the late twelfth century had become that of *magna Gillecruce* and *parva Gillecruce* by 1272.[20] Simple cross-referencing between different charter collections can also yield examples. Thus, in the Honour of Skipton, the "hamlet of Bradley" that was recorded in a document of 1278[21] was later transformed into High and Low Bradley.[22]

Most of the evidence presented so far has been circumstantial, relying on observable changes in the designation of townships by early charters. Whilst there is an impressive consistency about the way such evidence bears out Maitland's conclusion that many townships were split over the twelfth and thirteenth centuries, it cannot be taken as conclusive proof. Doubt can only be removed by more explicitly documented examples of splitting and fortunately, these are forthcoming. In some cases, townships can be seen being split tenurially and then, in subsequent documents, being split toponymically into different portions. Typical of such townships is that of Bourton in Oxfordshire; its description as Great and Little Bourtons followed the granting of three-quarters of the fee to Robert of Chacombe.[23] In the same county, the township of Chesterton emerges into the light of documentation initially as a single estate held in 1086 by Miles Crispin; its splitting into Great and Little Chesterton followed the acquisition of a portion of the original township by Thame Abbey in 1137, a portion which later became tagged as Little Chesterton[24] (see Fig. 11).

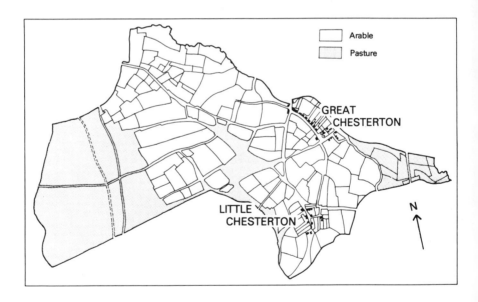

Fig. 11. Great and Little Chesterton, Oxfordshire (c. 1764-68). Based on M. D. Lobel (ed.), 'A History of the County of Oxford', vol. VI (London, 1959), p. 98. Despite the clear splitting of Chesterton into two settlements, there is no indication in early sources that its fields were likewise split.

An approach favoured by Maitland for placing the problem on a firmer footing was to establish the link between split settlements using personalized place-name elements and the individuals they actually commemorate, thereby setting such settlement groups in their chronological context. There are many examples with which to illustrate this line of approach. For instance, in Berkshire, the twin settlements of Letcombe Regis and Letcombe Basset possibly derive from when part of the original township of Letcombe — a township held by the King — was granted to the Basset family in the twelfth century.[25] Further east, in Essex, the triple settlements of Woodham Ferrers, Mortimer and Walter probably derived from the fact that the Domesday settlement of Woodham, already split tenurially into three estates, was soon after split into three physically separate estates, one held as part of the Ferrers Barony, another by the family of Robert de Mortimer and the remaining one by the family of Robert Fitzwalter.[26] The *Victoria County Histories* detail other possible examples. Thus, in Somerset, the settlements of Charlton Adam (or East Charlton) and Charlton Mackrell (or West Charlton) probably owe their nomenclature and existence as split settlements to tenants who together held the original settlement of Charlton of the mesne lordship in the late twelfth century.[27]

In other cases, the assumptions over splitting can be tightened further, thanks to legal processes or comments that deal directly with the matter. For instance, Thomas Habington's survey of Worcestershire refers unambiguously to the "Litlinton divyded nowe into three villages", or those of *Southe*, *North* and *Myddel*.[28] Doverdale, too, was described by him as divided into two parts or estates.[29] Early thirteenth-century *Curia Regis Rolls* concerning the partition of the Percy estates refer to seisin being given for the halves of *Litton* and *Bukeden*, both settlements which later appeared divided into East and West portions.[30] When three hides in Wick (Wiltshire) were partitioned at the start of the thirteenth century, it may well have produced the split settlement of Wick.[31]

Without question, the most valued illustrations of splitting are those which produced documentation of the very process or act of splitting itself. Given that the majority of English split townships were probably formed in the two or three centuries after 1086, we cannot reasonably hope for detailed charter coverage of these early examples. Those instances of partition cited in the previous paragraph may typify the sum total of recorded information we can expect for this early period, with their mere announcements that a partition or division of an estate or township was to be carried out. However, where splitting occurred later, more detailed documentation might be expected. An area where splitting did occur or continued to occur quite late, was that of Northumberland. Detailed documentation, including surveyor's reports, are available for a whole series of township fissions that took place over the fifteenth, sixteenth and seventeenth centuries. Taken together, they remove all doubt over what was involved in the process of splitting.

A richly documented example is that of Cowpen. When split in 1619, a division into two parts was discussed, but then a division into three adopted. The associated survey of the township declared that "after such devision of all in three partes, if the said parties in every severall third devision shall agree to sub-divide and partition . . . and observacion be used as before, that everie partie within such devision has his parte and purpoant according to the quantitie or number of acres due to him".[32] Extant plans show that "as before" meant sub-divided. Likewise, when the township of Harlow Hill was split in 1622 into "iiii partes or quarters and to every quartre two tenementes allotted . . . so as everie two tennantes have their arable meadowe and pasture divided from all other men"[33], it was still a sub-divided field(s) layout that remained, albeit a less complicated one. As at Cowpen, the use of the word *several* applied to the townships being created by the division and not to the holdings within them. Again, when it was agreed to "devyde the Towne of Chatton into 4 severall townes"[34], each landholder had "their land allotted rigg by rigg as is the custom in every husband towne, so that each should have land of the like quality".[35] Similarly, when the township of Rock was split into two halves in 1599, five tenants were allocated to one half and seven to the other. As E. Bateson remarked, "within the limits of each township, the common field system probably went on as before".[36]

The forementioned townships represent a sample of a large number of split townships in Northumberland. Some, like Hartford, were split during the fifteenth century,[37] and others, like Long Haughton[38] and Lesbury[39], were split in the sixteenth century. Still others, like Bilton[40] and Birlington[41] were not split until the seventeenth century. Some, like Hartley, were simply split in two.[42] Others, like Tugg near Bamburgh, were quartered.[43] Some even involved complex double splitting. Acklington, for example, was said to equal 36 husbandlands in 1498 but by 1616, it comprised two separate portions of 17½ husbandlands each; then, in 1702, part was sub-divided further into two portions of 8½ *farms* and 9 *farms* respectively[44] (see Fig. 12).

These Northumberland examples also shed light on exactly what splitting meant in terms of field and settlement layout. The distinction, it seems, between a single township — divided tenurially between two or more estates — and a split settlement group was not a sharp one. In some cases, splitting simply led to the division of a township's arable land into two or three discrete, self-contained cropping sectors. This appears to have been the case when Rock township was split in 1599. Alternatively, the settlement itself — its farmsteads and outbuildings — may have been split but not the fields. The splitting of Hartford in the fifteenth century seems to have fallen into this category, though not certainly so. However, that divisions of this sort were

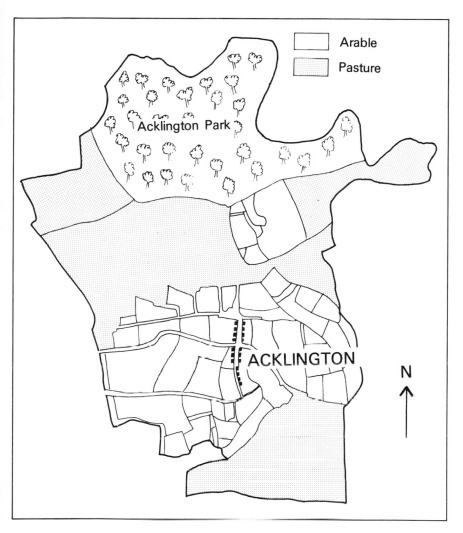

Fig. 12. *Acklington, Northumberland (c. 1624). Based on J. C. Hodgson (ed.),* 'A History of Northumberland', *V (Newcastle, 1899), pp. 372-3. Despite being split twice, once before 1616 and again in 1702, Acklington still appears outwardly — if not in tenurial terms — a single, coherent settlement.*

implemented can be testified for by other areas. In the Midlands, there were quite a number of townships that were split into two or more settlements, but which continued to share the same field system, settlements like East and West Langton in Leicestershire,[45] or the Baldons in Oxfordshire (Toot Baldon, Marsh Baldon, Baldon St Lawrence and Little Baldon). Of this latter group, it has been written that "the fact that the four Baldons shared a common field system suggests that three of the hamlets were later colonies, settled by men and women from the original village".[46] This interpretation of how the Baldons evolved touches on an issue of some importance. When settlements were split, it was often a case of one portion retaining the old settlement site and the other(s) acquiring a new one or ones: this was probably what happpened at the Baldons and it was also what happened at Thirston (Northumberland). Its twin townships of West and East Thirston were also known as Old and New Thirston respectively. Clearly, when Thirston was split during the mid-sixteenth century, East was created as a new settlement within its portion of the arable allotted to it from the land of the old township[47] (see Fig. 13). Likewise, when the Cumberland township of Clifton was split, possibly in the thirteenth century, its twin settlements became known as "Great Clifton, High Clifton or Kirk Clifton, and Clifton, Low Clifton or Little Clifton".[48] The fact that Little or Low Clifton was also known by the bald title of Clifton, suggests it formed the site of the original settlements and Great Clifton, the new one. This can be compared with the reasoning of other writers who, taking these prefixes literally, have tended to imply that a Great or *magna* must invariably have preceded a Little or *parva*, the two being set in a parent-daughter relationship.[49] Although it is possible that one settlement site was occupied later than the other, it is unlikely that we can draw a fixed relationship between the old and new on the one hand and the prefixes Great and Little on the other. Furthermore, even when new settlement *sites* were created, it does not follow that we are dealing with a new

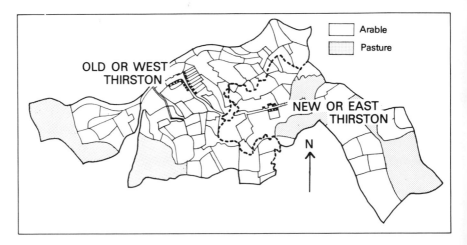

Fig. 13. East and West Thirston, Northumberland (1623). Based on J. C. Hodgson (ed.), 'A History of Northumberland', VII (Newcastle, 1904), p. 37.

settlement or township, but merely an old one split into new portions which, in consequence, created different needs as regards the siting of settlement.

To sum up then, there is a strong case to argue in favour of Maitland's ideas on this vital phase in settlement history. Not only can the whole notion of settlement splitting be validated, but so too can his proposed chronology. To restate this chronology, some splits were in existence by 1086, possibly as many as one quarter of all examples that were eventually to be found in England. However, the main period of their formation seems to have been over the two or three centuries after 1086, when — at a rough guess — as many as one half were formed. The remainder developed after c. 1400. Such a chronology, though, may need modification from region to region. Peripheral areas to the north and west — like Northumberland — may ultimately reveal a different chronology, one in which the main phase of their formation was weighted much later, perhaps during the late medieval and early modern periods.

This question of chronology is crucial when fitting the process of splitting into the wider evolutionary framework of settlement. As outlined earlier, recent work has stressed both the general fluidity of settlement layout and the particular transformation which occurred roughly over the eighth and ninth centuries when dispersed settlements were concentrated into larger, village-type units. On the face of it, the latter would seem a contrary trend to the fragmenting processes involved in splitting. Recognition of their differing chronologies, therefore, is critical. It makes it feasible to see both as part of the history of English settlement. The general fluidity of settlement layout established by recent work makes the addition of this fresh layer of change a fairly straightforward matter. Indeed, given that splitting was, in essence, a splitting of estates, there is no built-in assumption over how settlement itself, the farmsteads and outbuildings, should respond. A variety of solutions or changes were possible. Overall, there is no reason why, in one period, it could not have tended to concentrate settlement and, in another, fragment it.

Township splitting: the Scottish evidence

The evidence for the splitting of Scottish townships is again a trend which can be pieced together through a mixture of circumstantial and direct evidence. The circumstantial evidence derives from land charters and rentals, through which a view of townships at consecutive dates can be constructed. These sources have few of the problems which attend English sources like the Domesday book or the Hundred Rolls, partly because of their nature as documents concerned more with defining or listing townships *within* estates than with distinguishing between estates, and partly because of the much later date at which township splitting in Scotland took place. Broadly speaking, the main period of splitting appears to have been spread over the fifteenth, sixteenth and seventeenth centuries.[50]

There are many Scottish estates capable of illustrating the value of these circumstantial sources. For example, in the south-east, late fifteenth century rentals for Ettrick list *Eldinhope, Dauloriane* and *Montergeris* as consolidated townships or stedes.[51] Subsequent rentals, though, show them to have been split into Eldinhopeknow, Over Eldinhope and Mid Eldinhope; Easter and Wester D'Lorain; and East and West Muntbernger.[52] Across Scotland, further examples can be culled from charters and rentals for Islay. There, townships like Glenastell, Gartcossyn, Killenan and Ylistill all appear as single townships in a rental of 1509, yet they had been split into Upper and Nether Glenastell, Upper and Nether Gartcossen, Upper and Nether Killenan and Easter and Wester Elister by 1733.[53] In Angus, mid-fourteenth century references to "the lands of Kenny towards the West"[54] were replaced by references to *Kennymaior* and *Kennemekle* by the late fifteenth century.[55] Nearby, late fifteenth century references to Lethnotis, Aucharne and Inchedoury[56] were set beside mid-fifteenth century references to "the two Lethnottis Over and Neddir", "the two Aucharnes Ester and Wester" and "the two Inchedowriis Estir and Westir".[57] The name of the first of these townships, or Lethnot, is of particular interest because it suggests (Leth = half) a still earlier split had occurred. Up in the Braes of Angus, the townships of Lightney, Blairno and Tilliarblet all appear split into Easter and Wester portions between c. 1600 references to them[58] and late seventeenth and early eighteenth century references.[59] Two areas rich in examples are Strathavon and Glenlivet in Banffshire. Comparisons between rentals of 1600, 1610, 1698 and for the early eighteenth century suggest quite a number of townships, such as Dellivorar, Blairfindie and Dallaquhyis, became split over the relatively short period spanned by the records.[60] However, there is a cautionary note to be added. Inspection of mid-eighteenth century estate plans suggest that these rentals may not have disclosed the full picture of what existed on the ground, perhaps because of the prevalence of the tacksman system and the holding of clusters of townships by a single person.[61] Faith in their general if not their exact reliability, though, is restored by the late seventeenth century commentator on the region, Gordon of Straloch, who reported that farmers in the locality had previously lived in large villages, but that within recent times they had divided up their townships into smaller, more manageable units[62] (see Fig. 14).

Gordon of Straloch's description of splitting is not the only direct proof of the process available for Scotland. A search through estate paper collections has uncovered a fairly large number recorded examples[63] extending back into the fifteenth century. For instance, amongst the earliest was the division of

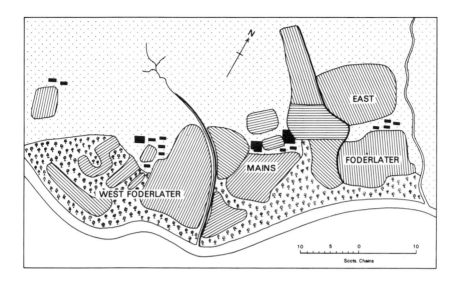

Fig. 14. The split township of Fodderlater, Banffshire (1762). Based on SRO, RHP 2488/3.

Blyth (Peebles-shire) in 1479 into two halves, one belonging to a Henry Levingstone and the other to a John Mertyn.[64] Some, like that of Blyth, were labelled clearly as divisions. This was the case with the division of Formall (Fife) in 1692. A hint as to the identifying prefix which each half of Formall adopted is provided by the fact that the division defined its task as a division into east and west ploughs.[65] In the case of other townships, the act of splitting was executed by means of an instrument of dissection, as with "the dissection of the lands of Haristayn" (Aberdeenshire) in 1547.[66] Not a few instances of splitting wore the disguise of a mere setting of boundaries, such as when Schethum (Fife) had the boundaries between its easter and wester halves fixed in 1491.[67] An agreement over boundaries between the three landholders of Blairquois (Lennox) in 1493/4 may also represent a splitting of their three shares into separate townships.[68]

If the Scottish evidence has any special merit, then it lies in the light it casts on the mechanics of splitting. In particular, it explains why prefixes like East/West and Nether/Upper were extensively used to identify split townships (see Fig. 15): it was because they formed part and parcel of the procedures by which townships were shared out between landholders, with shares being distinguished either through the language of a sun-division (sunny and shadow portions) or its equivalents, namely, east/west and upper/nether; that all these terms were equivalent is borne out by early Scottish legal texts.[69]

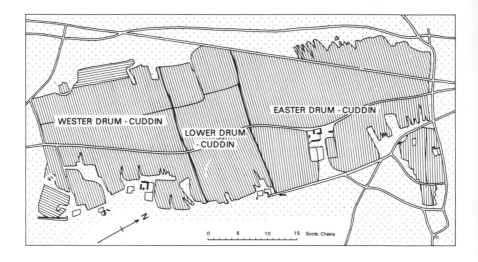

Fig. 15. The split township of Drumcuddin, Ross and Cromarty (1796). Based on SRO, RHP 1469.

It is also borne out by the way they were interchanged with each other in the description of split townships, as in the case of "Over or Easter Markinsh, call Kirk Markinsh", 1681.[70] What we have to envisage is a cosmographically-based scheme of differentiation which allocated sunny/east/over/upper/fore on one side and shadow/west/nether/lower/back on the other.[71] Its convenience is that it embraced all possibilities, from runrig to shares set apart as separate townships. Where shares were intermixed in runrig-fashion, then portions were commonly dubbed as sunny/shadow, east/west or upper/nether shares or ploughs of a township. Where split into discrete sub-townships, then they tended to become the East/West or Upper/Nether township. The nomenclature of shares, though, may not always be so legible in terms of what they represented on the ground. In some cases, shares designated as the east/west or upper/nether portion of a township could well have been disposed as separate units. Only where such terms intruded into the designation of townships, as opposed to the shares *within* townships, can we be absolutely certain of what they signify in terms of landholding.

This uncertainty over what the township shares recorded by charters or rentals actually meant arises from the prevalence of shareholding in Scotland. Because of shareholding, landholders constantly faced the problem of dividing out the property-holding of townships. If proprietors were involved, their decisions would have been relatively permanent. If tenants, then their decision may not have lasted beyond the duration of their tack before a fresh decision over layout was taken. Each decision was a choice between a runrig or split township layout. The point is starkly focussed by a charter of 1511 for the "terras et baroniam de Chamberlane-Newtoun at Roxburgh (Roxburgh-shire) which was to be "contigue jacebat cum principali villa ejusdem sive divise".[72] The choice was made in favour of a split township, with Roxburgh eventually comprising an East and West Mains, an Upper and Nether Roxburgh with the latter sub-divided into East and West parts, and the Newtoun of Roxburgh. The splitting of Scottish townships then, was not an unique or exceptional event in the history of landholding but one that was both widespread and recurrent: Indeed, it is just possible that there were townships in which tenant shares were shifted between runrig and split units on a regular basis. Only where proprietors intervened and stabilised the choice as one of split rather than consolidated — but internally runrig — townships, need it have surfaced in place-names.

Township splitting: the Welsh evidence

The Welsh evidence for splitting is potentially the richest. There is hardly a corner of the Welsh countryside which does not possess *prima facie* evidence for splitting in the form of place-name prefixes like East and West or, more abundantly, suffixes like *Isaf* and *Uchaf* or *Fawr* and *Mawr*. However, with the possible exception of the heavily Normanised/Anglicised areas in the south-east and along the southern coastlands, the character of township splitting in Wales differed noticeably from that of England and Scotland. It did so because many townships in west and north Wales lacked the singular coherence which their counterparts elsewhere possessed. Holdings within each township were rarely focussed around a common centre, but seem to assert themselves more strongly as independent units. We find them standing alone as discrete units or, if intermixed, to be only partially so or in parcels more than in strips or fragmented over sections rather than the entire territory of the township. This lack of cohesion reflected the tenurial conditions that prevailed in the Welshry, or those areas where the Norman and Edwardian conquests did not transform Welsh institutions of tenure and landholding in any radical way. Two particular attributes of tenure stand out as important for township splitting. The first consists of the custom of gavelkind or partible inheritance which continued to be practised in Welsh areas right up until it was abolished after the Union with England in 1536. Secondly, the general weakness of lordship in these areas as a force shaping the daily lives of landholders, coupled with the prevalence of freeholds derived from the old *gwelyau*, meant that there was less co-ordination in the development of landholding compared with townships in England and Scotland. These two factors — partible inheritance and the greater freedoms of tenure — imparted a definite character to the splitting of Welsh townships. Put simply, it meant that we are dealing not so much with the splitting of large sub-divided field townships into smaller sub-divided field townships (as in England and Scotland), but with the splitting of consolidated holdings into smaller ones. It is a difference of scale, but one that manifests the essentially different conditions of the north and west of the Principality.

The question of partible inheritance in Wales has already been aired in connection with the formation of sub-divided fields. The purpose of this reconsideration is to show that it could have a quite different effect, one equivalent in its form to split townships. That it could split estates in a tenurial sense is beyond dispute. A fine review of its role in this general fashion is provided by R. R. Davies' discussion,[73] which demonstrates admirably the extreme tenurial fragmentation that could overwhelm estates within two or three generations. Amongst the examples he cited was that of Iowerth ap Cadwgan who lived c.1220. In time, he had four sons, seven grandsons and 17 great grandsons. It can be established that by 1313, the land he held was shared between 27 direct descendants.[74] At root of the problem was the fact that inheritance amongst freemen operated within the framework of the *gwely*. Whether the *gwely* should be seen first and foremost as a patrilineal descent group or lineage[75] or as a joint proprietary unit[76] cannot be discussed here, though the writer's sympathies are with the former. What matters is that land was held through membership of a defined kin group, with both the kin group and its property holding becoming known as a *gwely*. The exact composition of the *gwely* requires careful definition, owing to the shaded differences which have arisen between scholars, differences based partly on standpoint or stress and partly on more fundamental matters of interpretation. Some, like T. P. Ellis or Glanville Jones, have defined the *gwely* as comprised of all males related to each other within four degrees of kin.[77] Concerned more with conditions over the thirteenth and fourteenth centuries, Davies defined it as a broader patrilineal descent group. The *gwely*, he argued, "was the social organism of the descent group".[78] It was meaningful or functional, in that access or entitlement to land depended on membership of a *gwely*. However, the four-generation group of kindred (*parentala*) around whom the joint possession and inheritance of land was based, is depicted by Davies as a narrower group of kin within the framework of the *gwely*.[79] As he put it himself, "title to land was determined by membership of descent-groups; inheritance of land was restricted within a four-generation agnatic kindred".[80] These differences arise from the fact that the *gwely* was not a stable but an evolving institution, its nature altering from one period to another.

A critical point of change seems to have occurred around the twelfth century. It is outwardly symbolized by the simple fact that most *gwelyau* bear topynomyns derived from individuals who lived around the twelfth century. No new *gwelyau* were formed after this date. Instead, established *gwelyau* simply expanded, gathering more members or descendants under their heading with each new generation and it is for this reason that Davies could rightly distinguish between the broad descent group or *gwely* and the narrower kindred group of four-generations depth that formed the unit of inheritance; the one had pulled apart from the other. Why they lost their coincidence can be variously explained. Possibly least acceptable is Jones Pierce's view that *gwelyau* were only established *de novo* around 1100. Prior to this date, Welsh free society was based on nomadic pastoralism. With the conversion to a more settled economy c.1100, there took place a process of land allocation between freemen. It was through this act of land allocation, that *gwelyau* based on the original landtakers, their sons or their grandsons emerged.[81] In sharp contrast, scholars like Glanville Jones see the *gwely* as of much older foundation. Its fossilisation c.1100 stemmed from a change in circumstances. For Glanville Jones, this change in circumstances developed from the progressive splitting of estates until eventually, a point was reached c.1100 at which this process of splitting (meant here in a purely tenurial sense) reached down to the scale of individual settlements. To distinguish between estates, the idea of the *gwely* — a social concept — was used to impose a tangible identity on its proprietary stake in the soil, so much so, that the social and proprietary dimensions of the concept became fused.[82] Davies, meanwhile, thought that the concern of English lawyers to stabilise the definition of an institution with which they were unfamiliar, one that could re-create itself every generation, may have been the reason why no new *gwelyau* were formed after the twelfth century.[83]

These changes to the *gwely* did not necessarily alter the rules governing inheritance within it. As Davies has made clear, there were still *gwely* after the twelfth century in which property devolved to kindred groups linked together across four generations. However, not all *gwely* proved so resilient in this respect. In fact, other writers have preferred to emphasize how the *gwely* began to dissolve from within after about 1300, with individual members asserting their several interests over the joint rights of the kindred.[84] Yet even where tenure was reduced to severalty on former *gwely*-land, partible inheritance could still be practised: the difference being that now it was confined to partition between immediate kin or sons. Not until 1536 did primogeniture finally establish itself as the rule in north and west Wales. Viewed overall then, there were powerful, divisive forces at work during the medieval period on the landholding of free communities in Wales. It would be no exaggeration to say that fission was the *dominant* theme in its history up to the Union.

There is still the thorny question of what this fission produced on the ground. Did it create more complex sub-divided field systems or did it split holdings into discrete units? There seems to be an entrenched belief that it invariably led to the former, with discussions of sharelands or *randiroedd* depicting complex patterns of strips or quillets. The sub-division and intermixture of holdings was certainly one end-product. Early references to the "mangling" of property are an adequate testimony of this.[85] Unfortunately, it is not always clear what was being implied. Part of their meaning possibly includes the spread of property across a number of different townships: this was certainly a feature of a number of *gwelyau*.[86] Part also, includes the division of landholding within townships in the form of strips and parcels, or what we would normally classify as sub-divided fields. Early references to the intermixture of holdings are often sufficiently explicit to remove all doubt over whether we are dealing with a pattern of sub-divided fields or not. For instance, an early seventeenth century reference to a dispute involving Sir John Wynne and various crown tenants in Caernarvonshire, talked of their land being "scattered by acres, half acres and little quillets".[87] However, there are serious difficulties when we try to establish the extent or importance of sub-divided fields in Wales generally. With the exception of the southern coastal belt and the March, the writer does not accept that we are dealing with a countryside filled with highly-developed sub-divided field townships. Early references are simply insufficient proof of this. A fairer guide consists of eighteenth century estate plans which show the sub-division of property to be localised in respect of the townships involved and, even within such townships, to be restricted.[88] It would require a veritable revolution in landscape to underpin the pattern depicted in such estate plans with an earlier pattern of sub-divided fields based on strips. Far easier would be to assume that there were many townships in west and north-west Wales which were composed largely of consolidated holdings or holdings which, whilst fragmented or parcellated to a degree, did not approach that of a genuine sub-divided field pattern, even back in the medieval period. Detailed analyses of landholding history, such as that by C. A. Gresham for Eifionydd, reveal a landscape in which holdings tended often to stand apart as separate entities within the townships and were not immersed anonymously under the collective identity of the township's sub-divided fields.[89] If holdings shared a common background, then it was more likely to have been because they had descended via processes of fission from once larger, integral estates or holdings. In a discussion of Cardiganshire townships, Melville Richards made the point that the further back in time we trace their history, the more they appear associated with a single family or settlement. In effect, the subsequent elaboration of landholding in such townships was a map of the family's growth, as co-parcenage and family arrangements divided it one way and then another.[90]

The writer hesitates to attach any definite proportion or balance to this relationship between townships or areas in which landholding was largely consolidated or severally-arranged, as opposed to those in which it was disposed more in the form of sub-divided fields. Rather has the main purpose of the discussion been to instate the idea that the Welsh countryside prior to the Union, particularly in the west and north-west, had a varied appearance, an appearance that must have ranged from consolidated estates or holdings to one of intermixture, an intermixture based either on large blocks or parcels of land to strips (see Fig. 16). Recognition of this has a two-fold importance.

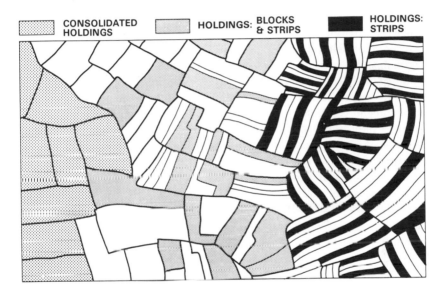

CONSOLIDATED HOLDINGS   HOLDINGS: BLOCKS & STRIPS   HOLDINGS: STRIPS

Fig. 16. Proposed continuum of Welsh field patterns, showing transition from sub-divided fields based on strips, through intermixed blocks and parcels, to several or discrete holdings.

First, it could conceivably reflect the subtle differences referred to earlier over how the different types of communities (free or bond) interpreted the constitution of their shares in either the township or the family patrimony (see pp. 36-7). Secondly, it prepares the way for making the vital point that partible inheritance could have a quite different effect to that of sub-divided fields. Where it operated on consolidated holdings, then it could have served to divide them in a manner directly analogous with the splitting of townships in England and Scotland.

There are, in fact, many case-studies we can cite showing how holdings became split into two or more parts, all of which were discrete units in the landscape. In the late fifteenth century, for instance, Madog ap Ieuan died and his holding in the parish of Pentryche (Caernarvonshire) was divided between his five sons whose shares formed separate *tyddyn* that became known as Tythyn Ieuen ap Madoc, Tythyn Howel ap Madoc, Tythyn David ap Madoc, Tythyn Robert ap Madoc and Tythyn Eignion ap Madoc. We also know that Tythyn Robert ap Madoc received the original farmstead for it was known alternatively as Tythyn yr Hendre.[91] Graham, in his study of Eifionydd, not only mapped the outcome of the partition[92], but cited a testimony by Madog ap Ieuan's grandson, William ap Robert ap Madog, which described how the holding had been split into five parts, for "the using & custom of the country was that all sonnes should at that tyme share and enioy all theire fathers lands as coheirs of the nature of gavell kynd, and further that division & partition was made between them by theire assent".[93] As Graham himself went on to state, the lands of Madog at this point "may be imagined as a series of scattered dwellinghouses with some fields cleared around each".[94] In actual fact, the process of splitting did not end there, for Tythyn Robert ap Madoc was later split yet again between coheirs.[95]

Given its micro-scaled perspective on landholding, Graham's work on Eifionydd naturally documents other examples. Thus, when the hamlet of Llecheiddor in the township of the same name was divided in the early sixteenth century between the three sons of Howel ap Madog ap Ieueu Fychan, it produced three separate estates, or those of Plas Llecheiddor, Llecheiddor Ganol and Llecheiddor Uchaf.[96] His discussion makes for an instructive comparison with the work of Jones Pierce on north-west Wales. Jones Pierce similarly drew attention to many examples of partition between co-heirs or *cyfran*.[97] But in contrast to Graham he tends to stress the complexity rather than the tidiness of the pattern produced, with holdings fragmented or broken down into scattered parcels and quillets. The description of individual shares of *gwely*-land as the *tir* of X or Y was seen by him as symptomatic of this fragmented condition. Yet when rentals begin to define such holdings in terms of their site or to give them a specific toponym over the fifteenth and sixteenth centuries, they manifest ample signs of splitting alongside the sub-division and intermixture of holdings in the form of strips or quillets.[98] Indeed, central to Jones Pierce's whole interpretation of landholding in the region is the idea of large estates (which he sees as initially being tribal holdings) becoming partitioned or split into townships, hamlets and holdings over the twelfth and thirteenth centuries.[99] That splitting played a part in this process is a *sine qua non* given the long catalogue of place names bearing the suffixes *Issa*, *Canol* and *Ucha* in the pattern produced. Further south, in Cardiganshire, fourteenth-century references to the *rhandiroedd* of Ruel, Wileirog and Kellan in Geneur y'Glyn parish or

Rhandir in Llangwryfon parish can be matched by later references to them in which each was split into *Issa* and *Ucha* portions.[100] In the case of Randir, the old focus of the estate is evidenced by the fact that there is a Randir Hen in addition to an Issa and Ucha. Also worth mentioning is the way the former granges of Strata Florida abbey in Cardiganshire became split into myriad smallholdings by the sixteenth and seventeenth centuries. The process probably began back in the fourteenth century, when the abbey began to farm out their property to tenants, but has to be seen as an ongoing process if the full extent of fission is to be grasped; this last point is well-made by those tenements which appear as tenements within tenements. For instance, a 1634 indenture refers to the tenement called Pen-y-lanwen, part of the ancient tenement of Llwyn-y-boydy-ucha, itself in the former grange of Mevenith.[101] Further south still, in Pembrokeshire, the *Black Book of St David's* 1326 anticipates the splitting of Kayrnedred and Llanygige, both in the Welsh area of Dewisland, and both later comprised of *Isaf* and *Uchaf* portions.[102] In the Lordship of Kemes, the holdings of Hendre (St Dogmaels parish) and Rosavarken (Nevern parish), both compact units in the fourteenth century, were split into Hendrey Issa and Hendrey Ucha by 1596.[103]

Although it was probably far more prevalent in areas where Welsh tenures survived strongly after the Norman and Edwardian conquests, splitting was not confined to these areas. Examples can be found in areas that were Anglicised, but they tend to be associated with other kinds of cause once Welsh tenures had been replaced. Usually, it was a simple case of part of a township being granted out or sub-infeudated to a different landholder. Two examples will suffice: in Pembrokeshire, the Barony of St Clear's became divided into thirds by the twelfth century, each of which was, for a time, held by a different landholder; these thirds became known as Trane Clinton, Trane March and Trane Morgan, the prefix *Trane* meaning a third.[104] In north-east Wales, the township of Stansty in the Lordship of Yale appears as a consolidated township in an extent of 1313 but arranged tenurially into two parts;[105] one half, however, was reported to have been given to Valle Crucis Abbey, a half which later appears as Stansty Issa, in contrast to Stansty Uchaf which remained in the hands of various Welsh tenants.[106]

The causes of splitting: a synthesis

As the previous section on Wales alone will have made abundantly clear, splitting cannot be reduced to any single, monolithic cause. A number of factors can be invoked. The purpose of this section is to draw together these various causes and to set them in their historical context. Broadly speaking, they can be grouped under two headings. First, there are those which involved the proprietary break-up of townships as a precondition, the physical separation of estates being the whole point and purpose of splitting. Secondly, and of crucial importance to the problem of field systems, there are those examples in which no fragmentation of proprietary rights were involved. Instead, splitting proceeded from a desire to make township layout smaller and more efficient.

The proprietary break-up of townships over the medieval period arose from a variety of causes: partible inheritance, family settlements, gifts, sales, mortgages, land grants, sub-infeudation and the like. All these were capable of creating a line of cleavage or weakness running through a township and, in the words of T. Aston, "all affected the nature of estates and villages . . . everywhere, if the process continued long enough; they led to the subdivision of the villages themselves".[107] The more precise timing of the process, though is critical. As Aston has explained, the process initially split estates and only during its later stages did it reach down to the level of individual settlements, as estates became divided into smaller and smaller blocks.[108] He implies that this second stage was reached during the century or so prior to 1066. In Wales, a roughly similar chronology can be pieced together through the work of scholars like Wendy Davies and Glanville Jones. In her work on the Liber Landavensis, the former argued that up to the eighth century, land grants were based on large estates or *unciae*. Thereafter, they tended to be based more on townships or *uillae*, having been reduced to this level by fragmentation or fission.[109] Presumably, the next stage, or the splitting of townships into two or more proprietary units, could have begun over the ninth or tenth centuries. For comparison, in north Wales, it is worth recalling Glanville Jones' suggestion that it was only towards the end of the eleventh century or c.1100 that estates or *gwelyau* began to cut across individual settlements on a widespread scale.[110] In other words, whilst the forces that led to the splitting of estates into smaller units operated deep in the medieval period, it may not have been until the eve of the Norman Conquest that they began to split individual townships or settlements on any extensive scale.

It must be emphasised that the proprietary break-up of a township did not lead automatically to its physical splitting into separate sub-townships on the ground. There was a choice: landholders could divide their shares in the form of sub-divided fields or they could split them into discrete units or sub-townships. These two options must be seen alongside each other as the options which shaped the history of landholding in Britain during the middle ages, A.D. 950-1350 and even beyond in the case of northern and western areas. Less common by far was a third option, or the farming of the township as a single unit with the produce only, not the land, being divided. Aston introduced this as one possibility in relation to Anglo-Saxon estates which became partitioned between co-heirs[111], but as a solution to the divisive effects of family settlements it was more likely to be found in Celtic areas.[112]

An unavoidable question is why landholders faced with a choice, opted to have their share of a township as a discrete or self-contained unit rather than intermixed with other shares. One possibility is that it served the administration of the estate better to have it demarcated as a separate unit, replete with its own settlement site; this was especially true where the split shares of a township carried a body of under-tenants and where the process of splitting led to the formation of new manors structured around the portions or sub-townships created by the split. Indeed, the writer would maintain that the creation of new manors by sub-infeudation prior to the statute of *Quia Emptores* in 1290 — which stopped sub-infeudation — was widely associated with the physical splitting of townships and settlements.[113] Splitting enabled the geographical jurisdiction of the manor to be cleanly defined on the ground, and made it far easier to administer manorial custom and work service. Of course, after the statute of *Quia Emptores*, the new settlements created by splitting could only form extra members within a fixed manorial framework. One further point to be kept in mind is that in all these cases of divided landownership, splitting dis-aggregated landholding at one level and one level only. It was still possible for under-tenants — at their level — to adopt a sub-divided field system as a solution to their shareholding problems. What the lord of the manor or barony did with his share or estate in a township, was quite different from what the customary tenants who held of him might do once the township had been split.

Quite different in character are those townships that were entirely subsumed under a single estate or landholder and which, without any division of proprietary rights, were still split. Many of the Northumberland examples fall into this category, some being held entirely by the Percy estate. So too do many Scottish examples, such as the group of townships on the Cupar abbey estate that were split during the fifteenth century.[114] In these instances, the nature of splitting compels us to seek a different explanation and fortunately, some sources provide this explanation. During the splitting of certain Northumberland townships, it was asserted that they had become too large and that smaller-size townships would be more convenient and more efficient. The case for their splitting is laid out in a letter to the earl of Northumberland that was written in 1656/7 when the splitting of Prudhoe was being discussed. In it, it was claimed that "everie towne hath a peculiar and proper disease, yett in generall the largeness and great distance of their cornefeilds and commons from the townes are the most effectual cawses of their weakness, th'one being thereby too chardgeable and costly to manure, and the utmost parte of th'other eaten up and depastured on by neighbours adjoyning".[115] Similar thoughts were expressed during the splitting of Long Haughton in 1567, the surveyor's report declaring that the "division was made in order that the tenants might enjoy greater convenience for the cultivation of their lands. Before the partition, in consequence of Long Haughton being 'a very long towne', the tenants had been obliged to travel long distances to reach their strips, scattered in outlying portions of the township, but, when the partition was made, the land was rendered more accessible to the tenants dwelling in the north and south ends of the village respectively".[116] But it was not entirely a case of the tenant's gain; lords gained also. At Chatton, its splitting in 1566 was prefaced by an agreement to "devyde the Towne of Chatton into 4 severall townes, by the advyce of such as have good knowledge therein and therby encrease the number of tenants making them wellthye and also encrease his 1p's service".[117]

Support for this idea that landholders were seeking smaller, more manageable units comes from Scotland. In his passing reference to the splitting of townships in north-east Scotland, Gordon of Straloch drew out the inconvenience of large, sub-divided field settlements. Having "so many neighbours" meant less provision for agriculture and more conflict between landholders.[118] A few documented examples of splitting also suggest that too many tenants were a source of inconvenience and conflict and that splitting reduced such problems. These were certainly the problems which promoted the splitting of Culcairny in Kinross-shire, 1611[119], Easter Moniack, 1609[120] and Baldornoch in Perthshire, 1629[121]. Surprisingly, despite their detail, there is little hint of why townships were split on the Cupar abbey estate during the fifteenth century, but since the evidence is contained in tacks or leases explaining to tenants how their mini-townships were to be arranged, it would seem that scale and the desire for more manageable units were at the heart of the matter.[122]

As a process of township re-organization, splitting could not fail to have a far-reaching impact on field layout. However, the added knowledge that some instances of splitting arose from a desire to rationalize field and holding layouts into more efficient forms makes the two sides of the problem — township splitting and field patterns — so inextricably linked that it is difficult to work out which was cause and which was effect. With this point made, the focus of discussion can now be shifted from splitting as an event in the history of township layout to a consideration of its particular association with field patterns.

References

[1] F. W. Maitland, "The Surnames of English Villages", pp. 84-95 in H. A. L. Fisher (ed.), *The Collected Papers of Frederick William Maitland*, Cambridge (1911), pp. 84-95.
[2] *Ibid.*, p. 86.
[3] *Ibid.*, p. 89.
[4] *Ibid.*, p. 91.

[5] *Ibid.*, p. 92.

[6] *Ibid.*, p. 93.

[7] M. Gelling, *Signposts to the Past*, London, 1978, pp. 206-8.

[8] Postan, "Medieval Agrarian Society in Its Prime: England", p. 563. For a researched example of a parent-daughter settlement relationship, see M. W. Beresford and K. St. Joseph, *Medieval England*, Cambridge (1958), pp. 83-91. The present writer, however, prefers to see the example which they discuss — that of Great, Little and Steeple Gidding — as a split settlement rather than a new projection into the waste from an old settlement.

[9] D. Bonney, "Early Boundaries and Estates in Southern England", pp. 72-82 in Sawyer (ed.), *op. cit.*, pp. 78-80.

[10] C. Taylor, *Dorset*, London (1970), pp. 49-72.

[11] R. A. Dodgshon, "The Origin of the Two- and Three-Field System in England: A New Perspective", *Geographia Polonica*, 38 (1978), p. 57.

[12] H. C. Darby and R. Welldon Finn (eds.), *The Domesday Geography of South-West England*, Cambridge (1967), p. 72. See also, pp. 8, 141-2 and 228-9 for identical statements by other contributors.

[13] Taylor, *Dorset*, p. 85.

[14] *Ibid.*, pp. 51-4.

[15] See, for example, Lennard, *op. cit.*, p. 9. Lennard talks of whole parishes being ignored because they could be subsumed under a single estate.

[16] Sir Frederick Pollock and F. W. Maitland, *The History of English Law*, I, Cambridge (2nd ed. 1958), p. 607.

[17] See, for example, Bracton, *De Legibus et Consuetudinibus*, III, pp. 395-7; J. P. Collas and T. F. T. Plucknett (eds.), *Year Books of Edward II, vol. XXIII, 12 Edward II, A.D. 1318*, Seldon Society, London (1950), pp. 1-2; W. C. Bolland (ed.), *Year Books of Edward II, vol. XI, 5 Edward II A.D. 1311-1312*, Selden Society, London (1915), pp. 125-9.

[18] P. H. Reaney, *The Place-Names of Essex*, English Place Name Society vol. XII, Cambridge (1935), pp. 94-5, 158, 203, 323-4, 328, 332 and 334.

[19] J. Wilson (ed.), *The Register of the Priory of St Bees*, Surtees Society, CXXVI, Durham (1915), pp. 413-5.

[20] *Ibid.*, pp. 542, 550-1 and 560-1.

[21] C. T. Clay (ed.), *Early Yorkshire Charters, vol. VII, The Honour of Skipton*, Yorkshire Archaeological Record Ser., Extra Ser., V (1947), p. 26.

[22] I. Kershaw (ed.), *Bolton Priory*, Oxford (1973), frontispiece map and p. 64.

[23] A. Crossley (ed.), *A History of the County of Oxford*, vol. X, London, (1972), p. 177.

[24] M. D. Lobel (ed.), *A History of the County of Oxford*, vol. VI, London (1959), pp. 94-5.

[25] M. Gelling, *The Place Names of Berkshire*, part 2, English Place Name Society, vol. L, Cambridge (1974), pp. 323-4.

[26] Reaney, *op. cit.*, pp. 231-2.

[27] R. W. Dunning (ed.), *A History of the County of Somerset*, vol. III, Oxford (1974), pp. 81, 84, 95 and 97.

[28] J. Amphlett (ed.), *A Survey of Worcestershire by Thomas Habington*, Worcestershire Historical Soc., vol. I (1895), p. 323.

[29] *Ibid.*, p. 190.

[30] *Curia Regis Rolls of the Reign of Henry III, vol. XIII, II to 14 Henry III (1227-1230)*, London (1959), pp. 271-3. See also, the reported partitions of the Honour of Bamber (Sussex) and the manor of Tetbury (Herefordshire) on p. 30 and the partition of the

manor of *Penigheston* (Yorkshire) into four parts on p. 85.

[31] W. P. Baildon (ed.), *Select Civil Pleas, vol. I, 1200-1203*, vol. 3, Selden Society, London (1890), p. 27.

[32] Craster (ed.), *History of Northumberland*, vol. IX, p. 325.

[33] Hope Dodds (ed.), *History of Northumberland*, XII, p. 184.

[34] Hope Dodds (ed.), *History of Northumberland*, XIV, p. 211.

[35] *Ibid.*, p. 212.

[36] Bateson (ed.), *History of Northumberland*, II, pp. 128-9.

[37] Craster (ed.), *History of Northumberland*, IX, p. 283.

[38] Bateson (ed.), *History of Northumberland*, II, pp. 369-70.

[39] *Ibid.*, p. 416.

[40] *Ibid.*, p. 458.

[41] J. C. Hodgson (ed.), *A History of Northumberland*, vol. V, Newcastle (1899), p. 202.

[42] Craster (ed.), *History of Northumberland*, IX, pp. 124-5.

[43] Hope Dodds (ed.), *History of Northumberland*, XIV, p. 354.

[44] Hodgson (ed.), *History of Northumberland*, V, pp. 372-3.

[45] J. M. Lee and R. A. McKinley (eds.), *A History of the County of Leicester*, vol. V, London (1964), p. 110.

[46] Lobel (ed.), *History of Oxfordshire*, V, p. 35.

[47] J. C. Hodgson (ed.), *A History of Northumberland*, vol. VII, Newcastle (1904), p. 37.

[48] Wilson (ed.), *Register of St Bees*, p. 355.

[49] Amphlett (ed.), *Survey of Worcestershire by Thomas Habington*, pp. 138-40; F. Kitchen, *Nettleworth Parva*, London (1968), p. 9.

[50] A general discussion of its chronology can be found in R. A. Dodgshon, "Changes in Scottish Township Organization During the Medieval and Early Modern Periods", *Geografiska Annaler*, 58B (1977), pp. 53-61.

[51] G. Burnett (ed.), *The Exchequer Rolls of Scotland, vol. XI, A.D. 1497-1501*, Edinburgh (1888), pp. 398-400.

[52] See, for example, the Buccleuch estate rentals in SRO, GD224/281/1.

[53] G. G. Smith, *The Book of Islay*, Edinburgh (1895), appendix III.

[54] SRO, GD16/14/2.

[55] SRO, GD16/14/4.

[56] J. B. Paul (ed.), *The Register of the Great Seal of Scotland 1424-1513*, Edinburgh (1882), p. 292.

[57] SRO, GD16/13/22.

[58] SRO, GD45/16/972, 1008 and 1019.

[59] F. Cruickshank, *Navar and Lethnot*, Brechin (1899), pp. 124 and 288-91. See also the estate plans for these townships compiled in 1766, SRO, RHP 1667/3 and 6.

[60] SRO, GD44/51/747; *The Miscellany of the Spalding Club*, 4, pp. 261-319; V. Gaffney (ed.), *The Lordship of Strathavon*, Third Spalding Club, Aberdeen (1960), pp. 192-5.

[61] SRO, RHP 2488 contains a number of fine estate plans for the area, which record the sum extent of splitting prior to Improvement.

[62] *Geographical Collections Relating to Scotland by W. Macfarlane*, II, Scottish History Society, LII (1907), p. 272.

[63] A list, and extended discussion, of them can be seen in Dodgshon, "Changes in Scottish Township Organization", pp. 59-61 and 65.

[64] SRO, GD150/187 (a) and (b) and 189.

[65] SRO, GD16/3/105.

[66] SRO, GD124/1/208.

[67] SRO, GD26/3/40 and 41.

[68] SRO, GD97/1/2.

[69] See Dodgshon, "Scandinavian 'Solskifte' and the Sunwise Division of Land in Eastern Scotland", pp. 11-12.

[70] SRO, GD26/3/950.

[71] See the splendid discussion in A. and B. Rees, *Celtic Heritage*, London (1960), pp. 176-185.

[72] Paul (ed.), *Register of the Great Seal of Scotland 1424-1513*, p. 778.

[73] R. R. Davies, *Lordship and Society in Medieval Wales*, pp. 358-77.

[74] *Ibid.*, pp. 367-8.

[75] *Ibid.*, p. 360.

[76] Jones Pierce, *Medieval Welsh Society*, p. 334.

[77] T. P. Ellis, *Welsh Tribal Law and Custom in the Middle Ages*, Oxford (1926), vol. 1, p. 224; Jones, "Post-Roman Wales", especially pp. 320-2.

[78] Davies, *Lordship and Society in Medieval Wales*, p. 366.

[79] *Ibid.*, p. 363.

[80] *Ibid.*, p. 366.

[81] See, for example, his detailed discussion of Anglesey in Jones Pierce, *Medieval Welsh Society*, pp. 251-87 or his more general discussion in *ibid.*, pp. 339-51.

[82] Jones, "Post-Roman Wales", p. 330.

[83] Davies, *Lordship and Society in Medieval Wales*, p. 364.

[84] Rees, *South Wales and the March*, p. 25; Jones Pierce, *Medieval Welsh Society*, p. 342.

[85] The reference to property being "mangled with division and subdivision of gavelkinde" was made by Sir John Wynn and is cited in C. A. Gresham, *Eifionydd. A Study in Landownership from the Medieval Period to the Present Day*, Cardiff (1973), p. 17.

[86] See, for example, those documented by Glanville Jones in "Field Systems of North Wales", Baker and Butlin (eds.), *op. cit.*, p. 449 and by Rhys Davies in *Lordship and Society in Medieval Wales*, pp. 371-2.

[87] Jeffreys Jones, *Exchequer Proceedings Concerning Wales in Tempore James I*, p. 58.

[88] National Library of Wales, Estate Plans, volumes 14 and 36 are illustrative of this.

[89] Graham, *Eifionydd*, pp. 1-380. See also, the detailed discussion in C. Thomas, "The Township of Nannau, 1100-1600, A. D.", *Jnl. of the Meirioneth Historical and Record Society* (1966), especially pp. 97-8 or the more general discussion in C. Thomas, "Peasant Agriculture in Medieval Gwynedd", *Folk Life*, 13 (1975), pp. 29-30 which likewise contrast dispersed or consolidated holdings with sub-divided field systems back in the medieval period.

[90] M. Richards, "Local Government in Cardiganshire: Medieval and Modern", *Ceredigion*, IV (1962), pp. 275-7.

[91] E. G. Jones (ed.), *Exchequer Proceedings (Equity) Concerning Wales Henry VIII— Elizabeth*, Cardiff (1939), p. 76.

[92] Graham, *Eifionydd*, p. 356.

[93] *Ibid.*, p. 355.

[94] *Ibid.*, p. 355.

[95] E. G. Jones, (ed.), *Exchequer Proceedings (Equity) Concerning Wales Henry VIII— Elizabeth*, p. 76.

[96] *Ibid.*, p. 205.

[97] See, for instance, Jones Pierce, *Medieval Welsh Society*, pp. 220-3 and 259-60.

[98] Rental transcripts are given in Jones Pierce, *Medieval Welsh Society*, pp. 92-101; Graham, *Eifionydd*, appendix II and III.

[99] Jones Pierce, *Medieval Welsh Society*, p. 222 contains a fair statement of his viewpoint in relation to a specific locality.

[100] Early references to Ruel, Wileirog and Kellan can be found in NLW, E. A. Lewis xerox facsimiles, no. 84, SC311/770/15 and to Randir in S. R. Meyrick, *The History and Antiquities of the County of Cardigan*, London (1808), p. 332. Later references can be found in NLW, Tithe Maps, Parish of Lanfihangel Geneu'r Glyn 1847 and Parish of Llangrwyddon 1844.

[101] Green (ed.), *Calendar of Deeds and Documents, vol. II*, The Crosswood Deeds, p. 58, 55, 67 and 69. The early grange structure of the abbey is detailed by S. W. Williams, *The Cistercian Abbey of Strata Florida*, London (1889), p. 1 *et. sec.*; T. Jones Pierce, "Strata Florida Abbey", *Ceredigion*, I (1950), p. 29.

[102] J. W. Willis-Bund (ed.), *The Black Book of St. David's*, Honourable Society of Cymmrodorion Record Series, No. 5, London (1902), pp. 53 and 105.

[103] Owen (ed.), *The Description of Pembrokeshire*, vol. 2, p. 405; F. Green (ed.), *West Wales Historical Records*, vol. II (1911-12, published 1913), Note on "Evan Lloyd of Hendre, Pembs.", p. 136 and into Rosavarken Issa and Uchaf by 1614 Owen (ed.), *The Description of Pembrokeshire*, vol. 2, pp. 469 and 526.

[104] Owen (ed.), *The Description of Pembrokeshire*, vol. 2, p. 387.

[105] T. P. Ellis (ed.), *The First Extent of Bromfield and Yale A.D. 1315*, Honourable Society of Cymmrodorion Record Series, no. XI, London (1924), p. 109.

[106] *Ibid.*, p. 109; A. P. Palmer and E. Owen, *A History of Ancient Tenures of Land in North Wales and the Marches*, Wrexham (1910), p. 202.

[107] T. Aston, "The Origins of the Manor in Britain", pp. 11-35 in W. E. Minchinton (ed.), *Essays in Agrarian History*, vol. I, Newton Abbot (1968), p. 29.

[108] *Ibid.*, p. 29-30.

[109] Davies, "Land and Power in Early Medieval Wales", pp. 11-12; Davies, *An Early Welsh Microcosm*, pp. 56-9.

[110] Jones, "Post-Roman Wales", p. 330.

[111] Aston, "The Origins of the Manor in Britain", p. 30.

[112] I have discussed this matter, and tried to assess its importance, in Dodgshon, "Runrig and the Communal Origins of Property in Land", pp. 192-3.

[113] The example of East and West Langton in Leicestershire is a typical illustration of this. See Lee and McKinley (ed.), *History of the County of Leicester*, vol. V, p. 196.

[114] A brief discussion of these can be found in Dodgshon, "Scandinavian 'Solskifte' and the Sunwise Division of Land in Eastern Scotland", p. 9; Dodgshon, "Changes in Scottish Township Organization During the Medieval and Early Modern Periods", p. 61.

[115] Hope Dodds (ed.), *History of Northumberland*, vol. XII, p. 110.

[116] Bateson (ed.), *History of Northumberland*, vol. II, p. 367.

[117] Hope Dodds (ed.), *History of Northumberland*, vol. XIV, p. 211.

[118] *Geographical Collections Relating to Scotland*, vol. II, pp. 272 and 463-4.

[119] SRO, GD224/78.

[120] SRO, Inventory of the Title Deeds . . . Estate of Easter Moniack, compiled by A. Mackenzie, 1796, xerox copy.

[121] SRO, GD16/5/126.

[122] The tacks are reprinted in C. Rogers (ed.), *Register of Coupar Abbey: Rental Book of the Cistercian Abbey of Cupar Angus*, London, (1880), vol. I, pp. 144, 188 and 200-1.

Chapter 6

Township splitting and the growth of field systems

It goes without saying that the splitting of townships meant a radical re-structuring of their layout. Although some confined this re-structuring to their settlements or farmsteads, the norm was for their fields as well as their farmsteads to be subjected to re-organization. It is this opportunity for the comprehensive ro planning of field layout that forms the prime interest of splitting for the history of field systems. In all probability, where it involved the re-creation of sub-divided fields, albeit on a smaller scale, it conferred a definite character on them. Whether earlier layouts had been tidy or untidy, regular or irregular, cohesive or anarchic, splitting must have created order. There was no other way of approaching the problem, for one could not reasonably re-create disorder or irregularity when dealing with a matrix of tenurial right and interest. The following discussion seeks to explore how this constrained approach affected the development of field systems, both in respect of sub-divided fields and communally-regulated cropping schemes.

Township splitting and sub-divided fields

As a point of reorganization, the splitting of townships offers conditions under which irregular sub-divided fields could have been cast into regular forms. Landholders or tenants probably abstracted a set of guidelines from the layout of their holdings prior to splitting which were then used to shape the re-constitution of their holdings after splitting. Seen in this way, it was obviously an important factor in the creation of regular layouts, but only in regard to areas like the Midlands where sub-divided fields tended to be stable in the long term. For areas like Scotland, where shareholding tenure tended to re-work sub-divided field layouts on a recurrent basis, splitting could have had no special significance in this respect.

Perhaps the strongest proof that splitting involved schemes for the systematic laying out of property, is contained in place-names. As mentioned earlier (see pp. 21-3), the use of prefixes like East and West — a use which is widespread throughout Britain and Ireland — can be linked to the adoption of systematic procedures for dividing land. The utility of these procedures is that they can be applied whether the shares of a township were to be cast into sub-divided fields or into split townships. The only difference was that in the case of the former, the designation of shares as East or West (Sunny or Shadow, Upper or Nether) had a relative meaning, whereas in the case of the latter, it had an absolute meaning (see Fig. 17). The intrinsically functional nature of such prefixes is perhaps best demonstrated by the way some landholders abandoned their use in favour of more personalised prefixes soon after the process of splitting was completed.[1]

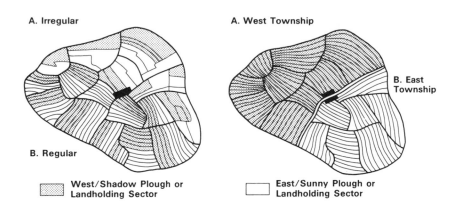

A. Irregular

A. West Township

B. East Township

B. Regular

▦ West/Shadow Plough or Landholding Sector

☐ East/Sunny Plough or Landholding Sector

Fig. 17. Diagram showing differences between east (sunny) or west (shadow) ploughs or halves which are either (a) subdivided and intermixed in regular or irregular form or (b) divided into discrete township units.

Given this overlap of method between the laying out of sub-divided fields and split townships, it follows that where the former were re-created in the context of the latter, then it is reasonable to expect the same systematic procedures to have been used at both levels; they need only differ in the choice being exercised and not in the method being used. Kibworth Harcourt in Leicestershire serves as an illustration of this point. As noted in Chapter 2, it was arranged into two sectors, one being the sunny and the other, the shadow sector. Tenants were assigned to one or the other.[2] The purpose of the arrangement was to facilitate the systematic laying out of customary holdings, with each sector denoting a relative location within each field. Kibworth Harcourt itself, though, was part of a split township pair, the other being Kibworth Beauchamp. Like similar pairs in the surrounding countryside, its twin portions probably began as magna/parva or east/west units. In other words, the same division procedures appear used between townships as within, once the broad equivalence between these various share designations is accepted.

Such reasoning reinforces the assumption that regular sub-divided fields were a by-product of township splitting, but it does not establish beyond doubt that this is when such fields made their pioneer appearance. If there is an answer to this question, then it might best be found in considering further how the division procedures employed — for both township splitting and regular sub-divided fields — originated. The whole notion of a classificatory scheme based on East/West, Nether/Upper, Fore/Back or Sunny/Shadow reflects a deep-rooted cosmographic scheme of ordering.[3] At first, such a scheme may have been used to order kin groups either between the different segments or quarters of a settlement or between different parts of an estate or tribal holding, and probably dealt in absolute rather than relative space. Used in this way, terms like East/West or Nether/Upper had an affective or symbolic value, locating kin groups to particular points in a cosmographic space. As landholding became stripped of its kin basis over the medieval period, such a system of ordering naturally lost its affective value, but not its utility as a scheme of spatial differentiation in the apportionment of land. Two levels of operation can be envisaged: that of large estates or units of lordship and that of smaller, individual holdings of bond or freemen. As regards the former, it is now an accepted feature of their history that many underwent fission during the medieval period. Indeed, the oldest use of place-name prefixes like East/West, Upper/Nether or *magna/parva* is in connection with split estates or territorial units as opposed to individual settlements.[4] As regards the latter, the assumption advanced in Chapter 2 (see pp. 41-3) was that individual holdings may have become progressively frag-mented over the medieval period. It is at this restricted level that the use of division procedures based on east/west shares may have first made the critical shift from dealing in absolute space to dealing in relative space, as co-heirs tried to preserve their proper share of the different types of land contained by their patrimony. Even so, such divisions dealt with holdings within townships not with entire townships, and it was only when the partition of estates reached down to the level of individual townships that a situation was reached in which entire townships might be subjected to *en bloc* systematic division procedures: thus, whilst the procedures were old-established, it may only have been at the point when township splitting first began that they were used to create regular sub-divided fields. Needless to add, their use at this point would have been to differentiate between relative not absolute space, or to fix the location of each person's strips within each sequence of allocation. All this may seem an exercise in speculative reasoning, but it is the direction in which the origin of regular sub-divided fields is most likely to be resolved. There is, however, one major proviso: as a direct source of regular sub-divided fields, it can only account for those conceived during the process of splitting. For other townships, though, the better-organized layouts of split townships may have served as an example, demonstrating how regular sub-divided fields reaped benefits in terms of efficiency and permitted scope for the systematic ordering of both livestock and crop husbandry.

Township splitting and the origin of two/three field cropping

Another substantial spin-off from township splitting may have been the development of two- or three-field cropping systems. As implied in the previous section, the radical changes of layout induced by splitting presented an opportunity to rethink — or perhaps to think for the first time — about what was a desirable or suitable layout of holdings or fields from the point of view of husbandry. Lords or communities could hardly have failed not to see it as an opportunity to devise layouts that assisted rather than hindered the primary tasks of cropping and grazing. What will be suggested in the following discussion is that the early examples of splitting, through their search for more efficient layouts, were a nursery for the emergence of two- or three-field cropping systems. From these pioneer layouts, they spread to other townships once their benefits of having a communally-regulated system had been demonstrated.

Undoubtedly the main argument in favour of a direct link between township splitting and the development of two- or three-field systems is the remarkable similarity between them as regards structure, nomenclature, purpose and chronology. Taking each of these aspects in turn, their similarity of structure requires very little in the way of corroboration since it is self-evident from much that has been said about them. Like the two- or three-field system, township splitting was most commonly based on the partition of townships into two or three separate units. That a few townships were split into four or more units is not an obstacle, for there were also field systems, such as those of Oxfordshire, that were arranged into four or more cropping sectors, sectors that carried the name of quarters or seasons. Looking at early estate plans, it is often well-nigh impossible to distinguish between them in morphological terms, since both have the obvious appearance of a once whole

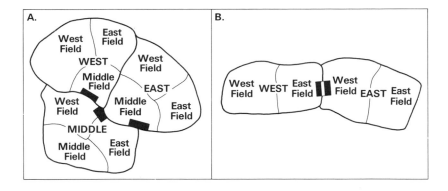

Fig. 18. Diagrams showing the parallelism that could exist between the two- or three-field system and split townships.

unit that had become split (see Fig. 18). From these appearances alone, we might conclude that split townships and the two- or three-field system were closely-related *species* of the same *genus*.

These bonds can be drawn still closer by considering their respective nomenclatures; both made extensive use of the prefixes East/West, Nether/Upper and the like.[5] Moreover, in both cases, the use of these prefixes appears flexible, with fields or townships called East or West in one source appearing as Great or Little in another. Where communities were dissatisfied with such standardised forms, they dispensed with them in favour of more personalised names at both the township and field level. The conclusion must be that two- or three-field systems were shaped by the same notions of differentiation as split townships. This parallelism can be extended still further by recalling the situation at Kibworth Harcourt, where the township was organized internally into two tenurially differentiated but physically intertwined sectors, as well as a two-field system.

To reiterate the conclusions reached earlier, these structural affinities between the different levels of township organization could well be due to the use of standard notions and procedures of spatial differentiation that had long been rooted in the folk mind. But in the case of the two- or three-field system, such a proposal needs examining carefully. As cropping schemes, the logical assumption would be to see their structure as a response to the needs of husbandry, in which case, their use of prefixes like East/West or Nether/Upper as field names would be no more than a matter of convenience. However, there are alternative possibilities that cannot be discounted. One is that two- or three-field systems wrapt themselves around older, more archaic sectors of the township that had been devised for other purposes, such as joint ploughing. A more persuasive alternative is to focus on the fact that prefixes like East/West or Nether/Upper are the language of a division. If so, then what did the two- or three-field system represent a division of? Given that with such cropping systems, holdings needed to be evenly distributed between the two/three fields if a landholder was not to have an unacceptable proportion of his land lying unproductive during the fallow year, the obvious division to introduce here is the one that accomplished this equitable spread of holdings. Where allied to a solskifte-type division of holdings, then each field (West/East or Nether/Upper) would have been further sub-divided into intermixed east/west, nether/upper or sunny/shadow ploughs or landholding sectors (see Fig. 18); the one complemented the other. Linking them together was procedure, a procedure in which the laying out of holdings began at sunrise in the East field and worked itself sunwise around to the West field by evening. It was a scheme that knitted relative space (the location of a person's strip in each sequence of allocation) and absolute space (the overall spread of holdings across the entire face of the township's fields) into a coherent framework. In fact, it is conceivable that two- or three-field cropping systems were adapted to this framework, not the other way round. Medieval rural communities may have been more inhibited by conventions than we realise. What makes this whole idea plausible is the tradition of argument that two- or three-field systems were not a novel way of cropping land or an innovative rotation so much as an organizational change which lifted a familiar cropping scheme from the level of the holding to the level of the township.

An additional problem concerning the structure of the two- or three-field systems is their distinct geographies. The former is mainly to be found in the central Midland and southern English counties, whilst the latter occurred in a broad belt on either side. Lumping these areas together for a moment, their association with the two- or three-field system was, as explained earlier, probably bound up with the fact that these were the areas in which assessed land took up the bulk of land available to townships. The nomenclature of their field systems, therefore, was designed to distinguish between the different sectors of a single cropping scheme, not between wholly separate cropping schemes as with infield-outfield. The question being posed now is why, within this broad area of distribution, some communities opted for a two-field and others for a three-field system? Their generally exclusive geographies suggest that there were very specific rather than random factors influencing their choice. The traditional view is that since the three-field version was more intensive and technically advanced relative to the two-field version, the underlying explanation for their respective geographies could easily be framed in terms of population pressure; such an approach forms what might be called a neo-Boserupian view.[6] Seen in relation to their detailed geographies, though, such a view appears unsatisfactory; it would presuppose that an area like the Welsh Marches, a three-field area, was more populated and more advanced farming-wise that counties like Leicestershire, where the two-field system predominated.[7] We need also to bear in mind the important qualification that little evidence actually exists for a shift from the two-field to the three-field system. It was the assumption that this shift was widespread that helped foster the idea of an evolutionary sequence of outfield/infield-outfield/two-fields/three-fields, a sequence underpinned by a scale of increasing intensity and population pressure. If rejected, their distribution becomes not a record of the conversion from one to the other, but a reflection of the different ways in which early communities *first* thought out their problems of field re-organization.

Given that population pressure forms the more obvious basis for explaining the geographical differences between the two- and three-field systems, the foregoing reservations over it create something of an impasse and they can hardly be said to clear the way for a new interpretation of why some communities preferred one to the other. If there is a need for an alternative approach to the problem, then it may be a case of looking again at the idea that the structure of the two- or three-field system was mediated through customary notions of spatial differentiation. What I am suggesting as a possibility is that the differences between the two- or three-field system may not be an expression solely of differences in basic agrarian needs, but equally of differences in custom and the way communities construed the structure of the personal space or territory around them. This may seem to trivialise the issue, but in actual fact, all it seeks to do is to balance agrarian needs with the force of custom more evenly, and perhaps more realistically, than earlier treatments of this aspect. An analogy might be drawn with the broad areal differences that existed over how townships constructed their land-unit framework. Over and above differences in the units of calculation (virgates, husbandlands, merklands, etc), further differences accrued from the way these were aggregated, some areas using multiples of 2, 4, 8, etc. and others using multiples of 3, 6, 9, etc. It is confessedly a hypothetical suggestion, but the contrast between diadic and triadic field structures may be rooted in the self-same notions of elemental order, and their subtle variations from one region to another.

The most telling comparison that can be made between the two- or three-field systems and split townships is over cause. The latter had a range of potential cause, from the proprietary break-up of townships to the search for more orderly and efficient layouts. Needless to say, the starting point for any comparison with the two- or three-field system in respect of cause must be this search for order. Two lines of argument can be juxtaposed: the first is that presented in the previous chapter which emphasised how the splitting of townships could occur in response to the growth or scale problems experienced by sub-divided field systems that had become too large and which, as a result, manifested serious dysfunctions; such instances of splitting formed an organizational change, an attempt to impose order and plan by both scaling down the size of townships and by laying out holdings and cropping sectors in a systematic fashion. The second line of argument is that much the same can be claimed for the two- or three-field system. Their adoption could quite easily have been a response to the growth problems felt by large, irregular, anarchic, sub-divided field townships. It introduced a sense of communal order where it was previously lacking, enabling gains to be made in the efficiency of work-routines, stubble grazing and cropping. Scholars like Thirsk have already characterized their adoption as being essentially an organizational change, but are content to highlight the particular gains it offered in terms of communally-regulated grazing rights over stubble (during a period when grazing was scarce) rather than the more general benefits that it also brought, though they fully recognize these extra benefits. But to disentangle the two levels of gain — the particular and the general — is well-nigh impossible, impossible as much for early communities as for us. If the two- or three-field systems were an exercise in reorganization, then communities must surely have anticipated the wider benefits which the disciplined and systematic laying out of holdings and cropping sectors meant. Once this is appreciated, their adoption and the splitting of townships can be aligned alongside each other as twin-solutions to the same basic problem.

The discovery of these twin-solutions probably flowed from the earliest attempts at township splitting, a process that was almost certainly initiated by their proprietary fission. The search for order which this enforced must have taken account not just of holding composition and disposition, but also, of what suited grazing and cropping. As intimated in the discussion of regular sub-divided fields in the previous section, these now better organized townships may have served as demonstration models, demonstrating in this case what could be gained by the splitting of large townships into smaller, more manageable units *and/or* by the adoption of communally-regulated cropping schemes embracing the entire township like those embodied in the two- or three-field system. Lords or communities could apply one or the other, or both, depending on the nature and scale of their growth problems: in other words, whilst the earliest phase of township splitting (a phase sustained by their proprietary fission) provided the nursery for the germination and maturation of the two- or three-field system, they could and did exist apart from township splitting. Just as the nature of township splitting itself altered by becoming a search for greater ease and efficiency of layout (as with Northumberland townships and presumably many others), so also could the idea of having communally-regulated systems of husbandry detach itself from the context of splitting and become a cause in itself. This forms a vital bridge in the argument because it links the two- or three-field system with townships *unaffected by splitting*, thus pathing the way for their diffusion from the special if widespread circumstances of splitting *to all townships*.

Finally, the plausibility of this supposed relationship between township splitting and the two- or three-field system is further endorsed by their overlap of chronology. To recap on what has been said already about chronology, the splitting of townships possibly got under way during the century or so before 1086 and became widespread over the twelfth and thirteenth centuries. However, as one moves towards the north and west of the country, into areas like the extreme north of England and Scotland, the process was retarded, with activity still occurring over the late medieval and even early modern periods. The chronology of the two- or three-field system depends on which authority is used as a guide. But those like Thirsk who see them as designed to secure more effective control over the tasks and resources of husbandry have tended to favour a date as late as the twelfth, thirteenth and fourteenth centuries for their inception. If correct, it would compare closely with the main phase of splitting, yet be sufficiently distanced from the earliest examples for their lessons (or advantages) to have been learnt. Equally at issue are the chronologies involved where townships applied both solutions — two- or three-field system and splitting — at different dates. This was the case with the Northumberland townships split over the fifteenth and sixteenth centuries, but which possessed two- or three-field systems *prior* to splitting. It could be that where both were used in this way, they were each designed to solve slightly different aspects of a township's growth problems. Perhaps the two- or three-field system was here a response in particular to the disorder of irregular sub-divided field systems, whilst splitting coped with the difficulties that derived from the sheer scale and complexity of large, sub-divided field systems, so each, therefore, would have had its own threshold even though each was a partial solution for the problems of the other.

Township splitting as a universal influence on field systems

Township splitting was widespread throughout Britain and Ireland. Its impact on field systems, therefore, cannot be confined to the role it played in the formation of the two- or three-field system. It had an impact, albeit a less profound impact, in other directions and in other areas. As will be shown, much depended on the precise context in which it operated.

For instance, in those parts of Wales where splitting acted on discrete or several holdings rather than large, sub-divided field townships, it could hardly have been used to inject a common order or purpose into the cropping and grazing of the township's fields; rather would it have served to emphasise the individual basis of farming. Its context in Scotland differed again. There, the splitting of sub-divided field townships either through their proprietary fission or as a means of combatting the problems of scale occurred widely, but it did so always in the context of shareholding. For this reason, the significance of splitting as an event was greatly reduced, since shareholding too afforded opportunities for reworking the layout of holdings and cropping sectors. The only difference was that splitting produced smaller townships in the process. This begs the question of whether such changes could have encouraged the innovation of communally-regulated cropping and grazing systems? The answer must be yes. Virtually all infields in lowland arable areas possessed organized cropping systems. Revealingly, they were *mostly* based on the grouping of shots into two/three cropping sectors, that were each subjected to the same two/three course rotation. In some cases, such as the very large proprietary runrig townships of the extreme south-east, the parallelism with townships south of the Border is even greater. The infield of townships like Newstead, Eildon and Bowden was structured around two large named *Fields*. They were not cropped as two-field systems nor was landholding evenly distributed between them, but then the eighteenth century material on which these statements are based may be a poor guide to earlier conditions. The fact of the matter is, that there must have been some purpose for this grouping of land into two large sectors or *Fields*, and the practice at some point in the past of a two-field cropping system seems the most likely explanation.[8] Yet no matter how important these two/three sectors or *Fields* were to the Scottish township economy, their distinction was smothered by the over-riding distinction between infield (assessed land) and outfield (non-assessed land). This smothering of infield cropping patterns, though, does not alter the essential fact that they possessed at their scale an order comparable with that of English townships, an order which splitting may have contributed to, if only in conjunction with the regular changes of township layout implicit in an active system of shareholding.

Taking a systematic approach, splitting may also have helped foster what might be called the illusion of communalism, an illusion which has shaped so many judgements on field systems. As a process whereby large territorial units could undergo a series of fissions into a veritable chequerboard of settlements and estates, splitting can be likened to a process of progressive differentiation, as the expanding population of the territory dis-aggregated itself into more and more discrete settlements and a finer mesh of landholding. Divorced from its context of splitting, these trends would be consistent with the ideas of scholars like Vinogradoff who saw the main historical drift of field systems as being from a condition of innate communalism towards one of severalism, as a case of undifferentiated rights becoming differentiated or clarified. This of course is counter to the conclusion presented in Chapter 2, which stressed instead the importance of seeing the so-called communalism of early farming communities as a set of arrangements into which they opted out of practical expediency rather than something which they inherited. An awareness of splitting can do much to resolve this conflict, for it explains why we can expect to find apparent but deceptive signs of an inherited communalism amongst early farming communities.

The argument is best developed through specific case-studies. In 1728, a disagreement arose between the Duke of Roxburgh and Lady Chatto over the grazing of harvest stubble in the Barony of Roxburgh (Roxburghshire). The Lady Chatto held the mains of Roxburgh and according to the Duke's lawyer, "a custom had crept in of pasturing the sheep of the mains of Roxburghe in the winter time upon the stibbles of the lands of the Barrony of Roxburghe pertaining to the Duke".[9] At issue were not the rights of stubble grazing within a single township, but the legitimacy of all the townships of the Barony intercommoning on each other's stubble. This is the sort of local practice that some would see as capturing the underlying sense of communalism that gave birth to sub-divided fields. An alternative, and more likely explanation, can be arrived at by invoking the all-important fact that the eighteenth-century pattern of townships in the Barony evolved through a complex series of splits. It is quite possible that this progressive differentiation of landholding left long-established customs, such as the grazing of harvest stubble, intact or without clarification. Only when the mains passed into different ownership to the rest of the Barony did it become a matter of concern to the Duke. This apparent overlap of interests between townships can be paralleled in other parts of Scotland, especially commonplace being the joint assessment of townships in terms of land units and their rent or service liabilities, a treatment only explicable through splitting.

It says much for the extent of township splitting in England that the two Oxfordshire townships used by Vinogradoff[10] and Maitland[11] in their dialogue on the supposed communal origins of sub-divided fields, both involved a background of township splitting. Part of their character almost certainly stems from this vital event in their history. Maitland's examination of Aston and Cote is especially interesting. It was administered — if that is not too strong a word — by an over-seeing body of landholders, with each of its 16 hides having one representative, hence its title of "the sixteens". The telling feature of the township's organization was that it embraced three physically separate manors. Had Vinogradoff been confronted with a situation in which a village assembly, "the sixteens", appeared to transcend the manorial domain, he would most certainly have read from it further proof of the autonomous, self-regulating character of early farming communities as communities. Maitland himself saw it as a township created fairly late through the co-operative efforts of three adjacent manors and which required an assembly of landholders — if not one of any real juridical authority — to administer the agreements and operations of husbandry. It poses fewer problems, though, if "the sixteens" is seen as an assembly of cultivators set up initially to oversee a single, integrated settlement, a settlement which later became split into three separate manors but which, through historical inertia or practical convenience, retained its original assembly as the main forum of discussion between those who actually farmed the land. Contrary to Maitland's own reasoning, there is really nothing *newish* about the appearance of Aston with Cote as a settlement; the very substance of its structure, or its framework of 16 hides or 64 yardlands (= 512 oxgangs), was identical to the land-unit assessment of Great Tew, the Oxfordshire settlement which Vinogradoff studied in depth. What is revealing, and perhaps suggestive of an archaic order, is not their exact accordance, but the fact that they both employed the same broad *scheme* of land assessment, a scheme which aligned them along a consistent scale both as regards the total number of land units which they contained (4, 8, 16, 32, 64, 128, etc.) and the relationship between the different levels of assessment (again, 4, 8, 16, 32, 64, 128, etc.). It may be chance, but there is a resemblance here with early schemes of land assessment to be found in parts of Scotland.[12]

Steeping back from the Vinogradoff v. Maitland debate, Oxfordshire generally is a very good county for illustrating the full and varied effects of splitting. Large, sub-divided field townships formed a complex intermesh of rights and customs. When splitting occurred, it could drive a clear and unambiguous wedge(s) through these rights and customs, creating two or more absolutely discrete townships: this is what happened in the case of Upper and Lower Horspath.[13] Alternatively, there were sites like the Baldons where the settlements were split but not the fields, which remained shared in a sub-divided field complex.[14] These two examples delimit the extremes of splitting. In between, one had scope for a whole range of possibilities. The survival of a landholder's assembly, such as "the sixteens" of Aston with Cote defines one of these possibilities, but there were a plethora of other rights and practices that could survive undifferentiated after splitting. Conversely, it may be a case of talking about the few rights that were differentiated. It could be that when settlement-groups like the Baldons are scrutinised closely, it will be found that whilst their fields remained intact as a single, consolidated system, there were other rights, such as those over grazing land or stubble, that were split or differentiated between the different settlements. Of course, the obvious example to cite of this sort of selective splitting would be the East Anglian fold course system, under which settlements shared by two or three manors had their grazing rights over the arable stubble split into an areallydiscrete fold courses, one per lord, but whose property rights in arable itself remained in an intermixed or sub-divided state.

To sum up then, splitting had a recognizable impact over and above its role in the evolution of the two- or three-field system. Both within the main area occupied by the latter and without, it came up against the whole gamut of rights and customs that invariably accompanied sub-divided fields. In some cases, it dealt with them in the same incisive, surgical manner in which it dealt with sub-divided fields. However, in other cases, its response to such rights and customs can be likened to that of a filter, differentiating some but not others between the split portions of the settlement. Where it operated in this selective way, splitting clearly had a potential for imparting considerable local and regional variety to the nature of early field systems.

References

[1] There are many examples of this to choose from. That of Charlton Adam alias East Charlton and Charlton Mackrell alias West Charlton in Somerset is typical. See Dunning (ed.), *History of the County of Somerset*, vol. III, pp. 81 and 95.

[2] Hilton, "Kibworth Harcourt", p. 30.

[3] Rees, *Celtic Heritage*, pp. 118-39; E. Durkheim and M. Mauss, *Primitive Classification*, trans. and ed. by R. Needham, 2nd English edition, London (1969), p. 68; P. Bourdieu, *Outline of a Theory of Practice*, Cambridge (1977), pp. 132-58.

[4] References to the fission or break-up of early estates, especially multiple estates, in both England and Wales can be found in G. R. J. Jones, "Multiple Estates and Early Settlement", pp. 15-40 in Sawyer (ed.), *Medieval Settlement*, p. 40. References to the splitting of shires in Scotland, such as *Magna* and *Parva* Blar, occur in W. F. Skene (ed.), *The Historians of Scotland, vol. IV, John of Fordun's Chronicle of the Scottish Nation*, Edinburgh (1872), p. 450. See also the highly relevant discussion of early *cantrefi* in Wales and their partition into commotes in M. Richards, "The Significance of *Is* and *Uwch* in Welsh Commote and Cantref Names", *Welsh History Rev.*, 2 (1964-5), pp. 9-18.

[5] Their use in relation to split townships can be gleaned from most ordnance survey sheets or gazetteers, such as H. C. Darby, *A Gazetteer of Domesday England*, Cambridge (1977). A systematic analysis of their use in relation to Scottish split townships can be found in Dodgshon, "Scandinavian 'Solskifte' and the Sunwise Division of Land in Eastern Scotland", p. 7 and Dodgshon, "Changes in Scottish Township Organization During the Medieval and Early Modern Periods", pp. 52-3. The most accessible list of field names associated with the two/three field systems is that published by Gray, *English Field Systems*, pp. 421-509. The scatter of references to North and South fields is matched by references to North and South townships, see Dodgshon. "Scandinavian 'Solskifte' and the Sunwise Division of Land in Eastern Scotland", p. 7. In all probability, they represent "modern" attempts to translate prefixes like sunny/shadow or nether/upper into a familiar form.

[6] E. Boserup, *Agriculture and the Conditions of Economic Growth*, London (1963).

[7] See, for example, the cautionary remarks of H. S. A. Fox, "The Origins of the Two- or Three-Field system in England", p. 116.

[8] The key source of data for these proprietary runrig townships is their division proceedings, mostly dating from the middle decades of the eighteenth century, which form part of the *Register of Decreets*, Roxburghshire Sheriff Court Records, Jedburgh. Sadly, the plans compiled have not survived. I have tried to summarise the evidence written for their layout in Chapter 1 of my doctoral thesis, see R. A. Dodgshon, *Agricultural Change in Roxburghshire and Berwickshire 1700-1820*, University of Liverpool, 1969.

[9] Roxburgh MS, Floors Castle, Memoriall and Claim His Grace John Duke of Roxburghe Against the Lady Chatto July 19th 1728.

[10] Vinogradoff, "An Illustration of the Continuity of the Openfield System", pp. 139-41.

[11] Maitland, "The Survival of Archaic Communities", pp. 313-65.

[12] I have reviewed such evidence in Chapter 3 of R. A. Dodgshon, *Land and Society in Early Scotland*, Oxford (1980), forthcoming.

[13] Lobel (ed.), *History of the County of Oxford*, vol. V, p. 180.

[14] *Ibid.*, p. 35.

Chapter 7

Conclusion

The foregoing discussion has tried to cast doubt on the widely held belief that field systems were designed solely in response to the husbandry needs of early farmers. A much more diverse range of influences and controls were at work, such that any review of their origin must impinge on the history of the rural community at large. In particular, three lines of argument would seem to be important.

The first concerns the basic problem of sub-divided fields, the hallmark of any field system as the term has been defined here. I have tried to explain why it is no longer tenable to see sub-divided fields as the product of a socially- or tribally constituted farming community in the sense conceived by Vinogradoff *et al.*, but that it is more likely that the former — helped by the impositions of feudalism — shaped the latter. This broad principle of argument naturally has repercussions on how we approach the problem. Thus, it seriously weakens the view that sub-divided fields must have been underpinned by a joint or common tenure in some original, pristine state. At the same time, it goes some way towards covering the otherwise awkward discontinuity of form between the field patterns of late prehistory and those evident in the later medieval period, a discontinuity that has become more prominent as the extent and nature of prehistoric fields has become more apparent. It is suggested that sub-divided fields and with them the formation of communities who farmed as one developed out of piecemeal colonisation and that their physical reorganization — for whatever reason — helped formalise their growing scatter of holdings into a share tenure. This two-stage or two-dimensional interpretation is almost essential if the morphological variety of sub-divided fields is to be adequately explained, with some townships having irregular, others regular and some, mixed systems.

The second line of argument proposed concerns infield-outfield; this type of field system has long been seen as a primitive system and the anchor for any evolutionary scheme of field systems. No better illustration of this exists than the way it has increasingly been used by model-building archaeologists to enrich their characterisation of late prehistoric society, and yet no scrap of documentary evidence exists for infield or outfield before the fourteenth century at the earliest. In fact, far from being a combination of the two most primitive forms of cropping (constant and shifting cultivation), it embodied a fundamental distinction in the basis of land tenure that arose fairly late. Infield formed assessed land, or that part measured in bovates, virgates, etc., and held by customary tenure. Outfield, meanwhile, was non-assessed land, or land measured in terms of its acreage and held by free tenure, usually for a cash rent; this distinction is valid for England no less than for Scotland and once seen in these terms, it also becomes clear that not all townships used it as the basis for infield-outfield *farming*; quite a few of them moulded farming and landholding patterns of a different sort around it. But although in the minority, these apparently *deviant* forms emphasise the point that infield-outfield derived its meaning primarily from the distinction between assessed and non-assessed land, not from any particular attribute of cropping. The extent to which this improves on traditional interpretations is highlighted by those Northumbrian townships which had two- or three-field systems developed on their infields and described their common pastures as outfield! Here clearly, the terms infield-outfield are being used overtly to capture the contrast between what lay within or without the assessed bounds of the township. Whilst this side to their distinction may have been more suppressed elsewhere, it was no less real nor was it any less important in determining their structural form.

The third line of argument which I have put forward as being crucial, concerns the relationship between the splitting of townships and the formation of the two- or three-field system. The extensive splitting of townships into two, three or more sub-townships has, of course, considerable historical interest for its own sake, since it is a process that has left its mark on virtually every corner of the British landscape. Its precise bearing on the two- or three-field system requires careful statement. It is not proposed that all two- or three-field systems were offspring of township splitting, only that the process provided a nursery for experimentations with layout — out of which the pioneer examples of the two- or three-field system may have emerged. Central to this argument is the indisputable fact that the process enables communities to rethink the layout of their holdings and presumably to ask questions about what sort of layout and husbandry were most beneficial to their individual and collective interests. Given that some scholars have argued for the two- or three-field systems being an innovation in organization or layout rather than in cropping, the splitting of townships would seem a propitious moment. Once the advantages of greater order and efficiency offered by the two- or three-field system over earlier irregular patterns had been demonstrated, it could have diffused on its own terms without being affiliated to splitting. As a process, splitting seems to have got under way around about the tenth or eleventh century. It is at this point, therefore, that the pioneer examples of the two- or three-field system may have appeared. It must be stressed however, that *estate*-splitting generally possibly had deeper roots than this. What was critical for any form of township reorganization was the point at which the township became a common unit of estate-holding, for this would have been the point at which the splitting of one led to the splitting of the other.

In my discussion, I stressed the parallelism between split townships and the two- or three-field system as regards their morphology and the schemes of land division employed to create them. This parallelism may be a vital clue as to why early communities chose a two- or three-field system as opposed to any other form of spatial order. The key to the point being made is the idea that the system may have been an innovation in the organization of townships, and no more. Its novelty could have been that it subjected the fields of the entire community to a standard concept of order and cropping, not that it used rotations which had not been seen before. Uppermost in the minds of these communities, therefore, may have been the problem of how to devise this order. It is at this point in the argument that the parallelism with split townships may be revealing: it admits the possibility that the rigid conventions of customary schemes of land division may have had a determinant role to play in shaping the precise structure of the two- and three-field system.

It has long been fashionable to dispense with the origin of field systems, or their geographical variety, in short pithy statements about their cultural or environmental basis. What I have tried to argue in this book lacks this sort of convenient simplicity; each of the three lines of argument on which my case rests comprises a small bundle of ideas, whose strands and linkages fan outwards into most dimensions of the early rural community and its economy. Simple classifications of cause, therefore, are not possible and have not been looked for. Likewise, there can be no single or simple answer to the question of chronology. A single township could conceivably experience the formation of sub-divided fields, their conversion to regular form, the formation of a two- or three-field system and then, the addition of an outfield-type system, the whole sequence of events starting in the early medieval period and finishing in the late medieval period. Explaining the geographical variety of British field systems also has no simple answer. Regional types in the sense of separately conceived and modelled systems did not exist. As I intimated at the outset, and as I have tried to demonstrate throughout my discussion, field systems everywhere were a response to the same basic set of problems. It was the way the different responses were combined and weighted that determined the regional varieties of form and function, not differences of a more substantive kind.

In looking at the possibilities for future research work, two areas of the problem require urgent clarification. The first concerns the link between the field patterns now being established by archaeologists for the late prehistoric and Romano-British periods and those studied by scholars working on the medieval period or later. Aided by the rapid growth of interest in this topic and the use of air photographs, the results of the former have undoubtedly shed valuable light on the nature of early field patterns and the all-important problem of when the countryside was first settled. However, there is a danger that amidst all the "total" landscapes now being resurrected for the late prehistoric and Romano-British periods, the real issues are being blurred. It is not sufficient to merely dovetail like-forms or morphological types together and, having matched them, to proclaim an early origin for this or that type. What I have tried to emphasise in the preceding chapters is that changes in the substance or composition of tenure, no matter how subtle, could have consequences for the growth of field systems. Nor am I referring here solely to the sub-division of property within fields which can rarely be apparent from field layout alone. Matters like the tenurial status of infield and outfield are just as critical. Until the prehistorian can introduce this notion of tenure or make allowances for it, then his comparison with later field patterns will be seriously incomplete; the same might be said of the prehistorian's attitude towards the use of early fields. By its use, I do not mean just its cropping or grazing, but also, the social context of its use, that is, the question of whether it was exploited by a community of farmers *acting together*. These reservations are not put forward so as to obstruct comparisons between prehistoric and medieval field patterns, but only to caution against too narrow an approach. Tenure or the social context of field use may not be so easily dug up as a field wall or bank, but their relevance to the interpretation of field patterns is no less vital. Given recent thinking on social archaeology, to call for discussion along these lines is not unreasonable, for only by adding clearer ideas on the tenure and social context of their use, can the field paterns of late prehistory and the Romano-British period be compared in any full sense with the field systems of medieval times.

The second area of the problem where a concentration of future work would be profitable, is on the general question of the catastrophic phases of township history. By the term catastrophic, I mean all those events which fundamentally recast the layout of a township's field, landholding and/or cropping patterns: they include those changes precipitated by the process of partible inheritance, township splitting, the adoption of new cropping courses, etc. Such changes stand as the decisive moments in the history of field systems, the moments when communities had the opportunity to rethink their field economy and when, in consequence, the evolved tended to give way to the planned. Despite their seminal importance to the whole concept of field systems, relatively little discussion has been published on such moments. This is due, in part, to the unwillingness of some scholars to accept that field systems could have passed through a revolutionary phase, preferring instead a more continuous and quiescent kind of development. It is also due in part to the scarcity of evidence explicitly documenting the occurrence of such events. However, circumstantial evidence may exist in some abundance once we open our minds to the possibilities involved, as with township splitting. From more systematic work on such evidence will flow not only a better grasp of its chronology, but also, a better and firmer understanding of how field systems were linked via these revolutionary phases to the wider processes at work in rural society.

I have tried to make this last point — or the idea that field systems focussed a wide array of issues and problems connected with rural society generally — the recurring theme of my discussion throughout this book. What it means is that far from being a simple cultural seal which early communities busily and mechanically stamped over the countryside of Britain, field systems represent a much more synthetic, more composite kind of institution, from whose form can be read the interwoven effects of a variety of processes and trends. Indeed, I would venture the conclusion that future work might find it more profitable to conceive of field systems in terms of these processes and trends that shaped their form, rather than in terms of the integral and generic *types* by which past scholars have sought to distinguish one part of the country from another. Admittedly, such a rigorously systematic approach could not do adequate justice to the way local custom (acting on tenemental units, terminology, etc.) and environment (acting on the crude balance between arable and pasture) contributed to the appearances and apparent diversity of field systems. But arguably the diversity which they imposed on the problem was cosmetic, a shallow veil over basic design features that were far more uniform across the country than previous discussion have admitted. The processes and trends which moulded these design features are the key to the whole problem, for it was their interplay and combination that caused any *basic* variation in the character of field systems. What this means is that field systems in Scotland and Wales can be explained in the same terms as those of England. There was but one type of British field system, articulated into different regional variants, rather than different regional types; this may seem a little tautological, but it emphasises that whilst the interpretation of field systems offered here may seem a cumbersome package in terms of the number of ideas or factors invoked to explain the problem, nevertheless, it has the merit of being one for all regions.

Select bibliography

P. Allerston, "English Village Development: Findings from the Pickering District of Yorkshire", *Transactions of the Institute of British Geographers*, 5, (1970), pp. 95-109.

T. H. Aston, "The Origins of the Manor in Britain", *Trans. Royal Historical Soc.*, 5th series, 8 (1958), pp. 59-83.

W. O. Ault, *Open-Field Farming in Medieval England. A Study of Village By-Laws*, London (1972).

A. R. H. Baker, "Open Fields and Partible Inheritance on a Kent Manor", *Economic History Rev.*, 2nd series, XVII (1964-5), pp. 1-22.

A. R. H. Baker, "Field Systems in the Vale of Holmesdale", *Agricultural History Rev.*, XIV (1966), pp. 1-24.

A. R. H. Baker, "Some Terminological Problems in Studies of British Field Systems", *Agricultural History Rev.*, 17 (1969), pp. 136-40.

A. R. H. Baker and R. A. Butlin (eds.), *Studies of Field Systems in the British Isles*, Cambridge (1973).

M. W. Beresford and J. G. Hurst (eds.), *Deserted Medieval Villages*, London (1971).

T. A. M. Bishop, "Assarting and the Growth of the Open Fields", *Economic History Rev.*, VI (1935-6), pp. 26-40.

H. C. Bowen and P. J. Fowler (eds.), *Early Land Allotment in the British Isles*, British Archaeological Reports No. 48, Oxford (1978).

R. A. Butlin, "Northumberland Field Systems", *Agricultural History Rev.*, XII (1964), pp. 99-124.

F. Cheyette, "The Origins of European Villages and the First European Expansion", *Jnl. of Economic History*, XXXVII (1971), pp. 182-206.

H. C. Darby and J. Saltmarsh, "The Infield-Outfield System on a Norfolk Manor", *Economic History*, III (1935), pp. 30-44.

R. R. Davies, *Lordship and Society in Medieval Wales 1287-1400*, Oxford (1978).

W. Davies, *An Early Welsh Microcosm. Studies in the Llandaff Charters*, Royal Historical Soc's *Studies in History* Series no. 9, London (1978).

F. W. L. Dendy, "The Ancient Farms of Northumberland", *Archaeologia Aeliana*, XVI (1894), pp. 121-56.

R. A. Dodgshon, "The Nature and Development of Infield-Outfield in Scotland", *Transactions of the Institute of British Geographers*, 59 (1973), pp. 1-23.

R. A. Dodgshon, "The Landholding Foundations of the Open Field System", *Past and Present*, 67 (1975), pp. 3-29.

R. A. Dodgshon, "Farming in Roxburghshire and Berwickshire on the Eve of Improvement", *Scottish Historical Rev.*, LIV (1975), pp. 140-54.

R. A. Dodgshon, "Towards an Understanding and Definition of Runrig: the Evidence for Roxburghshire and Berwickshire", *Transactions of the Institute of British Geographers*, 64 (1975), pp. 15-33.

R. A. Dodgshon, "Runrig and the Communal Origins of Property in Land", *Juridical Rev.*, (1975), pp. 189-208.

R. A. Dodgshon, "Scandinavian 'Solskifte' and the Sunwise Division of Land in Eastern Scotland", *Scottish Studies*, 19 (1975), pp. 1-14.

R. A. Dodgshon, "Changes in Scottish Township Organization During the Medieval and Early Modern Periods", *Geografiska Annaler*, 58B (1977), pp. 51-65.

R. A. Dodgshon, "The Origin of the Two- and Three-field System in England: A New Perspective", *Geographia Polonica*, 38 (1978), pp. 49-63.

R. A. Dodgshon, "Law and Landscape in Early Scotland: A Study of the Relationship Between Tenure and Landholding", in A. Harding (ed.), *Lawmakers and Lawmaking in British History*, Royal Historical Soc. *Studies in British History*, London (1979), pp. 127-45.

T. P. Ellis, *Welsh Tribal Law and Custom in the Middle Ages*, Oxford (1926), two volumes.

H. A. L. Fisher (ed.), *The Collected Papers of Frederick William Maitland*, London (1911), two volumes.

H. S. A. Fox, "Outfield Cultivation in Devon and Cornwall: A Reinterpretation", in M. Havinden (ed.), *Husbandry and Marketing in the South West 1500-1800*, no. 8, Exeter Papers in Economic History (1973), pp. 19-38.

H. S. A. Fox, "The Chronology of Enclosure and Economic Development in Medieval Devon", *Economic History Rev.*, 2nd series, 28 (1975), pp. 181-202.

G. L. Gomme, *The Village Community*, London (1890).

S. Göransson, "Regular Open-Field Pattern in England and Scandinavian Solskifte", *Geografiska Annaler*, XLIIIB (1961), pp. 80-101.

H. L. Gray, *English Field Systems*, Cambridge, Mass. (1915).

C. A. Gresham. *Eifionydd. A Study in Landownership from the Medieval Period to the Present Day*, Cardiff (1973).

H. E. Hallam, *Settlement and Society: A Study of the Early Agrarian History of South Lincolnshire*, Cambridge (1965).

A. Harris, *The Open Fields of East Yorkshire*, East Yorks. Local History Series, IX (1959).

M. Harvey, *The Morphological and Tenurial Structure of a Yorkshire Township: Preston in Holderness 1066-1750*, Occasional Paper no. 13, Dept. of Geography, Queen Mary College, University of London (1978).

R. H. Hilton, "Old Enclosure in the West Midlands: a Hypothesis about their Late Medieval Development", *Géographie et Histoire Annales de L'Est*, XXI (1959), pp. 272-83.

R. H. Hilton, *A Medieval Society: The West Midlands at the End of the Thirteenth Century*, London (1966).

R. H. Hilton, *The Decline of Serfdom in Medieval England*, London (1969).

R. C. Hoffman, "Medieval Origins of the Common Fields", in W. N. Parker and E. L. Jones (eds.), *European Peasants and their Markets*, Princeton (1975), pp. 23-71.

G. C. Homans, *English Villagers of the Thirteenth Century*, Cambridge, Mass. (1941).

G. C. Homans, "The Explanation of English Regional Differences", *Past and Present*, 42 (1969), pp. 18-34.

G. R. J. Jones, "Post-Roman Wales", in H. P. R. Finberg (ed.), *The Agrarian History of England and Wales*, vol. I, part II, Cambridge (1972), pp. 281-382.

T. Jones Pierce, *Medieval Welsh Society*, ed. by J. B. Smith, Cardiff (1972).

E. A. Kosminsky, *Studies in the Agrarian History of England in the Thirteenth Century*, Oxford (1956).

(Maitland), *The Collected Papers of Frederick William Maitland*, ed. by H. A. L. Fisher, London (1911), two volumes.

F. W. Maitland, *Domesday Book and Beyond*, London (1960 edition).

D. N. McCloskey, "English Open Fields as Behaviour Towards Risk", in P. Uselding (ed.), *Research in Economic History*, vol. I, Greenwich, Connecticut (1976), pp. 124-70.

E. Miller, "England in the Twelfth and Thirteenth Centuries: An Economic Contrast", *Economic History Rev.*, XXIV (1971), pp. 1-14.

J. S. Moore, "The Domesday Teamland: A Reconsideration", *Trans. Royal Historical Soc.*, 5th series, 14 (1964), pp. 109-30.

J. S. Moore, *Laughton: A Study in the Evolution of the Wealden Landscape*, Occasional paper no. 19, Dept. of English Local History, University of Leicester (1965).

K. Nicholls, *Gaelic and Gaelicised Ireland in the Middle Ages*, Dublin (1972).

F. D'Olivier Farran, "Run-rig and the English Open Fields", *Juridical Rev.*, 71 (1959), pp. 134-49.

C. S. and C. S. Orwin, *The Open Fields*, Oxford (1938).

W. Rees, *South Wales and the March 1284-1415*, Oxford (1924).

M. Richards, "Local Government in Cardiganshire: Medieval and Modern", *Ceredigion*, IV (1962), pp. 278-82.

B. K. Roberts, "A Study of Medieval Colonization in the Forest of Arden, Warwickshire", *Agricultural History Rev.*, 16 (1968), pp. 101-13.

B. K. Roberts, "Village Plans in County Durham", *Medieval Archaeology*, XVI (1972), pp. 33-56.

B. K. Roberts, *Rural Settlement in Britain*, Folkestone (1977).

J. H. Romanes, "The Land System of the Scottish Burgh", *Juridical Review*, 47 (1935), pp. 103-19.

T. R. Rowley (ed.), *The Origins of Open Field Agriculture*, London (1980).

P. H. Sawyer (ed.), *Medieval Settlement*, London (1976).

F. Seebohm, *The English Village Community*, London (1890).

F. Seebohm, *The Tribal System in Wales*, 2nd edition, London (1904).

J. Sheppard, "Pre-Enclosure Field and Settlement Patterns in an English Township", *Geografiska Annaler*, 48B (1966), pp. 59-77.

J. A. Sheppard, "Medieval Village Planning in Northern England: Some Evidence from Yorkshire", *Jnl. of Historical Geography*, 2 (1976), pp. 3-20.

A. Simpson, "The East Anglian Foldcourse: Some Queries", *Agricultural History Rev.*, IV (1958), pp. 87-96.

J. Storer Clouston, "The Orkney Townships", *Scottish Historical Rev.*, 17 (1920), pp. 16-45.

C. C. Taylor, *Fields in the English Landscape*, London (1975).

J. Thirsk, "The Common Fields", *Past and Present*, 29 (1964), pp. 3-29.

J. Z. Titow, "Medieval England and the Open-Field System", *Past and Present*, XXII (1965), pp. 86-192.

P. Vinogradoff, *Villainage in England*, Oxford (1892).

P. Vinogradoff, *The Growth of the Manor*, London (1905).

P. Vinogradoff, *Outline of Historical Jurisprudence*, Oxford (1920), two volumes.

P. Vinogradoff, *The Collected Papers of Paul Vinogradoff*, Oxford (1928).

D. M. Wilson (ed.), *The Archaeology of Anglo-Saxon England*, London (1976).

Index